HISTORY OF KANNUR AND NORTH MALABAR

HISTORY OF KANNUR AND NORTH MALABAR

Kolatiri, Arakkal and Mysore Sultans

LEENA MORE

MANOHAR
2026

First published 2024

Reprinted 2025, 2026

ISBN 978-81-19953-74-5 (hardbond)
ISBN 978-81-19953-90-5 (ebook)

Published by
Ajay Kumar Jain *for*
Manohar Publishers & Distributors
4753/23 Ansari Road, Daryaganj
New Delhi 110 002

Typeset by
Kohli Print
Delhi 110 051

Printed and bound in India

To

the loving memory of my mother,

MRS. KARUVATH SHANTHA

and my father,

MR. PUTHIYAPARAMBIL BHASKARAN

Contents

List of Figures

Foreword

Dr. Leena More had previously authored a book on the history of Attingal and the Travancore kingdoms with special reference to the English East India Company. It was published in the year 2004. It was a path-breaking study. It highlighted the historical roles played by the Attingal and Travancore kingdoms in the history of south Kerala. The most significant feature of the study was the vivid portrayal of the Attingal revolt of 1721, during which scores of Englishmen were massacred by the Malabaris.

In the present work, More focuses on the origins and early history of northern Malabar and Cananore until its annexation by the English in the year 1792, after which it became part of the Madras Presidency of British India as Malabar district. This work is also a path-breaking study, as hardly any scholar had undertaken such a specific study till now, except for a few exceptions like the French scholar, Geneviève Bouchon, and Prof. K.K.N. Kurup, who had worked on the Mamales of Cananore and Ali Raja of Cananore.

Of special significance is the fact that More had based her study on ancient Tamil and Sanskrit literatures, the Latin, Arabic, Chinese and Persian accounts since the ancient times up to the sixteenth century, as well as many records and works in European languages like French and English. She had especially put to good use the records in English and French found in the Bibliothèque Nationale de France, Paris and the India Office Library and Records, British Library, London.

On the basis of ancient Tamil literature like *Purnanuru* and *Akananuru*, she had established that north Malabar was part of Tamilakam or Tamil land. She had identified in no uncertain terms the Kingdom of Nannan and his descendants, who ruled north Malabar since ancient times. Her researches establish that Nannan was an independent ruler of his kingdom, and that it was never part of the ancient Chera kingdom. Nannan's dynasty seems to have given way to the Mushika dynasty, which was succeeded by the Kolatiri kings. She also does not find any irrefutable evidence of the Mushika and Kolatiri kings being the vassals of the Perumal rulers of the second Chera kingdom, though there were some interactions between them.

More, then, delves into the colonial period, when the Portuguese, Dutch, French and English established trading posts and constructed forts all along the Malabar coast. But contrary to what one might expect, the Malabaris were largely successful in restricting the Europeans to their trading posts and forts, which prevented them from colonizing the Malabar country, unlike what happened on the eastern coast of India, which served as the spring-board for European expansionism in India.

More also traces successfully the history of the rise of the Mamales of Cananore, who was subordinate to the Kolatiri as the principal trader and seafarer of the northern Malabar coast. She establishes convincingly that a Kolatiri prince of Cananore had converted to Islam during the thirteenth century or before, on the basis of the accounts of Ibn Battuta, and that this conversion got mixed up since the Portuguese period with the legend of the conversion of Cheraman Perumal to Islam.

The author also traces the rise of the Ali Rajas of Cananore from the early conversion, as noted by Ibn Battuta and the Mamales, as subordinates to the Kolatiri. But later they became rivals to the Kolatiri. It was Ali Raja who invited first the northern Kanarese chiefs, and then the Mysore Sultans into Malabar to help him in his tussle for power with the Kolatiri kings. This was followed by the entry of the English army from the east, which undid the Mysore Sultans and subjected the Kolatiri, Ali Raja and other princes and Nairs of Malabar to finally annex it with the Madras Presidency. Thus, northern Malabar including Cananore which was the seat of the Kolatiri for a long time as well as that of the Ali Raja became British colonial possessions in India.

On the account of originality of the approach as well as the various records and works consulted in several languages this study is no doubt a significant contribution to the history of northern Malabar and Cananore.

Paris
10 April 2022

J.B. PRASHANT MORE

Preface

Few studies have been carried out on the early and medieval history of Kerala and its interaction with the Europeans. But an exhaustive study of the origin and early history of north Malabar and Cananore was not attempted in a systematic manner by any writer. It is important to draw attention to the fact that north Malabar, including Cananore seems to have had a distinct history and socio-political evolution of its own since ancient times. As I hail from this region, I decided to take up this complex study pertaining to the history of Cananore and north Malabar since ancient times until its annexation by the British in 1792.

My journey of tracing the history of Cananore and North Malabar from precolonial times was particularly difficult due to the paucity of relevant materials. The history of Kolatiri ruler who ruled over this region and his prime officer, a Muslim trader, based in Cananore, is a prime concern of this book. The latter who played a significant role in the sea faring activity in the Arabian seas, and later evolved into Ali Raja, or sea king who gradually broke away from Kolatiri, and became an independent chief of Cananore, is adequately dealt within this work. I have tried to represent as accurately as possible the vicissitudes of the Kolatiri kingdom and Arakkal House in their relationship not only with the European powers, but also with the Canarese kings and Mysore Sultans.

In order to attain my objectives, I have mainly relied on the original records, documents, manuscripts and rare books, available at the various archives and libraries located across India, France and England. I am grateful to the prompt assistance rendered by the Tamil Nadu Archives, Chennai; Maharashtra State Archives, Mumbai; National Archives, Delhi; India Office Library and Records, London; Bibliothèque

Nationale de France, Paris; and the History Department Library, University of Calicut.

This work would not have seen the light without the inspiration and support that I drew from my professors. First, salvo was fired by Prof. Valsan, S.N. College, Kannur when he attended my first book release and asked me to write about the History of Kannur. Sir, my sincere gratitudes to you! I profusely thank Prof. M.G.S. Narayanan, the former Head of the Department of Calicut University and ICHR Chairman, who was my mentor and late Dr. Sreekumaran Nair, who was my thesis guide and supervisor. I am also thankful to Prof. K.S. Mathew, the founder of IRISH, Tellicherry, Dr. K.K.N. Kurup, former Vice-Chancellor of Calicut University. Prof. Kesavan Veluthat, Prof. Rajan Gurukkal and Prof. Warrier and Dr. Mujeebu Rahman of Calicut University.

My sincere gratitude to Dr. K.J. John, Dr. Mohamed Koya, Dr. Kunjali, Dr. Gangadharan Nambiar, who had left us. My special thanks to Mr. Shihad, the Director of Arakkal Museum for furnishing me with information related to Arakkal House.

I wish to place my profound appreciation and admiration to my husband Dr. J.B.P. More, for the overwhelming care he took to go through my transcript and giving valuable suggestions and even editing it, despite his busy schedule. I record my profound sense of gratitude towards my mother K. Shantha and my father P. Bhaskaran, who though no more, was the driving force behind this work. I am also grateful to my brothers, Sunil P.K., Sudeep P.K., and my sister Hansa Prakash, and my aunt Valsala Karunakaran for the moral support they rendered to me for accomplishing my goal. I am deeply indebted to my friends and colleagues, who stood by me with encouragement all these years. Finally, I wish to send a warm appreciation to my son Rahul More who followed me throughout this venture. He kept on asking me, 'Mama! Are you registering whatever you are typing in a USB?' His words always warmed my heart.

LEENA MORE

Abbreviations

AME	Archives des Missions étrangeres, Paris
BNF	Bibliothèque Nationale de France, Paris
IOL	India Office Library and Records, London
MAB	Maharashtra State Archives, Mumbai
TNA	Tamil Nadu Archives, Chennai
NAD	National Archives, Delhi

CHAPTER 1

Introduction

When I decided to write about the origin and early history of Cananore and north Malabar, I did not realize that it will be a daunting task. European travellers referred to it as 'Cananore'. Later, the British called it as 'Cananore'/'Cannanore'. Today, the anglicized Cannanore is known by its Malayalam equivalent, Kannur. In this study, I will be using the term Cananore all throughout. It was a passing remark made by Prof. Valsan, the former Professor of S.N. College, Kannur and the former Principal of Sree Narayana College, Cherthala, who was present during the launch of my first book entitled, *English East India Company and the Local Rulers of Kerala: A Case Study of Attingal and Travancore*, which made me sit up and think. The book was actually released by the eminent Kerala historian M.G.S. Narayanan, in the presence of Prof. K.S. Mathew, Prof. K.J. John, Mr. Moorkoth Ramunni, a renowned bureaucrat, Mr. Ramanunni, a reputed Malayalam writer, and the French historian Dr. J.B. Prashant More.

On that occasion, Prof. Valsan told me 'Leena, you have written about Travancore history. Now it's your duty to write about the history of Kannur'. I presume he said that because I was a native of Cananore, I was indeed fascinated by his idea, I pondered over it for quite a while, while I was residing in France. As time passed by, this idea got rooted in my mind and finally I decided to take up this challenge to delve into the history of Cananore and north Malabar from its origin until its annexation in 1792.

Kerala, as we know it today, comprises of the narrow strip of land that lies on the southwestern coast of India between the Western Ghats and the Arabian Sea. In the antiquarian days, it was part of Tamilakam region (roughly the present States of Kerala and Tamil Nadu) as it was known then, when the Cheras were reigning supreme there. In this study, I intend to deal only with Cananore and the north Malabar region in which it is located. Generally, historians of Kerala, with some exceptions, have paid scant attention to the study of northern Kerala and its regions and towns and its rulers and kingdoms.

The State of Kerala, as it is known today, is the result of the reorganization of States in 1956, instituted by the Government of India after it independence. This State of Kerala comprised of the Travancore and Cochin kingdoms, as well as the Malabar district of the former Madras Presidency of British India.

As far as the history of north Kerala or Malabar is concerned, it all seems to have begun with Revd. Gundert, a German Missionary of the Basel Mission, during the second half of the nineteenth century. He took a keen interest in the study of Malayalam manuscripts, grammar and history and produced several historical works. Similarly, we have the officers of the British Indian Civil Service like William Logan, Evans, Innes and Robert Sewell who throughout their lives pursued relentlessly the task of tracing the history of Malabar. William Logan had produced the *Malabar Manual* (1886). Following these studies by British scholars and officials, various studies on Kerala history was undertaken by scholars of Kerala.[1]

These studies focus mainly on the history of central and south Kerala and neglect to a considerable extent the history of north Kerala. Some of those studies are the *Thiruvithamkur Charithram* by Pachu Muthatha, published in 1867, *History of Travancore* by Shungoony Menon, published in the year 1878, and the *History of Cochin*, by K.P. Padmanabha Menon which was published in 1912. During the twentieth century, scholars like Elamkulam P.N. Kunjan Pillai, K.M. Panikkar, K.V. Krishna Ayyer, C. Achutha Menon, K. Achutha Menon, T.K. Krishna Menon, L.A. Krishna Ayyer, T.I. Poonen, Sreedhara Menon, K.N. Panikkar, Prof. M.G.S. Narayanan, Ibrahim

Kunju, K.K.N. Kurup, Raghava Varier, Rajan Gurukkal and Kesavan Veluthat have carried out important studies on the history of Kerala since ancient times. But here too, we find that less attention or scarce attention has been paid to the history of north Kerala, i.e. Malabar region. Kunjan Pillai and M.G.S. Narayanan treated north Malabar as a political sub-division of the ancient and medieval Chera kingdoms. Other than this, there were very few studies by Kerala historians which focused exclusively on north Kerala, or Malabar.[2]

More generally, historians have neglected the history of ancient Kerala, both north and south up to the eighth century at least and even up to the medieval period with some exceptions like that of the study of the Perumals of Kerala by M.G.S. Narayanan. This seems to be mainly because the Malayalam language itself seems to have taken shape only after the sixteenth century. Further, there are no in-depth historical studies on the famous towns and cities of Kerala or Malabar, with of course, some exceptions like that of a study of Calicut by Narayanan.

Nevertheless, whenever studies have been undertaken on northern Kerala, the focus has always been the Muslims of Malabar and the Malabar revolt of the 1920s. Panikkar, Roland Miller, Stephen Dale, Ibrahim Kunju, P.A. Saythu Muhammad have all paid their attention to the study of the Muslims of Malabar. J.B.P. More, however, has produced a complete work on the *Origin and Early History of the Muslims of Keralam*, with special focus on north Kerala. But never did anyone attempt any general study of the history of north Kerala or Malabar since ancient times in a systematic manner. It is because of all the preceding reasons, it becomes more important to study the history of Cananore and north Kerala. It is important to draw attention at this juncture to the fact that north Malabar including Cananore seems to have had a distinct history and socio-political evolution of its own since ancient times, until its annexation by the English in 1792.[3]

The writing of the early history of Cananore, or Malabar until about the fifteenth century is never an easy task, owing to the fact that systematic compilation of historical events during this early period was not available, given that history writing and record-keeping did not exist in the traditions of south India and Kerala. Voluminous literature in Tamil and Sanskrit, the two oldest languages of India, pertaining to religion, philosophy and literature were produced in abundance during this early period till the medieval age. These may contain some historical features and information related to the Malabar region. But they are absolutely inadequate.

Hence, in the course of this study, I have relied upon the primary and secondary sources that I have consulted in the various libraries and archives in India, United Kingdom, and France. The complexity of undertaking this study pertaining to the history of Cananore and Malabar since ancient times until its annexation by the British is difficult for more than one reason. Primarily, as there is hardly any written record related to Cananore, either inscriptional or literary in Malayalam before the fifteenth century, one has no other alternatives, but to rely on ancient Tamil literature of the Sangam period and also Sanskrit literature, if available, to reconstitute as far as possible the ancient history of Cananore and the north Malabar region in which it is located. It is good to remember at this juncture that Kerala was part of Tamilakam during the ancient times until about the twelfth century, when the former parted company with the latter. Moreover, to undertake the study of the ancient period, I have also relied on certain accounts left by the ancient Greeks, Romans, and Chinese. Besides, from the eighth century onwards, we do have references to Malabar and even Cananore in the travellers' accounts of the Chinese, Arabs, and Persians. Hence, I intend to utilize such material to reconstitute the old history of Cananore and the Malabar region.

As far as the history of north Malabar region is concerned, we have at our disposal, the Sanskrit work of the eleventh century called *Musakavamsakavya*, which is a *vamsacharita* or the genealogical description of Musaka kingdom composed by Atula, the court poet of the Mushika King Srikantha. This poetical work, largely mythological, discovered by Gopinatha Rao, does provide ample historical information concering the Malabar region.[4]

But from the fifteenth century onwards, there exist, abundance of written records in the various European languages such as Portuguese, French, Dutch, and English. I intend to exploit these early records to the fullest extent in our study. Some local sources like the *Kerala Mahatmayam* and *Keralolpatti*, probably belonging to the late seventeenth century or eighteenth century though largely mythological, composed in Malayalam will also be put to good use in the reconstruction of north Malabar history. Thunchattu Ezhuthachan is believed to be the author of *Keralolpatti*. *Keralolpatti* is the history of the origin of Kerala from the Brahmanical point of view. These works are largely legendary in character, and it is extremely difficult to sort out the truth from the falsities and mythologies that we find in them. These works have been dismissed largely as figments of imagination of their authors by British historians like Robert Sewell. Sewell, however, admitted that there might be some germs of truth found in this literature, which are hard to identify and isolate so that they might become authentic historical material.[5]

Apart from the preceding literature, there exists an Arabic text, produced by Sheikh Zainuddin al-Malabari in the late sixteenth century. This text contains a lot of historical, geographical and sociological contents regarding Kerala, which we will put to good use in the elaboration of this work. Sheikh Zainuddin wrote in Arabic in order to please his benefactors in the Bijapur Sultanate. It seems that he did not produce a Malayalam version of it simply because a developed Malayalam written script did not exist at that time. Zainuddin's work sheds lot of useful information about the north Malabar society and political struggles.[6]

Otherwise, we have the *Malabar Manual* produced by the colonial bureaucrat William Logan (1886) giving a historical outline of north Kerala, or Malabar. Narayanan had written about the history of Kozhikode in south Malabar. Kurup wrote about the Ali Rajas of Cananore. M. Gangadharan had written about *Mappila Padanangal* in Malayalam, K. Balakrishnan had written about *Kannur Kotta* in Malayalam, Saythu Muhammad on *Kerala Muslim Charithram* in Malayalam, Chirakal T. Balakrishnan Nair, who belonged to the Chirakkal family has provided historical insights and has identified most of the places, rivers, and temples depicted in the *Musakavamsakavya* in his work. Sreedhara Menon has compiled and edited *Kerala District Gazetteers* (including Malabar and Cananore). C.A. Innes and F.B. Evans have produced the *Malabar District Gazetteers*. We have other authors and writers like Francis Day (1863) and Revd. Samuel Mateer (1871), who produced works on Kerala.[7]

Over and above these works, I intend to make use of all primary and other secondary sources, records and documents available especially at the Tamil Nadu Archives, Chennai; National Archives, New Delhi; British Library (India Office Records), London; Maharashtra Archives, Mumbai; Bibliothèque Nationale de France, Paris; Richlieu Manuscript Library, and Calicut University Library, Kozhikode. The hitherto unexploited documents and records obtained from the British Library and the National Library of France, dating back to the seventeenth and eighteenth centuries are particularly significant to this study.

On the whole, while using all the preceding sources, I intend to adopt a chronological order in order to retrace the history of Cananore and north Malabar. But before delving any further into this subject, we must have first an understanding of the historical evolution of north Malabar and Cananore since its origins in order to achieve this objective.

NOTES

1. H. Gundert, *Keralolpatti: The Origin of Malabar*, Mangalore, 1868, 1961 (reprint); *Malayalam English Dictionary*, Mangalore, 1961; William Logan, *Malabar Manual*, vol. I, Madras, 1951; C.A. Innes & F.B. Evans, *Malabar Gazetteer*, Madras, 1951; Robert Sewell, *List of the Antiquarian Remains in the Presidency of Madras*, Madras, 1882.
2. Vaikathu Pachu Moothathu, *Thiruvithamkur Charithram*, Cochin, 1867, 1986; P. Shungoony Menon, *History of Travancore from early times*, Madras,1878; K.P. Padmanabha Menon, *A History of Kerala* (4 vols.), Ernakulam, 1924, 1929, 1933, 1937; Elamkulam P.N. Kunjan Piliai, *Kerala Charithrattile Irulatanja Etukal*, Kottayam, 1953, 1963 (reprint); K.M. Panikkar, *Malabar and the Portuguese*, Bombay, 1929; K.V. Krishna Ayyer, *A History of Kerala*, Palghat, 1965; K.V. Krishna Ayyer, *The Zamorins of Calicut*, Calicut, 1938; K.N. Pannikar, *Against Lord and State-Religion and Peasant Uprisings in Malabar, 1836-1921*, Delhi, 1989; C. Achutha Menon, *Cochin State Manual*, Ernakulam, 1911; K. Achutha Menon, *Ancient Kerala*, Trichur, 1961; T.K. Krishna Menon, *Dravidian Culture and its Diffusion*, Ernakulam, 1937; L.A. Krishna Ayyer, *Social History of Kerala*, Madras, 1970; T.I. Poonen, *Dutch Beginnings in India Proper, 1580-1615*, Madras, 1933; T.I. Poonen, *Dutch Hegemony in Malabar and its Collapse, AD 1663-1795*, Trivandrum, 1978; A. Sreedhara Menon, *A Survey of Kerala History*, Kottayam, 1967, Madras, 1984; M.G.S. Narayanan, *Perumals of Kerala: Political and Social Conditions of Kerala under the Cera Perumals of Makotai (AD 800-1124)*, Calicut, 1996; A.P. Ibrahim Kunju, *Medieval Kerala History*, Trivandrum, 1975; K.K.N. Kurup, *The Ali Rajas of Cannanore*, Calicut, 2002; Raghava Varier and Rajan Gurukkal, *Cultural History of Kerala*, Trivandrum, 1999; Kesavan Veluthat, *Brahman Settlements in Kerala*, Calicut, 1978.
3. Roland Miller, *Mappila Muslims of Kerala: A Study in Islamic Trends*, Madras, 1976; Stephen, Frederick Dale, *Islamic Society on the South Asian Frontier*, Oxford, 1980; P.A. Saythu Muhammad, *Carita Keralam* (Malayalam), Kottayam, 1957 (third edition); J.B.P. More, *Origin and Early History of the Muslims of Keralam, AD 700 -AD 1600*, Calicut, 2011.
4. Cf. N.P. Unni, *A History of Mushikavamsa*, Trivandrum, 1980.
5. Ibid., p. 21; Robert Sewell, *A Sketch of the Dynasties of Southern India*, Madras, 1883, p. 55.

6. M.J. Rowlandson (tr.), *Tohfut-ul-Mujahideen*; historical work in Arabic Language, London, MDC CXXXIII; J.B.P. More (ed.), *Offerings to the Muslim Warriors of Malabar*, Chennai, 2015.
7. M.G.S. Narayanan, *Kozhikodinde Katha* (Malayalam); *Ottappalam*, 2001; cf. *Kozhicode Charithrathilninnu Chila edukal* (Malayalam), *Kozhicode, 2011:* K.K.N. Kurup, *Kannurile Ali Rajavamsam*, Calicut, 2008; M. Gangadharan, *Mappila Padanagal*, Calicut, 2007; K. Balakrishnan, *Kannur Kotta* (Malayalam), Kottayam, 2008; Chirakkal T. Balakrishan Nair, *Tiranjedutha Prabhanthangal*, Thrissur, 1981.

CHAPTER 2

Historical Background of Malabar

Keralam or Kerala, as it is known today, had been in contact with the seafaring people of the west from the earliest times. Walled off by the Western Ghats and watered by the Arabian Sea, this tiny strip of land had come into the limelight of the world for its spice trade since ancient times. The region that came to be known as Malabar district during British rule is located in the northern part of the present-day Kerala State. This narrow coastal belt of Kerala or Malabar attracted foreigners for a number of reasons. The chief products of this region were pepper, whereas cardamom and cinnamon and silk cotton trees were the other main products of foreign trade. The entire Malabar region and its country side was also covered with coconut trees, jackfruit and banana plantation.[1]

Pepper was widely used in Europe for preserving meat, flavouring food and was also considered to have medicinal properties. It was also given as offerings in churches. Pepper had great influence not only in Europe's economy, but also in politics and warfare. After a war, pepper was included among the items to be exchanged. Similarly, this item was also given as presents and bribes. In fact, it is for this pepper trade that Malabar, or more precisely Calicut and Cananore came into the spotlight from time immemorial.[2] Thus, the easy availability of pepper in the Malabar and the ready market it had in Europe, made it the prime article of trade.

EARLY HISTORICAL REFERENCES TO KERALA/MALABAR

The origins of Kerala as related in the *Kerala Mahatmayam* and *Keralolpatti* of the eighteenth century is largely legendary.

The Parasurama legend recounted in them from the Brahmanical or rather the Nayar/Nambutiri point of view, according to which Keralam was retrieved from the ocean by Parasurama is an attempt to cut off Kerala from its past history and historical consciousness and give it a divine status, when actually Kerala or rather a good part of it was part of the Chera kingdom. This kingdom along with the Pandyan and Chola kingdoms were the three southern kingdoms that constituted Tamilakam, as noted by the eminent historian, Narayanan. According to K.N. Ganesh, this mythological attempt to obliterate the past was successful. Had it been so, it had done a great disservice to the writing of the genuine past history of the Cheras, which is part and parcel of present Kerala, or Malabar history.[3]

During the year 334 BC, Alexander the Great crossed Indus and Jhelum rivers, fought several battles in India and conquered the Indus Valley. He was accompanied by archers, astronomers, philosophers, geographers, historians and cavalry during his voyage. Onesicritus, a student of Greek Philosophy, who was the pilot of Alexander's fleet and who accompanied the latter during his voyage to India, had sung praises of India as a southern land, where spices were produced. This land could be nothing else, but the Chera country. Onesicritus has described the land of *Musicanus*, which according to him was the southernmost-part of India. He had described the banyan and cotton trees and pepper vines grown there.[4]

Later, in the fourth century BC, the Greek ambassador, Megasthenes came to India through the northwestern passes. He had mentioned about the western coast and its ruler. Further, in the edicts of Emperor Ashoka of 250 BC, we find the Cheras and Cholas mentioned as the southern kingdoms. The Roman geographer Strabo confirmed that during 31 BC, there was great increase in Roman trade with south India. According to him, during normal period, only around 30 ships sailed to southern India every year. However, by 31 BC, the scenario changed drastically. Larger fleets comprising of hundreds of vessels were sent out as far as the Coromandel coast to bring back Indian products. As a result of this brisk commercial activity, Roman and Egyptian gold flowed into India conti-nuously. Much of this gold would have landed in the Chera country on the western coast. Thus, during this early period, there were three major dynasties, notably the Chera (kingdom of Keprobotos), Chola and Pandya, who were ruling the southern parts of India. All of them spoke Classical Tamil or some dialects of Tamil, if we rely on *Sangam* literature, which was common to the three dynasties.[5]

The Chera, Chola, and Pandya dynasties figures incidentally, in the ancient Sanskrit texts like the *Ramayana*, and the *Mahabharata* too. It is very important to specify at this juncture that the pre-Islamic Arabs had settled in Sumatra and Ceylon by the first century AD. They also had a settlement or colony in Canton as early as AD 300. It is also known that the Persians were also trading with China since the fourth century AD. By the beginning of seventh century, there was a foreign colony in Canton consisting not only of Arabs, but also Persians.[12] These Arabs and Persians would have most certainly traded with the Malabar region on their way to China. It is true that Arabs were the first navigators of the Indian Ocean, and the first carrier of the Indian produce to the rest of the world. Actually, it appears that it was the Arabs who introduced oriental spices into Pharaonic Egypt and Roman Palestine.[6]

Acccording to O.K. Nambiar, it was from the Arabs that the Greeks, Egyptians, and the Romans learnt to establish commercial ties with Malabar and rest of the *Hind* (India). Later, during the reign of the Roman Emperor Nero, around AD 70, Pliny was extremely worried about the trade balances with India. He complained that the Roman Empire was being drained of its currency gold to the value of nearly a million pounds a year, in exchange for perishable wares like pepper, which were sold at a hundred times their cost. Roman contacts with India during this period were mainly with the Malabar and Coromandel coasts. In the ancient Tamil literature *Tolkappiyam* and *Manimekalai*, there are ample evidences of

Roman or Greek presence in southern India. They were generally known as *Yavanas.*[7]

Generally speaking, maritime activity increased in the Indian Ocean during the first century AD. This was mainly due to the fact that at that time, Hippalus, discovered the usage of the monsoon winds to cross the Arabian Sea to Malabar and southern India directly. Thenceforth, ships from the west regularly visited Indian ports in large numbers in search of Indian products like the spices of Malabar. According to Strabo, the Roman geographer, Hippalus is said to have boldly stood out to sea from Cape Fertak in Arabia and sailed with the southwest monsoon and reached Malabar in less than four weeks, with far less labour.[8]

According to the Peutingerian tables of this period, which were sort of maps reproduced from the fresco paintings in Rome, there was a temple of Emperor Augustus at Muziris in central Kerala or Malabar (Kodungallur, or Pattanam village) with a garrison of two cohorts and 1,200 men. Besides, the rulers of the Pandya and the Chera kingdoms seem to have sent more than one embassy to Rome. The one to Augustus was noticed by Strabo. However, with the dissolution of the Roman Empire from the fourth century onwards, Roman and Greek Maritime trade expeditions to the Indian Ocean area literally came to an end. The Persians reasserted themselves in the third century AD through the Sassanians, who defeated the Romans in AD 260 and managed to banish the Roman vessels from the eastern waters.[9]

The Chinese had knowledge of the Chera country and Malabar in the early part of the fifth century. During the year AD 414, the Chinese pilgrim, Fa-Hien left a record of his voyage to India and Ceylon. In Ceylon, he had noticed the wealth of the 'Sa-po traders' who was in all likelihood Arabs from the Hadramaut and Omani coasts. Though Fa-Hien did not allude to Malabar directly, he had met people from *Po-lo-man*, i.e the Malabar Coast. He also mentioned about his meeting with the people of *Po-lo-man* in a ship bound from Java to Canton. *Po-lo-man* was a name used during those days by the Chinese to designate the west coast of India from Quilon, or Kollam to the mouth of Indus. This would imply that the ancient Chera Kingdom, which flourished on the southwest coast of India upto about AD 500 had a direct trade relations not only with West Asia, but also with Southeast Asia and East Asia, i.e. China. This seems to give the lie to the contention that Indians did not travel across the seas to foreign countries for the purpose of trade during the ancient period.[10]

In the sixth century, Cosmas Indicopleustes had mentioned in his book a port named 'Male', where pepper was traded. Actually, Indicopleustes gave a twist to the earlier *Meli* and *Mili* of the Greeks and called the country, where pepper was grown as 'Malé'. He also drew attention to the ports of Mangarouth (Mangaluru), Salapatana, Nalopatana and Poudopatana on the coast of *Kottonariké*, i.e. the pepper country. The latter three ports were definitely in north Malabar and were not parts of the Chera Empire, which had ceased to exist around AD 500. Poudopatana seems to be the Poudoperoura of Ptolemy and *Kottonariké* was of course the country of pepper.[11]

Indicopleustes also gave an account of the horse-trade carried on between Persia Gulf and Malabar. He further referred to a settlement of Nestorian Christians, which proved that Christianity had arrived in Malabar already. He also referred to Ethiopia and Aden which was a principal port in West Asia from where ships set sail to Sind India and China. The Nestorian Patriarch Jesujabus (Ishoyahb III) who died in AD 660 had made a special mention of Quilon (Columbum) in his letter to the Simon, Metropolitan of Fars (Persia). He contended that India extended from the coast of the kingdom of Fars to Colon (Quilon).[12] Moreover, there is ample evidence to show that regular trade relations existed between the Cheras and China even before the end of the Chera period.

But in none of the preceding accounts do we find any reference to the geographical extension of the Chera country. We do not know if it included all parts of today's Keralam or just the southern or middle parts of it.[13]

About a century later after Cosmas, in the year AD 629 the Chinese pilgrim Huan-Tsang visited India. He had reached the Cholamandalam coast and called the Malabar country as *Mo-lo-ku-tsa* which in Sanskrit meant *Malakuta* (group of mountains). The form *Mo-la-ye* or Malaya became popular at about the same time. During the Sung Period, Quilon was called by the Chinese as *Ku-lin*, and during the Yuan period it was known as *Ku-lan*. However, Huan-Tsang was not aware of the intercourse existing between Malabar and Ceylon and the countries to the East, like Sumatra, Java and Indo-China. Huan-Tsang spent 17 years in the country.

Huan-Tsang was followed by an another Chinese pilgrim during the later part of the seventh century, I-tsing. He mentioned about the Chinese junks going to south India during this period from Canton. According to the records of the Tang dynasty (618-913), Quilon was the chief port of the Chera land for the Chinese traders. However, the Chinese travellers and accounts before the seventh century do not throw any light on the northern part of Malabar, which included Cananore, Ezhimala and Kasaragod.[14]

We find from the narratives of the celebrated Arabian traveller and historian al-Masudi, who wrote at the beginning of the tenth century, and that of Ibn Haukal, also an Arabian traveller, who visited India shortly after al-Masudi, that the Arabs in the course of seventh and eighth centuries made several descents upon the coasts of Guzerat (Gujarat), the gulf of Cambay and Malabar, and had a limited commerce with the country.

Sindbad the sailor in his fourth voyage described an island (all the countries were regarded as island by him). Though he gave no name to the island, however, he recounted that he found there 'men gathering pepper'. This most certainly represented the coast of Malabar.[15]

REFERENCES TO KERALA IN ANCIENT TAMIL LITERATURE

In ancient Tamil literature, *Keralan* was one of the glorious Tamil titles of the kings of the Chera kingdom. As a matter of fact, the word *Keralam* itself seems to have been derived from *Keralan*, which means 'Master of the country of Keralam'. Maridas Poullé, the pioneer Indologist of the eighteenth century, who preceded William Jones, has noted this historical fact in his work.[16] However, the territorial limits of Keralam or *Cheranadu* were never clearly specified in olden times.

The Tamil anthology *Pathirruppattu* (the Ten Tens) was composed or compiled about 2,000 years before. It is a historical account of several kings of the Chera dynasty and their deeds and achievements. The author has divided the entire work into ten books, of which the first and last are unavailable. It sang the glory of the various Chera kings till about AD 300. Though the geographical extent of the Chera Kingdom, included the southwestern coastal lands of present-day Keralam as well as parts of western Tamil Nadu, there is nothing in the *Pathirruppattu*, which allows us to affirm invariably that all parts of northern Keralam, or Malabar were included in the ancient Chera Kingdom. It is worth mentioning that Ilango Adigal, was the brother of the famous Chera king Cenkuttuvan and the second son of King Ceralathan reigning at Vanji (presently identified with Karur in Tamil Nadu), who composed the *Cilappatikaram* around AD 200. However, even in this Sangam era Epic, the exact geographical extent of the Chera Kingdom has never been specified.[17]

Astonishingly, a king or chieftain of northern Malabar called *purikho* had patronized a collection of short love poems attributed to as many as 205 Tamil poets under the title, *Kurunthokai*. Even the *Aingurunuru*, meaning 'short five hundred', was compiled at the instance of the Chera king, Cheraman Irumporai.

On the contrary, in other Tamil anthologies like the *Akananuru*, it has been expressly stated that a king or chief called Nannan ruled from Ezhilkunram in northern Malabar. We do not know if *purikho* was the same as *nannan*, or two different chiefs/kings of northern Malabar. While historians like Elamkulam Kunjan Pillai claimed that *nannan* was at the head of a kingdom, others like Gurukkal, Ganesh and Raghava Warrier reduced *nannan* to the status of a tribal chief at the head of chiefdom. It should be noted that Romila Thapar considered the Chera, Chola and Pandyan kingdoms of the Sangam period as mere chiefdoms though this appears to be a bit far-fetched and without literary or epigraphic foundation.[18]

Whatever may be the truth, Ezhilkunram has been identified by historians with the more recent Ezhimala on the northern Malabar coast. It is believed that Nannan's kingdom comprised most certainly of many neighbouring regions like Madayi, Sreekantapuram, Taliparamba, Payyanur, Cananore and Valapattanam. These regions were made up of hilly slopes, forests, wet lands, pastoral tracts, fertile paddy lands, streams, fresh water channels and river belts.

In another Tamil anthology of 583 lines called *Malaipadukadam*, or *Kuttararruppadai*, the achievements of Nannan were portrayed vividly. There are references to his ancestors as well as his court. This work also referred to a Siva shrine in Naviram hill in the Kingdom of Nannan, and also the agricultural products, mountains and gardens found therein. However, the Tamil anthologies do not give us the geographical extent of *nannan's* kingdom or chiefdom, except for the fact that it was situated in northern Kerala or Malabar, with Ezhilkunram as capital.

I do not think that the Tamil anthologies would have given so much importance to *nannan* had he not been a powerful ruler of a kingdom at the northwestern end of Tamilakam. Further importance was also given to a hill named Naviram, where there was a Siva shrine on the hilltop, which threw light on the prevalence of the Siva cult in the area about 2,000 years back. In the ancient Sangam literatures that date back to more than 2,000 years like the *Tolkappiyam* and *Purananuru*, Lord Siva is mentioned. It could be said that the Shaivaite cult was prevalent in northern Malabar even before the penetration of the Nambudiris and the Brahmanical literature into the area.[19]

EZHILKUNRAM OF NORTH MALABAR (KOLATTUNADU)

Ezhilkunram, which in Tamil would mean 'beautiful hill', was always jutting into the sea and its valley was always washed by the waves of the sea. The *Akananuru* tells us that there was a harbour near to the hill, known as *Perumthurai* (meaning big port), which was frequented by numerous foreign ships. It also tells us about the presence of pirates to the south of Ezhilkunram above Muziris who plundered the ships in distress, which inadvertently encroached into other territories deviating from their original route. This has been confirmed during the first century AD by the Roman writer Pliny, who had alluded to the port of Muziris in the country of the Caelobothras (Cheras). He recounted that it was not a desired place of call as its neighbourhood, known as *Nitrias* was infested with pirates. Over and above this pitfall, the approach to the shore and transloading facility at that port was also not efficient. Another disadvantage was that this shore was not equipped with supplies of wares for sea traffic. As a result, the ships had to anchor far off the coast, which was a glaring drawback.

Pliny the Elder also mentioned the seaport of Sigerus on the Malabar Coast. In Arabia, we find the Syagros promontory (Ras Fartak) which was pointed out by Strabo and also mentioned in *The Periplus of Erythrean Sea*. It is quite possible that Pliny had chosen to use a similar name—Sigerus to refer to the Ezhimala cape, which was the promontory of spices. It is also possible to equate Sigerus with Meli-Zeigara of *The Periplus* and the Mili-Zegyris of Ptolemy. *Meli* and *Mili* could have been derived from *mala*, which meant hill or mountain, or else it could be a corruption of *ezhi* in Ezhil-kunram or Ezhimala; though Zeigara and Zegyris resemble the Syagros promontory of Arabia region.

Clearer indications emerge from *Periplus* written about AD 80 that all the ports on the western coast carried out flourishing trade in local products like peppercorns, other spices, coir, and coral with foreign countries. Though their principal item of export was of course pepper which according to *The Periplus* was abundant in the *Kottonariké* district, i.e. Malabar. Similarly, Pliny too mentioned the pepper country as *Cottonara*. A.C. Burnell had identified Cottonara with Kolatta-*nadu*, i.e. north Malabar (Kannur-Kasaragod region), while Dr. Buchanan had preferred to equate it with Kadatta-*nadu*, which was south Malabar, on either side of Calicut. *Nara* in Cottonara may be derived from *nadu* meaning country while there is greater possibility of Cotto being a corruption of Kolatta. The suffix *ké* in *Kottonariké* meant 'land' or 'country' in Greek language.

It is also significant to note at this juncture that in ancient Tamil, *Kolakam* meant 'long pepper'. Thus, it is quite possible that the country of *kolakam* became Kolatta-*nadu*, and one who ruled that *nadu* became Kolatiri, i.e. 'Lord of Pepper'.[20]

It is quite obvious from the above that the Greek, Roman, and Arab sailors who came to the Malabar Coast from Persia, Egypt and the Arab heartlands, were familiar with Ezhilkunram or Ezhimala, which meant the same thing. Though *ezhi* might have been a difficult word to retain for these sailors in Ezhimala, they seem to have definitely retained the word *mala* or *Eli*, not just to signify Meli-Zeigara or Mili-Zegyris, but also to signify the entire pepper country and coast in the course of time. Thus, Meli-Zeigara or Mili-Zegyris seems to have given birth to the words *mali* or *male* or *mala* in the course of time.[21]

The Periplus had also mentioned the port of Barake or Ela Baraké which was much frequented on account of pepper and betel nuts procured in great quantities there. This pepper was known as pepper of Cottonara. The port of Ela Baraké might possibly be identified with Elimala, though we do not have much further evidence for that.

The Periplus also referred to the ports of Naura, Tyndis and Muziris as the first marts of Damiriké; *Ké* in Greek would mean land or nation, as we have seen. Therefore, Damiriké could signify lands of the *Damirs*, i.e. the *Tamizhars* (Tamils).

Naura is identified with Cananore of *Damiriké* in the northern Malabar coast.[22]

Towards the north of Naura, the *Periplus* mentioned the port of Meli-Zeigara, Balepatna, and beyond that Mandagara. Besides, Ptolemy (AD 150) had described Madai. We have seen that Melizeigara could signify Ezhimala. Mandagara might be Mangaluru. Ptolemy too has mentioned Mandagara. Further south of Naura, beyond Tyndis were Muziris and Nelcynda. Tyndis has been identified with Tondi or Ponnani and Muziris had been equated with Muyirikotta, or Kodungalur. They were located within the limits of the Chera kingdom of Cerobothros (Ptolemy) or Keprobotos (*Periplus*) or Caelobothras (Pliny), Nelcynda belonged to the Pandyan kingdom. No doubt the kingdom of Cerobothra was the Chera country, with the inland town Karur, which stood opposite Muziris as its capital. Muziris belonging to the kingdom of Keprobotos (the kingdom of the Cheras) was a flourishing port to which traders from west Asia came in ships. These traders who were generally Greeks, also included Arabs during the pre-Islamic era.[23] Obviously, the Cheras were one of the three legendary fraternal Tamil ruling dynasties of south India. Naura, which was located to the north of Tyndis and south of Ezhilkunram or Ezhimala was out of the limits of the Chera kingdom. It was known to have been an active port in the days of the Roman trade as it has yielded one of the most important finds of Roman coins of the reigns of Tiberius, Claudius and Nero.[24]

Ezhilkunram was the name given to the coastal Malabar town in classical Tamil anthologies like *Akananuru* and *Purananuru* by Tamil Sangam poet, Paranar. However, they do not give us much information about King Nannan himself or his ancestry and the origin or the extent of his power over the people of the region and the lands. The terms, such as *Nannan nalnadu* and *Nannan parambu* that appears in *Akananuru* could mean that Nannan ruled over those lands. We do not find any instances in the anthologies about the inhabitants paying taxes to King Nannan. However, the latter was portrayed as extremely rich and resourceful. He has been described in the *Akananuru* as a ruler who possessed much gold and his city *Pazhi* on top of Ezhilkunram, was known for its gold treasure. P.N. Kunjan Pillai thinks that *Pazhi* was the *pattanam* or capital of Nannan, though he provides no corroborating evidence to buttress his assertion.[25]

It will be worth noting that besides the Tamil anthologies, the writings of *Periplus* and Ptolemy revealed that Nannan's kingdom, situated in northern Kerala, in the area that later evolved as the Kolatiri kingdom, was not part of the Chera country from the very beginning. It seems to be the earliest independent political entity of northern Malabar. As Nannan's kingdom was wealthy owing mainly to its trade contacts with foreigners through its own ports, and due to piracy in the vicinity of Muziris, it seems to have invited the attention of the southern Chera ruler Narimudi Cheralathan who seems to have put an end to Nannan's power. But there is no record or literature that clearly established the over lordship of the Chera king over north Malabar, though Naravu, i.e. Naura seems to have come under the control of the Cheras at least temporarily. As a matter of fact, the *Akananuru* tells us that Nannan's dynasty continued even after his death and his kingdom was never annexed by the Chera king. In fact, the anthologies reveal that after the demise of Nannan of Ezhilkunram, his son Nannan Uthiyan succeeded him. Murkot Ramunny thinks that Nannan's kingdom of northern Malabar extended to the Western Ghats including Wayanad and Gudaloor, upto the present Coimbatore in Tamil Nadu, though he provided no corroborative evidence. [26]

Whether the latter became a vassal of the Chera king or was independent like his father has not been established. Looking back, it is very important to take note of the wealth comprising of gold of Nannan and Ezhilkunram. It is also noticed that no wealth (income) was yielded from land, in the absence of land records. Over and above, there is no evidence about gold being produced in Ezhilkunram region, though in nearby Wayanad region, gold seems to have been mined in ancient times. However, the bulk of the gold discovered there must have been brought in by foreign traders. The Roman gold coins of first century AD found in Kottayam Poyil, near Koothuparamba in Kannur district and the more recent findings of gold remains in Naduvil stands testimony to the fact that Ezhilkunram had trade relations with foreign countries.[27]

As a matter of fact, Pliny was particularly worried that gold worth about a million pounds a year was finding its way to southern India from Rome. Some of this gold definitely found its way to Ezhilkunram. This fact seems to account more for its wealth and opulence than any other factor. As far as the wealth obtained from piracy and looting of foreign ships were concerned, we do not have any records to prove that Nannan had a major share in the loot and even if it was so, it could not account for such immense wealth of north Malabar.[28]

As far as the etymological origin of Ezhimala is concerned, it appears certain that the ancient Ezhilkunram of north Malabar had evolved into Ezhimala or even into Elimala in the course of time. Ezhilkunram, or Ezhimala simply meant 'beautiful mountain' or 'high mountain'. Its identification with *Sapta-saila* or seven hills as found in the Sanskritic text *Kerala Mahatmayam*, and with the 'rat hill' are meaningless and without foundation and was a later interpolation. Elimala was actually a long narrow hill about two and half miles long from north to south, and half-a-mile broad, jutting out into the sea, with its highest peak at 851 feet. The king of this region, i.e. north Malabar during early times was Nannan and his descendants. But later in the sixteenth century, it was the Kolatiris and the language spoken then was 'Maliama'.[29]

FROM NAURA TO KANNUR

During the later years, Francis Buchanan who visited Cananore and Malabar noted that the proper name of Cananore was *Canura*. This was in accordance with the findings of Ptolemy who mentioned Naura which might be Cananore. The French traveller Auguste Toussaint had remarked at the end of the eighteenth century that the last port before arriving at the tip of Mont Deli, where the coast of Kanara began was Cananore or *Kanoura* at the bottom of the small bar with the same name. He alluded to *Kanoura* being the same as the Naura in Ptolemy. He further mentioned that *Kanaura* was a city very vast and densely populated.[30]

Kanaura today is just about 18 miles south of Ezhilkunram. However, there is no corroborating evidence in literature or in inscriptions to attest that Naura or Kanaura was Kannur itself. There seems to be a strong possibility that Naura was within the independent domains of Nannan in north Malabar, as it was located near Ezhilkunram, the classical name of Ezhimala. Naravu appears in the *Patirruppattu* as a port city were plundering tribal groups were active. This Naravu might be the Naura in Pliny's work.[31]

It is also interesting to note at this juncture that in Tamil, the word *kanna* would also mean 'long pepper' and *ur* in ancient Tamil meant town or dwelling place. If we put together '*kanna*' and '*ur*', it gives Kannur, which as we know is a town, situated in the vicinity of Ezhimala, which might just mean 'pepper town'. Besides that Kannur could also be derived from Kannanur, which meant 'the town of Lord Krishna'.

Naura which had been identified with Kannur (or Cananore) by Schoff and Majumdar was within the southern limits of north Malabar. However, it must be noted at this juncture, that apart from the reference in the ancient Greek literature to Naura, and the reference to *Naravu* in *Patirruppaattu*, there is no other inscriptional or literary evidence in Tamil or Sanskrit to attest that the modern Kannur town actually existed as a port in ancient times.

Nevertheless, from the preceding, it appears certain that Nannan's kingdom or north Malabar had been always historically an independent political entity from the earliest times, if we take into account all the ancient literature available in Tamil and the accounts of the Romans and Greeks. There is dearth of literary or inscriptional evidence to establish that it was part of the ancient Chera Empire, whose kings have been enumerated in the *Pathithiruppaattu*. Even Paranar, who had sung the glories of the Chera king, Senguttuvan, had never uttered a word about Nannan being a vassal of the Chera kingdom Nannan.

NOTES

1. Anjengo Factory Records 1704-49, Simon Cowse, Anjengo to the Court of Directors, June 1704, p. 5, TNA; O.K. Nambiar, *Our Seafaring in the Indian Ocean*, Bangalore, 1975, pp. 8-14 ; Jacob Canter Visscher, *Letters from Malabar*, Madras, 1862, p. 153; James Forbes, *Oriental Memoires*, London, 1813, 1834, vol. I, pp. 219, 221.
2. Murkot Ramunny, *Ezhimala, the Abode of the Naval Academy*, New Delhi, 1993, pp. 8-9; S. Krishnasami Aiyangar, Commemoration volume, Madras, 1936, p. 233; Louis Renou and Jean Filliozat, *l'Inde Classique*, vol. I (French), Paris, 1947, p. 20.
3. H. Gundert, *A Malayalam and English Dictionary*, Germany, 1970, p. 318; M.G.S. Narayanan, *Perumals of Kerala: Political and Social Conditions of Kerala under the Cera Perumals of Makotai (AD 800-1124)*, Calicut, 1996, p. vi; Wilfred Schoff, *The Periplus of the Erythrean Sea*, New York, 1912, pp. 44-5, 204-8; K.N. Ganesh, 'Writing the History of Pre-Modern Kerala: A Study in the Transition of Historical Consciousness', in Mujeebu Rehman, K.S. Madhavan (eds.), *Explorations in South Indian History*, Kottayam, 2014, pp. 48-9.
4. Truesdell S. Brown, *Onesicritus: A Study in Hellenistic Historiography, Periplus of the Erethrean Sea*, Berkeley, 1949, pp. 22, 54, 58 (fn.), 100-2; Iliff Robson, B.D. (tr.), *Arrian: Anabasis Alexandri*, in 2 vols., Cambridge, 1933, 1949, 1958, 1966, MCMLXVI, p. 151.
5. G.W.B. Huntingford, tr. & ed., *The Periplus of the Erythrean Sea*, London, 1980, p. 50; R. Caldwell, *A Comparative Grammar of the Dravidian or South Indian Family of Languages*, New Delhi, 1987, p. 14; E. Iliff Robson (tr.), *Arrian, Annabasis of Alexandri*, in 2 vols., op. cit., p. 329; O.K. Nambiar, *Our Seafaring in the Indian Ocean*, Bangalore, 1975, p. 31; Robert Sewell, *A Sketch of the Dynasties of Southern India*, Madras, 1883, pp. 1, 13.
6. William Vincent, *The Periplus of the Erythrean sea*, vol. II, London, 1807, pp. 60-1; R. Beagley, *Dawn of Modern Geography*, London, 1897, p. 490; Hirth and Rockhill, tr. with annotations, *Chau Ju Kua:*

His Work on the Chinese and Arab Trade in the 12th and 13th Centuries, entitled Chu-fan Chi, St. Petersburg, 1911, pp. 9, 14, 16; G.F. Hourani, *Arab Seafaring in the Indian Ocean in the Ancient and Medieval Times*, Princeton, 1951, p. 61; Ahmed Nafis, 'Arab Knowledge of Ceylon', *Islamic Culture*, XIX, 1945, p. 224; Dabry de Thiersant, *Mahometans en Chine*, vol. I, pp. 86-7; E.O. Winstedt, *The Christian Topography of Cosmas Indicopleustes*, Cambridge, 1909, pp. 119, 365.

7. G.F. Hourani, op. cit., p. 29; P.T. Srinivasa Iyengar, *History of the Tamils from the Earliest Times to AD 600*, Madras, 1989, pp. 298, 305-12, 317; Pliny the Elder, *Natural History* VI, tr. W.H.S. Jones, Cambridge, 1989, p. 26; Strabo, *The Geography of Strabo* VII, London, 1966, p. 5; O.K. Nambiar, *Our Seafaring in the Indian Ocean*, Bangalore, 1975, p. 28.
8. R.H. Major, *India in the Fifteenth Century*, op. cit., pp. vi-vii; O.K. Nambiar, ibid., pp. 11, 30; O.K. Nambiar , *An Illustrated Maritime History of the Indian Ocean*, Delhi, 2013, p. 11.
9. Nagam Aiya, *The Travancore State Manual*, Madras, 1989, p. 242; P.T. Srinivasa Iyengar, op. cit., p. 312; Jouveau-Dubreuil, 'The Temple of Augustus in the South of India', *The Quarterly Journal of the Mythic Society*, 19, 1929, pp. 180-1; E.H. Warmington, *The Commerce between the Roman Empire and India*, Cambridge, 1928, pp. 60-2, 137-8; H.G. Rawlinson, *Intercourse between India and the Western World*, Cambridge, 1916, pp. 121-56; David Morgan, *Medieval Persia 1040-1787*, London, 1988, pp. 1, 10.
10. Colonel Yule, (tr. & ed.), *Cathay and the Way Thither*, vol. I, London, MDCCCLXVI, p. xvvii; Rockhill and Hirth, *Chau-Ju-Kua*, St. Petersburg, 1911, pp. 2-8; Sayed Mohammed Husayn Nainar, *Arab Geographers: Knowledge of Southern India*, Calicut, 2011, p. 16.
11. J.W. McCrindle, tr. & ed., *Ancient India as Described in Classical Literature*, Amsterdam, 1971, pp. 161, 161fn., 165; O.K. Nambiar, *Our Seafaring in the Indian Ocean*, Bangalore, 1975, p. 32; K.P. Padmanabha Menon, *History of Kerala*, vol. 1, Madras, 1989, p. 1; O.K. Nambiar, *An Illustrated Maritime History of Indian Ocean*, New Delhi, 2013, op. cit., p. 12.
12. Tan Ta Sen, *Cheng Ho and Islam in South East Asia*, Singapore, 2009, p. 144; Hirth and Rockhill, trs., op. cit., pp. 2-4, 7, 12; James Legge (tr.), *Fa Hien, A Record of Buddhist Kingdoms*, New York, 1965, pp. 12, 111-15; E.O. Winstedt, *The Christian Topography of Cosmas Indicopleustes*, Cambridge, 1909, pp. 3-4, 6, 244, 338, 345, 354, 355, Nagam Aiya, Ibid., p. 243.

13. G. Bouchon, *L'Asie du Sud à l'époque des Grandes Découvertes*, vol. III, London, 1987, p. 9; Robert Sewell, Ibid., pp. 1, 1fn., 240; A. Sreedhara Menon, *A Survey of Kerala History*, Kottayam, 1967, p. 123; M.G.S. Narayanan, *Perumals of Kerala: Political and Social Conditions of Kerala under the Cera Perumals of Makotai (AD 800-1124)*, Calicut, 1996, p. vi.
14. F. Hirth and W.W. Rockhill (tr.), *Chau-Ju-Kua*, St. Petersburg, 1912, pp. 8-9; Nagam Aiya, *The Travancore State Manual*, Madras, 1989, p. 244; G.F. Hourani, op. cit., p. 62; Tan Ta Sen, op. cit.; Hirth and Rockhill (trs.), op. cit., pp. 2-4, 7, 12; James Legge (tr.), *Fa Hien, A Record of Buddhist Kingdoms*, New York, 1965, pp. 12, 111-15; E.O. Winstedt, *The Christian Topography of Cosmas Indicopleustes*, Cambridge, 1909, pp. 3-4, 6, 244, 338, 345, 354-5; Nagam Aiya, Ibid., p. 243.
15. R.H. Major, *India in the Fifteenth Century*, op. cit., pp. xxxiii-xiv; E.F. Oaten, *European Travelers in India*, Madras, 1991, pp. 14-15.
16. J.B.P. More (ed.), *La Civilisation Indienne et les Fables Hindoues du Panchatantra* (by Maridas Poullé), Pondicherry, 2004, p. 61.
17. Cf. Caminatayer, U.Ve. (ed.), *Patirruppattu*, Madras, 1980; Ramachandra Dikshitar, *Studies in Tamil Literature and History*, Madras, 1936, pp. 28, 70; R. Parthasarathy (tr.), *The Cilappatikaram of Ilanko Adikal: An Epic of South India*, Columbia, 1993; Revd. Robert Caldwell, op. cit., p. 11.
18. Elamkulam P.N. Kunjan Pillai, *Studies in Kerala History*, Kottayam, 1970, pp. 41-50; *Keralam Anjum Arum Nootandukalil*, Kottayam, 1961, pp. 70-91; Romila Thapar, 'Early Mediterranean Contacts with India: An Overview', in F. De Romanis and A. Thernia (eds.), *Crossings: Early Mediterranean Contacts with India*, New Delhi, 1997, p. 20; Rajan Gurukkal and Raghava Varier, *Cultural History of Kerala*, I, Thiruvananthapuram, 1999, p. 200.
19. Ibid.; K.V. Zvelebil, *A History of Indian Literature: Tamil Literature*, Wiesbaden, 1974, pp. 49-50; Cf. R. Nagaswamy, *Mirror of Tamil and Sanskrit*, Chennai, 2012.
20. R.H. Major, op. cit., p. vii; K.P. Rajesh, 'Agro-Pastoralism and the Early Chiefdom of Ezhimala, North Kerala', in Mujeebu Rehman, K.S. Madhavan (eds.), *Explorations in South Indian History*, Kottayam, 2014, pp. 191-214.
21. *Akananuru*, 258: 6, 345:7-8, 152: 6, 13, 4-7; J.W. McCrindle., tr. & ed., *Ancient India as described in Classical Literature*, Amsterdam, 1971, pp. 111, 111fn., 112; F. De Romanis and A. Thernia, eds.,

op. cit., pp. 85, 87, 104-5; William Vincent, trs., *The Periplus of the Erythrean Sea*, London, 1807, p. 182; R.C. Majumdar, *The Classical Accounts of India*, Calcutta, 1968, pp. 297, 311, 337; cf. Louis Renou, *La Géographie de Ptolemée*, Paris, 1925; J.B.P. More, *From Arikamedu to the Foundation of Modern Pondicherry*, Madras, 2014, pp. 14, 163.

22. G.W.B. Huntingford (tr. & ed.), *The Periplus of the Erythrean Sea*, London, 1980, pp. 50, fol. 85, 115; J.W. McCrindle (ed.), *The Commerce and Navigation of the Erythrean Sea*, London, 1870, fol. 126, fol. 130; W.H. Schoff (ed. & tr.), *The Periplus of the Erythrean Sea*, New York, 1912, pp. 43-4, 204-5, 208; R.C. Majumdar, op. cit., pp. 305, 312, 365, 381, William Vincent, tr., *Periplus of the Erythrean Sea, The Commerce and Navigation of the Ancients on the Indian Ocean in Two Volumes*, vol. II, London, 1807, pp. 456-8.
23. Wilfred Schoff (ed. & tr.), *The Periplus of the Erythrean Sea*, London, 1912, p. 32; Hirth and Rockhill (tr. with annotations), *Chau Ju Kua: His Work on the Chinese and Arab Trade in the 12th and 13th Centuries, entitled 'Chu-fan Chi'*, St. Petersburg, 1911, pp. 1-2; G.W.B. Huntingford (tr. & ed.), *The Periplus of the Erythrean Sea*, London, 1980, pp. 50-3, William Logan, *Malabar Manual*, I, Madras, 1951, p. 147; A. Sreedhara Menon, *Kerala District Gazetteers*, Trivandrum, 1972, pp. 62-3; William Vincent (tr.), op. cit., p. 429; J.W. McCrindle, Ibid., London, 1870, p. 6, 132, fol. 132, fol. 133.
24. W.H. Schoff (ed. & tr.), op. cit., pp. 43-4, 204-5, 208; R.C. Majumdar, Ibid., pp. 305, 312, 365, 381.
25. *Tamil Lexicon*, vol. 2, Madras, 1982, pp. 693, 1194-5; *Akananuru*, 349: 8; 356: 8; 15 (*Palai* song), 208 (*Kurinji* song) and 396 (*Marutham* song); 15: 10-11, 396: 1-3; K.P. Rajesh, op. cit., p. 203; Elamkulam P.N. Kunjan Pillai, op. cit., 1970, pp. 45-7; W.H. Schoff, op. cit., pp. 44-5, 221; R.C. Majumdar, op. cit., 1968, pp. 305, 339; *Tamil Lexicon*, II, pp. 693, 1194-5; G. Bouchon, *Mamale de Cananor—Un adversaire de l'Inde Portugaise (1507-1528)*, Paris, 1975, p. 2.
26. J.W. McCrindle, op. cit., pp. 48-50; *Akananuru* 199: 19-24; 258: 1-5; K.P. Rajesh, op. cit., pp. 205-6, 208; Elamkulam P.N. Kunjan Pillai, op. cit., 1970, pp. 50-1; F. De Romanis and A. Tchernia, (eds.) op. cit., pp. 90-8, 103-5; *Patirruppattu*, 60, 11-12; 85, 7-8; K.N. Sivaraja Pillai, *Chronology of the Early Tamils Based on the Synchronic Tables of their Kings, Chieftains and the Poets Appearing in the Sangam Literature*, Madras, 1932, pp. 137, 172; Murkot

Ramunny, *Ezhimala—The Abode of the Naval Academy*, New Delhi, 1993, pp. 1-3.

27. Robert Sewell, *A Sketch of the Dynasties of Southern India*, Madras, 1882, p. 240.
28. K.P. Rajesh, op. cit., pp. 203-4; Pliny, the Elder, *Natural History*, VI, tr. W.H.S. Jones, Cambridge, 1989, p. 26.
29. M.L. Dames, *The Book of Duarte Barbosa*, vol. 2, 1921, pp. 1, 6; cf. also, Yule and Burnell, *Hobson-Jobson*, 1903; *Tamil Lexicon*, Madras, 1982, p. 539; S. Koumareeshwari (ed.), *Aganannuru, Purananuru, Sanga Ilakkiyam*, vol. 3, Chennai, 2012, p. 243.
30. Francis Buchanan, *A Journey from Madras Through the Countries of Mysore, Canara and Malabar*, vol. II, London, 1807, p. 553; August Toussaint, *L'Ocean Indien au XVIIIe Siecle*, Paris, 1974, p. 121.
31. E.H. Warmington, *The Commerce Between the Roman Empire and India*, New Delhi, 1995, p. 57; J.W. McCrindle, *Ancient India as Described by Ptolemy*, New Delhi, 1884, pp. 6-10, 47-50, 111; Elamkulam P.N. Kunjan Pillai, op. cit., 1970, p. 49; M.P. Kumaran, *Kolathupazhama*, Trissur, 1998, pp. 24-9; K.P. Rajesh, op. cit., p. 204; *Akananuru*, 60, 7; *Kuruntokai*, 128, 2; *Patirruppattu*, 60, 11-12; 85, 7-8.

CHAPTER 3

Mushika Nadu

A major historical event occurred during the seventh century AD, which was the birth and spread of Islam across the world. Arab tribes unified and energized by this religion seized Persia, Syria, Palestine, North Africa, and Spain and made themselves masters of the trade routes to India. Thenceforth, Arab seafaring became more extensive and regular in the Indian Ocean.[1] Between AD 622 and 632, the Prophet Muhammad is believed to have written to the crown heads of several countries with which the Arabs had close trade relations. According to some historians, such a letter was also dispatched to the Malabar king. However, there is no credible evidence for this. During this period, the second Chera dynasty had not even come into existence and the first Chera dynasty had ceased to exist.[2]

The ancient Chinese were totally ignorant of the country of origin of certain products that came to their ports in those days. They thought that all the products from the East came from Persia. Even black pepper and long pepper (known as *Kola*), which came to their shores was thought to have come from Persia (*Po-ssi*). In reality, those were the products of Malabar. As noted already, Nannan and his successors in north Malabar were already trading from their territories in Malabar in these products.[3]

The second Chera kingdom (AD 900-1124) of the Perumals of Kerala came into existence with its capital in Makotai or Mahodayapuram (Kodungallur). It did not comprise of Kongunadu (western Tamil Nadu) like the ancient one. It was founded by Rajasekara in the first half of the ninth century, who was known by the title Cheraman Perumal Nayannar, typically a Tamil title, denoting his origin. Narayanan had claimed that the new Chera kingdom comprised of North Kerala or Malabar also. This new Chera dynasty seemed to have continued till the year AD 1122 at least, when it disappeared mysteriously. He claimed further that the last Perumal, Rama Kulasekhara disappeared under mysterious circumstances, making it impossible to provide for accession to the throne. Narayanan has pointed out that there was no reason to reject the old tradition that the Chera King (Rama Kulasekhara) embraced Islam and went to Mecca. According to him, they need not have concocted such a tale which in no way enhanced the prestige or furthered the interest of the Brahmins of Keralam.[4] We will go into these assertions later in the course of this work.

NORTHERN MALABAR IN ARAB AND PERSIAN ACCOUNTS

Several travellers had visited Kerala and Malabar during the ninth and tenth centuries. Of them the most renowned were the Arab merchants Sulaiman al-Tajir, al-Masudi and Ibn Khordadbeh.

As cited earlier, Onesicritus, the pilot of Alexander's ship had mentioned about the land of Musicanus. Surprisingly, the word 'Musicanus' is frequently used in the Greek accounts. It is pointed out that it is really the name of a people rather than the name of a King. Hence, there is a probability that this word might be Hellenized form of the Indian 'Mushika', the southern part of India.[5]

Sulaiman al-Tajir's (AD 851) travelogue gives us a glimpse into the socio-political, cultural, religious and economic conditions in India. Al-Tajir is said to have explored the Indian Ocean and rounded the entire coastline of India. He emphatically stated that he did not know any single Chinese or Indian, who had embraced Islam or knew Arabic. But in another place, he added that the princes of India were kind and affectionate and friendly towards the Arabs. This is a standing testimony of the presence of Arabs on the Malabar Coast during the ninth century.[6]

Sulaiman further asserted that it took a month to cross the Arabian Sea from Muscat to Kaukammali. The latter seems to be nothing, but Quilon or Kollam with the suffix-*mali* added to it as it had become the tradition since Ptolemy's time. He referred to a famous king on the west coast of India called Balahara, who had his ears bored. This might be the monarch of the second Chera dynasty of Mahodayapuram, or Kodungallur. He claimed that many other neighbouring kings were at war with him. Despite of this, the Arabs enjoyed great favour in his dominions. He actually visited Koulam (Quilon) and proceeded to visit the house and church of Saint Thomas in Maliapur (Mylapore), where Saint Thomas, the Apostle of Jesus Christ, was said to be buried.[7]

Sulaiman particularly referred to the King of Harez whose dominions were on a promontory. This kingdom situated on the promontory jutting into the Arabian Sea seems to be nothing, but the old Ezhimala Kingdom of Nannan in north Malabar. Sulaiman claimed that this kingdom was rich with numerous forces and had more horses than the other princes, but was unfriendly with the Arabs. Sulaiman's account testified that the ruler of Ezhimala was not subject or tributary to the Chera king, but was an independent king in his own right in north Malabar. Therefore, it is apparent that in the ninth-century north Malabar, or Harez was not part of the Chera kingdom.[8] Unfortunately, we do not have any further details about the rulers of Harez in the literature of the period concerned, though it seems that they might be the descendants of Nannan's successors.

The Arab historian al-Masudi (AD 890-966) of Baghdad in his work *Muraj al-dhahab wa ma'adin al-jawahir* related that the principal centre of civilization was at Canooj, and its Prince was known by the title, 'Balahara'. This Balahara seems not to be the one above mentioned by Sulaiman at Tajir. There is a strong possibility that al-Masudi never visited the Malabar

Coast. Or else, he would have mentioned the king of Harez or Ezhimala or at least Kulam Male. Actually, he had met Abu Zaid of Siraf at Basra in AD 916 and exchanged information about India with him. However, he had mentioned that the ships engaged in the Sino-Arab trade passed through Kulam Male (Kollam/Quilon).[9]

From the narratives of al-Masudi and of Ibn Haukal of the tenth century who visited India briefly after al-Masudi, it could be understood that though the Arabs made several visits upon the Guzerat, Gulf of Cambay and Malabar they did not make any fixed stay at these coasts. But they erected mosques and were in the habit of publicly celebrating their five prayers in a day. According to them, the Arabs were held in high esteem in the country where Islam had begun to grow.[10]

Ibn Khordadbeh (AD 844-8), who belonged to the Iraqi school of geographers of the ninth century, in his account written in AD 846-7 titled, *Kitab al-Masalik wa'l-Mamalik* (Book of Roads and Kingdoms) where he mentioned 'Mali', where pepper and bamboo were found. *Mali* was nothing but Malabar or the mountain country. He actually alluded to the northern kingdom of Malabar and emphasized that Babattan was in that kingdom. Babattan had been identified as Baliapatam or Valarpattanam, where rice was grown. If Babattan was really Valarpattanam, then it is quite possible that the descendants of Nannan or his successors were still ruling the area. The Cananore region could have been within their domains.[11]

Al-Biruni (AD 970-1039) called the southwestern coastal region as *Melibar*. Later, al-Idrisi (AD 1153) who was born at Ceuta in Morocco travelled to India, where he wrote the *Kitab Nuzhat-ul-Mushtaq fi Ikhtiraq al-Afaq*. He affirmed in his work that in all the countries of Sindh and Hind, there were Muslims. This could mean that the Muslim community had come into existence by then in the Malabar Coast.

Further al-Idrisi in his accounts also mentioned Kulammali (Quilon) and Babattan (Valarpatnam). He further referred to the island of Malay, which according to him was an elevated plateau covered with vegetation where pepper is grown. This might be the Maldives. He also referred to Kandarina/Fandarina, which had been identified as Pantalayini, about 16 miles north of Calicut. He claimed that it was a wealthy port-town built at the mouth of a river which flowed from *Manibar*, where foreign ships anchored. Beyond Pantalayini, towards the north, he located another populous port-town called Jirbattan. He wrote that the land was fertile at Jirbattan where rice and other grains were grown. He remarked that Jirbattan exported provisions to Serendib (Ceylon). Similarly, Pepper was also available at Jirbattan which was grown in the neighbouring mountains. It is clear from this account that Jirbattan was a coastal port. This place has also been reasonably identified with Cananore.

Al-Idrisi also wrote about the southern prince called Balahara, who welcomed Arab merchants and travellers and gave them all facilities for trade, honoured their religion and treated them with respect. This Prince seems to be the Chera king (possibly Vallabha rajas), or a king belonging to the Rashtrakuta dynasty, or even north Malabar. During these years Arab merchants had settled in considerable numbers on the coast.[12]

In the late tenth century, Persian account *Hudud-al-Alam*, four towns or lands along the western coast were known by the same name Malai. This only goes to confirm that the suffix '*mala*' in Ezhimala has been systematically used to name the other west coast towns too as '*mala*' or '*mali*' by foreign travellers since the time of Ptolemy and Sulaiman al-Tajir. King Balharay, or Balahara was paramount in the Malai lands.

This king seems to be none other than the Chera ruler of Mahodayapuram. However, it is not claimed in the *Hudud* that the northern kingdom of Ezhimala was subject to the Chera king. In another work of the early eleventh century by Sharaf al-Zaman Tahir Marvazi, a king called al-Saylaman has been mentioned. This king was claimed to be greater than the Pandya and Chola kings and was credited to possess the most numerous army. Al-Saylaman might be identified with the Cheraman title of the Chera dynasty. But Marvazi does not say if the sway of the Chera kings extended to the Ezhimala kingdom of north Malabar.[13]

MUSHIKAVAMSA

Mushikavamsakavya is the earliest known historical *mahakavya* in Sanskrit language, which dealt with the regional history of North Kerala, or Malabar which pre-dated Kalhana's *Rajatarangini* of Kashmir. It was a combination of largely mythical and probably some historical references about the origin and development of Mushika Nadu or Mushika country that existed in Northern Malabar during the early medieval period since the eighth century.[14]

Mushikavamsakavya was composed in the eleventh century by Atula, the court poet of the Mushika King Srikantha of Kolam. He is assumed to be a contemporary of the great eleventh century Chola ruler Rajendra. The poem traced the history of Mushika dynasty of *Mushikaparvata* from the time of its mythical founder Ramaghata Musaka, a contemporary of Parasurama, the legendary founder of Keralam to that of Srikantha, patron of the poet Atula. Parasurama is believed to be the mythical originator of Keralam including its northern part. The Mushika kingdom was situated at the north end of Malabar near Eli hills comprising of the territory from Kasaragode to Cananore, according to M.G.S. Narayanan.[15] The founder king of the Mushika dynasty is mentioned as Ramaghata Mushika in the poem. Thus, *Mushika* became the title of the Kings of the line.

The word *Musakaparvata* is found in the *kavya* has been identified by Narayanan with Ezhimala or Elimala, which existed some 1,000 years back as Ezhil Kunram. Mushikas with the Eli Hills as their capital facing the Arabian Sea seems to have flourished for a period of three centuries from the ninth to the twelfth century AD.[16]

We have different legends about the origin of Mushikas in *Udayavarmacarita* of Ravivarman, *Keralolpatti* and *Kerala*

Mahatmayam. The term Mushika Nadu meant simply the *Nadu* of Mushikas or the country of *mushikas*. In historical studies, Mushika Nadu has been closely identified with Kolathunad of the later period. At the same time, *Mushikavamsakavya* and the *Tiruvattu* inscriptions mentioned the term Mushika Raja of Mushika denoting the name of the country and the ruling family respectively.

According to the French scholar, Geneviève Bouchon, *Mushikavamsa* owed its origin to the promontory which was believed to be infested with rats, which according to tradition were the ancestors of the Musaka sovereigns. However, all said and done, the Mushika dynasty might be after all the successors of Nannan's dynasty, though we do not know the exact connection between them in the present state of research.[17]

Atula provided a mythological origin of the Mushika dynasty tracing its descent to a Heheya queen, whose family was killed during Parasurama's slaughter of the Kshatriya rulers. The pregnant Queen initially wanted to commit suicide, but her family preceptor dissuaded her from doing so encouraging her not to destroy her unborn baby. With the help of the preceptor, the Queen fled southwards and came to the coastal region that later became the Mushika kingdom. There she was attacked by a huge rat (*mushika*), who was actually the divine spirit of the Eli mountain (Ezhimala) and had been cursed by the sage Kaushika to become a rat. The Queen burned the rat to ashes with the flame emitted from her eyes. The rat was, thus, redeemed, and became transformed into its original form. At the request of the divine spirit, the Queen started living in a cave of the mountain protected from Parasurama. There she gave birth to a boy who received education from the preceptor. By the time the Prince grew up, Parasurama had wiped the Kshatriyas from the earth 21 times. Feeling sorry for the widows, he decided to absolve himself from the sin of killing the Kshatriyas by taking refuge at Eli mountain. In one instance, during one of the sacrificial ceremonies, he required a Kshatriya prince. The divine spirit of the mountain brought to him the Heheya prince, who belonged to the Lunar Dynasty. After the end of Parasurama's ceremony, the prince was crowned as a king and thus, became the founder of the Mushika dynasty. Since Parasurama performed his consecration with the holy water from a *ghata* (earthern pot), this king came to be known as Rama Ghata Mushika.[18]

Though the preceding legend appears to be entirely fanciful, yet it serves to establish that the Mushikas were either elevated to the status of Kshatriyas originally or belonged to the Kshatriya caste, who was nevertheless, subjected to Parasurama or rather the Brahmins and were consecrated as kings by them. Atula, in all probability, was a Brahmin, as he wrote in Sanskrit, a language that was the preserve of the Brahmins in those days. It is noteworthy at this juncture that there were 32 Brahmin settlements in Kerala and one or more of those settlements were situated in *Mushikanadu*. Perhaps, Atula being a Brahmin seems to have spun a legend involving Brahmins and Kshatriyas in his poem.

It was also believed that the pregnant Queen who fled from legendary Hehayas came by sea route along with her perceptor in a country boat called *kolah* and reached the western slope of the Ezhi, or Eli Hill. 'The Queen' made a hut under the *musika* tree (known as *vaka* in Malayalam, and *sirisa* in Sanskrit), and lived in it. The legendary Parasurama who consecrated her son as the king was supposed to have given the symbol of the tree and its flowers as the royal emblem, as well as a sword to the royal line at the time of coronation. It was claimed that the Kolatiris, who succeeded the Mushikas in later times inherited these royal insignia. The flag sign was also given. It comprised of the crescent moon along with a country boat, a lamp and a bunch of flowers of the *vaka* trees. Thus, according to the above story, the name of Kolam was derived from the country boat used by the Queen, and the word Mushika from the tree having the same name.[19]

The ancestral home of the Mushikas before migration to northern Malabar was believed to be Ramgad near the Vindhya

Mountains on the banks of River Musi, which gave them the dynastic title of 'Ramaghata Musika'. Their earliest headquarters in Malabar was Ezhimala or Elimala. The Mushika kings built their capital which was called Kolam near the Eli Hills. It was built at the mouth of River Prathana. It was considered as *Kularajadhani*. Kolam, probably derived from the word *kolah*, is not be confused with Pantalayani Kollam and Quilon further south. According to the *Mushikavamasakavya*, Ramaghata Musika is credited with the establishment of the capital at Kolam, which was then considered as the foremost city in the world. The kings of the line used to reside there. The River Killa flowed washing the ramparts of the city. The capital was protected by ramparts having tall towers and a deep moat which surrounded the fort that made the city unassailable. The waters of the River Prathana which flowed nearby reflected the skyscrapers of the city. It is said that so numerous were such buildings that the skyline was often cluttered. The royal streets were frequented by visiting royalties every day. In addition, the bazaars contained the merchandises brought from different regions and islands. The business community was so rich that they were compared to the lord of wealth. There was religious harmony despite the existence of different religions like Jainism and Buddhism besides Brahmanism. Thus, the overall picture we have of Mushikanadu from Atula was that of a very prosperous country.[20]

The Ramantalli stone dated Kali 4029/927 bears the oldest inscriptions taken from its slopes. It revealed the name of a port called Illangopattanam on the north Malabar Coast, which was prosperous enough to have attracted members of the merchant guild *manigrammam*. Besides, *Mushikavamsakavya* affirmed the existence of a commercial centre named Acalapattanam. This town was supposed to be established by Acala, son of Arya Gupta near the Eli Hill. The locality was originally identified with Cachalpattanam, a settlement of foreign traders in the neighbourhood of Elimala. Immense archaeological remains collected from the banks of River

Elimala upheld that the city must have extended inland from the coast between Kunimangalam and Payyannur. Besides, we also have the *Payyannur-pattu*, which had extolled about the merchants of Kachilpattanam. During this period it is understood that the Muslims did not settle down in the area, but their presence was only as members of the shipping crew.[21]

Further, the etymology of Eli has given rise to several hypothesis owing to the confusion generated by two words in Malayalam, *ezhu* and *mala*. Terms, *ezhu* meant 'seven' and *mala* means 'mountain', referring to seven mountains. In other words, Eli country was also referred to as *Sapta Saila* or seven hills in Sanskrit. But this reference seems to be erroneous as no travellers' accounts had mentioned the existence of seven hills in the Eli region. Ezhimala is one lone mountain that served as a landmark since ancient times as it was the only promontory about 855 feet high jutting into the sea from the northern Malabar Coast and even the entire west Indian coast as already mentioned. It was said to be visible to sailing vessels at a distance of 25 miles.[22]

Moreover, significant information about the rule of the Mushikas was reflected in the Jewish copperplates. They revealed that in anticipation of a major invasion in the year AD 1000, the rulers of Malabar had assembled at the capital at Mahodayapuram at the command of the Cheras to offer their council and service. It is also cited that during this event, the Musikas from the extreme north came to the south to participate in the meetings and offered their allegiance to fight for the Cheras. This is a testimony to the power they exerted over the north Malabar region which allowed them to offer military assistance to the Cheras in times of need. It also showed that the Mushikas were never the vassals of the Chera kingdoms.[23]

The poem, had also given a beautiful description of the prosperous Mushika country. It was covered with green vegetation which was a beautiful sight to behold. Plantations heavy with fruits was a common feature. Gardens abounding in coconuts, arecanuts, sugarcanes, cardamom plantations and rice fields were found throughout the length and breadth of the country. Besides, the *kavya* even referred to the course of rivers, location of temples, monasteries, villages of Brahmans, its capital at Eli Hills and other institutions.

In addition, this poem gave a mine of information on Mushika Kings. Actually, it contained an account of 118 rulers starting with the legendary founder Ramaghata Mushika and ending with Srikantha, the patron of the poet Atula. King Nanda, the first Mushika King described in four *sargas* (sections) of the *kavya*, following the mythical founder, might be identified with Nannan of Elimala celebrated in the Sangam literature. The city of Kolam described as the capital in the later *sargas* of the *kavya* must have given the name to the principality in the later period. The *Mushikavamsakavya* of which the really historical portions begin with the twelfth *sarga* spelt out the intimate relations between the Cheras and the Mushika from the time of Isana II Mushika and the Chera King Jayaraja Vijayaraga. The Chera conquest of the Mushika country was not openly acknowledged in the *kavya*. It is suggested by the course of events narrated. However, the triumphant entry of Chera King Jayaraja into the Mushika capital and the tributes he received all along, showed that the Mushikas were under the influence of the Cheras for sometime at least.[24] This, however, has no corroborative evidence. It did not establish conclusively that Mushikas were the vassals of the Chera king.

Atula also brought forth the information that towards the end of ninth century. Mushikas switched from patriliny to matriliny probably due to the influence of the Cheras. He also threw light on the foundation of cities like Kolam, Valabhapattanam and Madayi. In addition to it, mention was made about the renovation of several temples and about the Mushika wars against the Gagas, Cheras, Chedis and Cholas, and on the occasional revolts in the state. He referred to the marriage alliance entered into with the Cheras, Chedis and Cholas. Atula also gave some detailed information of Mushika policy towards Buddhism and Brahmanism. Shaivite cult was also prevalent in the area like in the previous Nannan's kingdom. Thousands of Brahmins were fed by Mushika kings like Udayavarman.[25] The fact that the Brahmins, who were generally admitted as migrants and settlers in the area from the northern regions, were held in high esteem in north Malabar society during this period shows us that the society had adopted the Brahmanical ordering of society with the Brahmins at the top of the hierarchy, followed by the indigenous Nair militia, and the others like the traders and astrologers. The *Mushikavamsakavya* does not shed much light on Malabar society, and its social divisions. Brahmanism seems to be the dominant religion, while Buddhism and Jainism too was allowed to flourish by the Mushika rulers.

Later, the accession of Vallabha II to the throne of the Musika heralded a new era for the dynasty. He was interested in promoting trade and adopted many progressive measures. He built the city Marahi (Madayi) for the development of foreign trade. Fleet of ships anchored there and brought plenty of merchandise from distant islands which, in turn, accelerated export of goods to foreign shores. He also fortified the city called Valabhapattana (Valarpattanam or Baliapatan) erecting high walled forts having lofty towers surrounded by deep moats. The king also promoted religion through the construction of temples. Vallabha had a well-organized naval power with which he seems to have conquered and ruled over several islands in the Arabian Sea like Laccadives, perhaps with an eye for promoting trade. Atula hinted that the great King Rama had subdued only a single island named Lanka, whereas Vallabha had controlled several islands. These islands must have included the Lakshadweep and Maldives islands. Vallabha himself seems to have crossed over the seas to accomplish this feat. After a glorious reign lasting for several years, Vallabha died attaining a ripe old age. His demise was mourned by all.[26]

However, the most glorious chapter in the history of the Mushika dynasty began with the last ruler Srikanta. He was supposed to be very benevolent. He showed keen interest in literature and poetry and had a soft corner for scholars. But he was ruthless on his enemies. He protected his country with the might of his arms. He was credited with the renovation of three famous temples. Atula further mentioned that the flag sign of his patron was *garuda* or eagle. Later on, the capital of *Mushikanadu* seems to have shifted to Karippattu near Taliparamba.

Scholars like Rao, Aiyer, A.G. Warrier, Narayanan, N.P. Unni, etc. have considered *Mushikavamsakavya* as the dynastic chronicles of Kolathunad. Almost all studies have treated Mushikanadu to be the same as Kolathunad. Hence, the rulers of Mushika lineage have been depicted as rulers of Kolathunad. Narayanan in his book on Perumals of Kerala was emphatic about Mushika rulers being rulers of Kolathunad.[27] However, Atula himself had never identified Mushika with Kolatiri. In the light of this, at the most, we can consider the Kolatiris of Kolathunad as the successors of the Mushikas, as there is no mention of any other dynasty ruling the area in the intervening period of succession.

It is further elucidated that Ezhimala was bathed by four rivers: to the North were the Kavai and the Elimala, a southern branch of which skirts the promontory to the south of Taliparamba and Valarpattanam, where wild cinnamons were grown in abundance on its cliffs. Commonly recounted narratives were that there was no proper port in the Eli country, yet there were great rivers with good estuaries wide and deep. It is said that the approach to this kingdom was so strong by nature that this country was impregnable and unassailable.[28]

As a matter of fact, Atula referred to Cheras only few times in his poem. The first reference was in connection with an attack launched by them on the sovereignty of Kolam during the legendary period. After the death of a certain Brahatsena, the country of Mushika was facing anarchy. Ugrasva, the senior-most member of the race, had already retired to the forest for a peaceful life. It was at that time that the Cheras crossed the border threatening the sovereignty of Kolam. He returned from the forest and chased away the Chera forces. Before retiring again to the forest, he married and begot a son who was consecrated as the King of Kolam. However, there is no historical veracity for the invasion by the Cheras. Besides, even the name of the Chera king was not mentioned. An interesting point to be noted in the *kavya* is that during the Mushika period, marriage alliances took place between the families of different kings who hailed from different regions of Malabar. Atula's work narrated about the marriage of Chera king Jayaraja to the daughter of Kuncivarman Mushika during the ninth century. Jayaraja (Vijayaraga) the Chera ruler, was the son-in-law of Sthanu Ravi. It is said that immediately after the marriage, Jayaraja led an expedition against his brother-in-law Isana II Mushika to chastise him for having joined the Chedi-Rashtrakutda group of powers in the Deccan.

A ferocious battle was waged between the Mushika King Isanavarman and the Chera King Raghupathi alias Jayaraja, who were related to each other. Mushika's army with their elephants marched and reached the banks of River Parussini where they camped and awaited the arrival of the Chera army. Atula related that the entire region echoed with the din of the war drums. Fierce battle was fought by both sides, and soon the war field was flooded with carcasses, and streams of blood flowed towards the River Parussini to provide food for the crocodiles. Both sides suffered heavy loss of men and materials and no king was victorious. Finally, both the kings decided to fight each other in a duel, but owing to the arrival of king's son Godavarman, who interposed between his father and uncle, the combat was stopped. Both the kings returned to their camps nursing their wounds, while learned counsellors of the respective kings succeeded in patching up the differences. Thus, the invader and the defendant felt ashamed and the Mushika King decided to show their goodwill by inviting the Chera King to spend a few days at his capital Kolam, where the Chera King was honoured and presented with valuable gifts. After this event the Chera King returned to his home country.[29] What is clear from the preceding is that the Mushika king and the Chera king were related to another and the former was not subject to the latter. River Parussini, on whose banks the war was fought between Mushika and the Chera kings, is identified presently with the Parassini Kadavu, a region through which the great River Valarpattanam flowed.

It is very clear from Atula's accounts that the Mushika kings of northern Malabar indulged in maritime trade and there were foreign settlers in the region under their control since the ninth century. These foreign settlers must have been Arab Muslims or Muslims from Persia or Gujarat or even Jews and Chinese. Unfortunately, there are no inscription evidence to ascertain the presence of Muslims in the area, apart from a lone inscription on a plaque listed by Sewell with regard to the foundation of a mosque called al-Madaji at Matayi at the mouth of the Taliparamba River on the northern banks in Kolathunad, or the Kannur-Kasaragode region, with an Arabic inscription commemorating its foundation in 518 AH (AD 1124). This mosque was believed to contain large blocks of Arabian marble brought by the original legendary preacher of Islam Malik bin Dinar himself. But J.B.P. More, in his work on the origin of the Muslims of Keralam has attested the non-existence of such an inscription and the Arabian marbles in the mosque premises. Matayi was believed to have been founded by the Mushika ruler Vallabha himself.[30]

KOLLAM AND FURTHER TRAVELLERS ACCOUNT

The history of Mushikavamsa cannot be wound up without unfolding the mystery of its capital Kollam. Even today, no one seems to know what happened to Kollam. Perhaps, this capital of the Mushika kings which existed in Eli *mala* or in its vicinity seems to have completely disappeared from the map just like the Chera capital at Makotai had disappeared.

I wish to point out that since ancient times; we have several cities referred to as Kollam. The earliest name in Malabar was Pantalayini Kollam which was identified as Quilandy.

Besides, Pantalayini Kollam (Quilandy) we have a second Kollam or Quilon which actually was situated in Travancore. This was referred to as Kulam Male or Kulam or Kualom by the Arab travellers. It was reputed as the second capital of the Chera kings from ninth to twelfth century. In fact, the city of Kollam (Quilon) seems to have been in existence even before AD 825. Thus, it is quite clear that Kolam, the capital of Mushikavamsa built at the mouth of river Prathana (this river does not exist presently) cannot be Pantalayini Kollam (Quilandy) or Quilon, because they were not situated in the Eli hills.[31]

At this juncture, it will be noteworthy to go through the accounts of the travellers who passed by the Malabar coast during the twelfth and thirteenth centuries to have an accurate notion of the strength of certain kingdoms existing during the period. Most of them mentioned the Eli kingdom, and Eli or Ezhi promontory.

The Venetian traveller Marco Polo (1271-94) visited the Malabar Coast towards the end of the thirteenth century. He noticed that the dialect spoken was different from that of the Tamil country (Malabar). This seems to attest that Malayalam language was gradually parting company with Tamil, due to the great admixture of Sanskrit words in the language during the rule of the second Chera dynasty, whose kingdom had cut itself off from western Tamil Nadu, unlike the first one.

From Kollam (or Quilon), Marco Polo sailed straight to Ezhimala, without stopping at Jirbattan (Cananore), which was already a port of some importance as mentioned by al-Idrissi. Cananore was part of the Eli kingdom, at that time. For Marco Polo, this kingdom formed the northern parts of Malabar proper, though traditionally the country extended further north upto Gokarnam. This kingdom seems to be nothing, but the Mushika kingdom or its successor.

Marco Polo stated that the Eli kingdom was ruled by a king who spoke a peculiar coastal dialect and was an idolater who paid no tribute to any other sovereign. This observation of

Marco Polo established that the ruler of Eli, or rather the Mushika king was independent and not a tributary to any other sovereign of the central or southern parts of Kerala or elsewhere. However, Marco Polo made a unique observation about the port. He reported that there were no ports in this kingdom, but there were only river mouths and fairly unsafe beaches. Nonetheless, there was a great river which opened into the sea where several ships came. Peppercorns and ginger were grown in abundance in the region besides other spices. The king of this country was supposed to be very 'rich in treasure but not strong in the number or valour of his people'.

Marco Polo was in agreement with the remarks made by contemporary travellers about the pirates and sea robbers near Elimala. Marco Polo gave an account of the pirates of Eli. He even mentioned about how the natives plundered the ships that entered their waters by accident or storm. At the same time, the ships that came to their port as per the fixed schedule, were received with full honour and given due protection.[32]

Following Marco Polo came Rashid-ud-Din (AD 1247-1381), and Al Qazwini (AD 1263-75), and the Arabian geographer Abul Fida (AD 1273). The latter mentioned about the abundance of pepper grown in Malabar. He had mentioned about Eli as *Ras Haili* in his work. We have, then, the famous Fransisan Friar Odorico Di Pordenone (1286-1331), who visited Malabar and noted with interest the pepper trade there. John of Monte Carvino (AD 1291), Friar Jordanus (AD 1320), and Marignolli (AD 1320) were unanimous in commenting about the pepper produced in Malabar region. Though Kolathunad and Cananore probably existed then, none referred to Cananore or Kolathunad by name. Of all the preceding travellers, it was Marco Polo who had given us a vivid account of certain food habits, palm wine drink and other customs and traditions of the Malabar people. His striking narration of pepper cultivation down to the minutest details till they were loaded in ships in bulk was precise and exhaustive.

It also appears that after his visit to the Mushika or Eli kingdom, the Mushika dynasty sank into oblivion and disappeared totally from the Malabar horizon. In this connection, the historian N.P. Unni had maintained that the Mushika period almost came to an end towards the close of thirteenth century or even a little earlier leaving no information about the later rulers. The Arab navigator, Ahmad ibn Majid had mentioned Ezhimala as *Hili Ras* during the fifteenth century.[33]

EMERGENCE OF KOLATHUNADU

By the fourteenth century, the old Mushika kingdom ceased to exist. It was followed by a kingdom known as Kolathunadu. A new line of rulers known as Kolatiris (known as Colastri to European writers) came into prominence in north Malabar or Kolathunadu. Probably, the Kolatiris were the descendants of the old Mushika Kings. But there is no conclusive evidence in support of this view. However, there are some traditional or legendary accounts of the origin of Kolatiris.

William Logan reiterates the story of three women (one Kshatriya and two Shudra), strangers from northern land being stranded in a local boat in Elimala. Cheraman Perumal took all three as his wives. To the descendant of the Kshatriya woman, he conferred the title of Eli *bhupam* (King of Eli) and he built for her the Eli King's house at the foot of Elimala. Logan also indicated that the Kolatiris were descendants from a matrimonial alliance between the last of the Chera Perumals and a lady of the stock of the great southern feudatory, the Raja Travancore (Southern Kolatiri). Besides, there is another story narrated in *Udayavarmacaita* about King Ravi Varma of Kolathunad in the beginning of the sixteenth century, according to which the founder of Kolatiri family was one King Kerala Varma, son of the legendary Cheraman Perumal. All the above-mentioned theories of the origin of Kolatiri are purely conjectural and have no historical moorings.[34]

Besides these traditional accounts, the manuscript collected by Col. Colin Mackenzie while he was serving in the English East India Company as Surveyor-General between AD 1810 and

AD 1815 contains very interesting information pertaining to the local history of Kolathunad. Written in Telugu, the text contains a genealogical description of the Kolatiri Raja, and how Cheraman Perumal installed Udayavarman Kolatiri Vaddtakkam Perumal as Maharaja of the entire Malabar kingdom, before his departure to Mecca.

While Cheraman Perumal was ruling over Keralam, a Kshatriya princess of Ayodhya was carried away by the River Ganges and thrown into the sea. She was washed ashore on the coast of the Malabar country near the Eli Hills. Cheraman Perumal married her on the promise that he would make their son an independent ruler. In a short time, a son was born to her and he was named Udayavarman. At that time Krishnaraya invaded the country of Malabar. Udayavarman, who had grown up, was sent against the invader. Udayavarman returned with glory upon which Cheraman Perumal made him ruler of the northern part of his dominions called Kolathunad of which the chief city was Valarpattanam. At the time of his coronation, the Brahmins bestowed upon him the title 'Kolatiri Vaddakkan Perumal'. His kingdom extended from Perumbalam in Tulu region to Pudupattanam. The preceding account is again largely legendary without any supporting historical evidence. But it is worth noting here that the manuscript admitted that the Mushika rulers preceded the Kolatiris.[35]

Again, Kolathunad appeared in the *Keralolpatti Granthavari*, which gave detailed account of the partition of the Chera kingdom, giving the area and military strength of the small principalities which were liberated and transformed into successor states with the liquidation of the central power. Thus, the Cheraman kingdom of 160 *kalam* between Pudupattanam in the North and Kanneeri in the south was partitioned into 17 principalities. Kolathunadu was first given to Kolatiri Udayavarman which included 35,000 Nairs of Valarpattanam, Cheraman's palace in Kotta, Ventrikkovil (Taliparamba) temple, Perincellur Grama and two chieftains called Culanna Kaymal and Nerpetta Kaimal.

Mackenzie's manuscript also dealt with the branching of

the Kolatiri family into several groups. The different princely houses founded were: (1) Pallikkolagam alias Ambukkolagam, (2) Puduppallikkolagam, and (3) Udayamangalattukkolagam. A further branching of the family alluded to in the manuscripts gives the following five family groups: (1) Cerakkalkkolagam, (2) Panirinjarikkolagam, (3) Cenjanakkolagam; (4) Kavaniri-scerikkolagam, and (5) Tevanangottu dayamangalamutiilek-kolagam.

In later times, the first among the five families controlled the region. Thus, the family originally known as the Vaddakkam Perumal Kolatiri Swarupam was later succeeded by the members of the Cerakkalkkolagam. Narayanan holds that *Musakavamsa* was only a Sanskritization of Eli which was a popular name of the region, and that the geographical extension of *Mushikanadu* lay roughly between Kavvayipuzha and Valarpattanampuzha in the south extending to Madayi creeks. But K.V. Subramanian Iyer on the contrary has accepted the version which located Mushika kingdom between Perumpula and Puduppattanam. Based on the geographical and historical information gleaned from Atula's poem, he had once for all maintained that the Kolathnadu region in the north Malabar was the country of the Mushikas.[36]

Ibn Battuta, the fourteenth-century Moroccan traveller had left us a vivid account of the Malabar. In it, he has mentioned about Cananore (Jurfattan) and about a king or prince of the area. We will deal with this more extensively in the next chapter. Furthermore, Duarte Barbosa, the Portuguese factor in Cananore had remarked at the beginning of the sixteenth century that there were only three Kings in the great country of Malabar. The Zamodry (Zamorin), who was named Benatetiry, the King of Cananore who was named Colestry, and the King of Coulam. Besides them, there were many other lords in the country of Malabar who wish to call themselves Kings, but could not claim the title as they could not officially mint money or cover their houses with roofs. In normal course, whoever dared to do such things were penalized. It is also revealed that the Kings of Kolam and Cananore defied the law and struck coins for a certain time in their countries without having the power to do so. Besides, Barbosa was surprised to see so many 'Moors' and 'Gentiles' in Cananore who were merchants and possessed many large and small ships.

Even Tomé Pires who followed Barbosa to Malabar Coast had noted the presence of the Zamorin of Calicut and the Kolatiri of Cananore and other kings and chiefs. He had also mentioned about the ports of Calicut and Cananore. The ports of Cananore, Dharmapatnam, Madayi, Nileshwaram, Kottakulam, Hyeri (Elimala), and Baliapatam belonged to the Kolatiri king. Pires also noted the presence of Moorish merchants in Cananore. One of them called Mamale was the most prominent. The Dutch Commander Henrick Adriaan van Rheed too mentioned about 'Colastri of Collettenade of Mallabaer'.[37]

According to Duarte Barbosa, Dharmapatnam was the last town held by Kolatiris whereas Tomé Pires believed Mahe was also included in their kingdom. The oldest member of the entire royal family including all its branches was the rightful heir to the throne. The law of succession followed the *marumakkatayam* system, which only took into account of matrilineal descent. We have seen earlier that it was the Mushika dynasty which adopted this system. Furthermore, Kolatiris seemed to have had several capitals at different places and at periods of time. They did not have any permanent capital. Successive rulers chose their capital according to their political and strategical needs. Besides, Kollam and Dharmapatnam, they also had capitals at Valarpatnam, Taliparamba and Madayi. Apart from this, Kolatiris had several other traditional residences which had probably been abandoned by the beginning of the sixteenth century. In the course of time eight distinct centres of their power was identified. The Ezhi Fort at Ramanthali, Madayi Fort, Kollam Fort at Pantalayini, Sreekandapuram near Taliparamba, Kadalayi Fort at Cananore, Valapatnam Fort, Karipaat Palli Palace at Taliparamba and Chirakkal Palace. The palace of Karipaat in the region of Chirakkal was supposed to be older than the

Eli Kovilagam. The ancient palace of Madayi and the citadel of Valarpatnam, where the Kolatiri seemed to have settled during the Portuguese period were reserved for the reigning sovereign. The sanctuary of Madayi Kavu and Kalarivathukkal both dedicated to Bhagavathi were attached to these two royal residences.

The topography of the royal residences followed the same movement. The oldest of the residence, the Eli Kovilagam, overlooked the Payyanur site. The fortified palace of Matayi was situated in Payangadi on the banks of the northern basin and the palace at Valarpatnam situated near Valarpatnam site was the favourite residence of the Kolatiri during the Portuguese period.[38]

One interesting fact that emerges was the control that the *Purohitas* or *poojaris* had over the Raja and his retinue. The influence of these *poojaris* over Kolatiri was so discreet that it went unnoticed even by the Portuguese observers. On the other hand, the influence of the soothsayers was more apparent as they had a hold over the decisions of the King. But as most of them belonged to Kaniyan caste; they were never admitted into the royal residence, but were received only in the palace gardens.

Kolatiris possessed a strong army of Nayars. Right from the medieval period, they were bestowed with considerable social privileges in return for unconditional devotion to their King. The Nayars were sworn 'to protect the cows and Brahmins'. In times of war, they fought on foot, they protected themselves with shields, swords and daggers, they were skilled in the use of lances, bows and arrows. They were renowned for their military prowess and their bellicose attitudes. These soldiers were trained from an early age in the military academies. The chosen ones accompanied the sovereigns in all his public appearances during which they performed their skill in front of the crowd.

It is interesting to note that by the late seventeenth century, in Malabar, the most powerful ruler was the Kolatiri, Raja of Cananore and the other Rajas honoured Kolatiri, the Crown

King of Cananore, This information is given in the accounts of Dellon, a French doctor who was in Malabar at that time. Besides, it was only after the defeat of Tipu Sultan and between 1792-1800 that the English East India Company took absolute control of the region.[39]

NOTES

1. William Vincent, *Commerce and Navigation of the Ancient in the Indian Ocean–Periplus of the Erythrean Sea*, 2 vols., London, 1807, pp. 60-2; Sayed Mohammed Husayn Nainar, *Arab Geographers Knowledge of Southern India*, Calicut, 2011, p. 17; Tan Ta Sen, *Chengo Ho and Islam in South East Asia*, Singapore, 2009, p. 157.
2. O.K. Nambiar, *Our Seafaring in the Indian Ocean*, Bangalore, 1975, pp. 37, 39; A.P. Ibrahim Kunju. 'Origin and Spread of Islam in Kerala', in Asghar Ali Engineer (ed.), *Kerala Muslims: A Historical Perspective*, Delhi, 1995.
3. Colonel Yule (tr. & ed.), *Cathay and the Way Thither*, vol. I, London, MDCCCLXVI, p. xvvii; Rockhill and Hirth, *Chau Ju Kua*, St. Petersburg, 1911, pp. 2-8; Sayed Muhammad Husayn Nainar, *Arab Geographers: Knowledge of Southern India*, Calicut, 2011, p. 16fn.
4. M.G.S. Narayanan, *Perumals of Kerala, Political and Social Conditions of Kerala Under the Cera Perumals of Makottai, AD 800-1124*, Calicut, 1996, pp. vi, 65, 91-4.
5. Truesdell S. Brown, *Onesicritus, A Study in Hellenistic Historiography*, Berkeley, 1949, p. 54.
6. Cf. E. Renaudot, *Ancient Accounts of India and China by Two Mohammadan Travellers in the Ninth century AD*, London, 1733; J.B.P. More, *Origin and Early History of the Muslims of Keralam*, Calicut, 2011, p. 46.
7. Gabriel Ferand (tr.), *Les Classique de L' Orient Voyage du Marchand Arabe Sulayman en Inde et en Chine Redege en 851 suivi de remarques par Abu Zayd Hassan*, Paris, 1922 , pp. 18, 48.
8. E. Renaudot, *Ancient Accounts of India and China by Two Muhammadan Travellers in the Ninth Century AD*, London, 1733, pp. 185-8; Muhammad Husayn Nainar, op. cit., p. 48.
9. Elliot and Dowson (eds.), *The History of India as Told by its Own Historians*, vol. I, 1867, pp. 1-2; G.R. Tibbetts, *A Study of Arabic Texts Containing Material of South East Asia*, London, 1979, p. 75; Ahmad

Maqbul, 'Al-Masudi on the Kings of India', in *Al-Masudi Millenary Commeration Volume*, Aligarh, 1960, pp. 18-25, 97-112.

10. R.H. Major (ed.), *India in the 12th Century*, London, MDCCCLVII, p. xiv; Elliot and Dowson (eds.), *The History of India as Told by its Own Historians*, vol. I, London, 1867, pp. 2-3, 18-25; G.R. Tibbetts, op. cit.
11. Elliot and Dowson (eds.), op. cit., I, book II, pp. 12-13, 13 fol., 15; G.R. Tibbetts (tr.), *Arab Navigation in the Indian Ocean Before the Coming of the Portuguese, Being a Translaton of Kitab al-Fawa'id fi Usal al-Bahr wa'l-Qawa'id of Ahmad bin Majid al-Nadji*, London, 1981, p. 2; cf. also Ibn Khordadbeh, *Al Masalik wa'l-mamalik*, ed., M.J de Goeje, Leiden, 1889.
12. S. Maqbul Ahmad (tr.), *Al Idrisi, Indian and the Neighbouring Territories in the Kitab Nuzhat Al-Mushtaq Fikhtiraq Al-Afaq*, Leiden, 1960, pp. 11-12, 63, 68-9, 85; Syed Mohamed Husayn Nainar, *Arab Geographer's Knowledge of Southern India*, Calicut, 2011, p. 28; Elliot and Dowson, (eds.), op. cit., I, 1867, pp. 85, 89-90, 95; C. Defremery and B.R. Sanguinette, *Ibn Battuta Voyages Inde, Extreme Orient Espagne and Soudan*, vol. III, Paris, 1858, 1986, pp. 203, 206.
13. V. Minorsky (tr.), *Hudud al-Alam, 'Regions of the World', a Persian Geography, AD 372 -AD 982*, London, 1970, pp. 57, 88, 238; Sharaf al-Zaman Tahir Marvazi (tr.), *On China, the Turks and India*, London, 1942, ch. xii, p. 46.
14. M.G.S. Narayanan, *Perumals of Kerala*, Calicut, 1996, pp. 11-12; N.P. Unni, *A History of Mushikavamsa*, Trivandrum, 1980, p. 10fn.; G. Rao, 'Extracts from the Mushaka Vamsam and "Mushaka Vamsa": A Study', *Travancore Archaelogical Series*, II, I, no. 10.
15. M.G.S. Narayanan, *Perumals of Kerala*, Calicut, 1996, p. 91.
16. N.P. Unni, *A History of Mushikavamsa*, Trivandrum, 1980, p. 1; M.G.S. Narayanan, op. cit., K. Balakrishnan, *Ezhimala, Kannurinde Samakalika Charithravum Puravrithavum*, Kozhikode, 2019, p. 161; G. Rao, op. cit.
17. K.Balakrishnan, op. cit., pp. 161, 165; N.M. Nambutiri, *Kerala Samskaram Akavum Puravum*, University of Calicut, 2002, pp. 200-5; Geneviève Bouchon, *Regent of the Sea, Cannanore's Response to Portuguese Expansion 1507-28*, Delhi, 1988, p. 6.
18. N.P. Unni, op. cit., p. 89; K. Balakrishnan, op. cit., p. 163.
19. Unni, op. cit., p. 157; Vanidas Elayavoor. *Lore and Legends of North Malabar*, tr. Ashvin Kumar, Kottayam, 2019, p. 428; Cf.

also, Kesavan Veluthat, *Brahman Settlements in Kerala*, Calicut, 1978.

20. N.P. Unni, op. cit., pp. 90, 155; M.G.S., op. cit., p. 92; K. Balakrishnan, op. cit., p. 164; G. Rao, op. cit.
21. G. Bouchon, op. cit., pp. 6-7; N.P. Unni, *History of Mushikavamsa*, Trivandrum, 1890, p. 160.
22. S. Maqbul Ahmad (tr.), *Al-Sharif al-Idrisi—India and the Neighbouring Territories*, Leiden, 1960, p. 83; G. Bouchon, op. cit., p. 5; J.B.P. More, *Origin and Early History of the Muslims of Keralam (AD 700-AD 1600)*, Calicut, 2011, pp. 38, 66, 73; *Tamil Lexicon*, Madras, 1982, p. 539.
23. G. Bouchon, op. cit., p. 244; M.G.S. Narayanan, op. cit., p. 105.
24. N.P. Unni, op. cit., pp. 1, 8, 11, 229; K.P. Rajesh, 'Regional Formation in North Kerala: 'A Study of the Mushikas', Calicut University, 2005 (unpublished thesis), p. 1.
25. M.G.S. Narayanan, op. cit., pp. 12, 83; N.P. Unni, op. cit., pp. 98, 121-2.
26. M.G.S., Narayanan, op. cit., p. 92; N.P. Unni, op. cit., pp. 120-3; G. Rao, op. cit.
27. M.G.S. Narayanan, op. cit., pp. 11-12; K.P. Rajesh, op. cit., pp. 16-17; N.P. Unni, op. cit., G. Rao, op. cit.
28. G. Bouchon, op. cit., pp. 5-6; William Logan, *Malabar*, vol. 1, Madras, 1989, p. 282.
29. N.P. Unni, op. cit., pp. 134-5, 153, 235; M.G.S. Narayanan, op. cit., pp. 46, 91, 170.
30. William Logan, op. cit., I, p. 194; G. Bouchon, op. cit., p. 8; cf. also J.B.P. More, op. cit., pp. 57-8; N.P. Unni, op. cit., 120.
31. S. Maqbul Ahmad, op. cit., pp. 89, 162; R.H. Major, *India in the 15th Century*, London, MDCCCLVII, p. xxv; M.G.S. Narayanan, op. cit., p. 16; N.P. Unni, p. 158.
32. Robert Sewell, *Archaeological Survey of Southern India*, vol. II, Madras, 1882, p. 243; K.P. Padmanabha Menon, *History of Kerala*, vol. I, New Delhi, 1989, p. 14; William Logan, *Malabar*, vol. 1, Madras, 1989, p. 282; A.C. Moule and Paul Pelliot, *Marco Polo-Description of the World*, vol. 1, London, MCMXXXVIII, p. 416 ; Innes and Evans (eds.), *Malabar Gazetteer*, vol. I and II , Trivandrum, 1997, p. 3.
33. N.P. Unni, op. cit., p. 11; A.C. Moule and Paul Pelliot (trs.), op. cit., pp. 414-16; Cf. A.C. Moule and Paul Pelliot (trs.), *Marco Polo*,

Le devisement du Monde, Le livre des Merveilles, Paris, 1996; G.R. Tibetts, op. cit., 1981, p. 252.

34. William Logan, *Malabar*, vol. 1, Madras, 1989, p. 234; A. Sreedhara Menon, *Kerala District Gazetters, Cannanore*, Trivandrum, 1972, p. 73.
35. N.P. Unni, op. cit., p. 18; G. Rao, op. cit.
36. Cf. K.V. Subramana Iyer, *Historical Sketches of Ancient Deccan*, Madras, 1917; N.P. Unni, *A History of Mushikavamsam*, Trivandrum, 1980, pp. 7, 17-18; M.G.S. Narayanan, op. cit., pp. 11-12, 66; K.P. Rajesh, op. cit., pp. 16-17.
37. Tomé Pires, *The Sumo Oriental*, New Delhi, 1990, vol. I, p. 65; Hendrick Adriaan Van Rheede, *Commander of the Malabar, Canara and Wingurla Coast, Selections from the Records of the Madras Govt. Dutch Records No. 14, (Dutch) Memoires Written in the Year* AD *1677*, Madras, 1911, pp. 3, 81; Henry E.J. Stanley (tr.), *Duarte Barbosa, A Description of the Coasts of East Africa and Malabar in the Beginning of the 16th Century*, Madras, 1995, pp. 103, 146; Cf. The book of Duarte Barbosa (tr.) M.W. Dames II, London, 1921; G. Bouchon, op. cit., pp. 23-4.
38. G. Bouchon, op. cit., pp. 12-16; Vanidas Elayavoor, *Lore and Legends of North Malabar*, tr. Ashvin Kumar, Kottayam, 2019, p. 422.
39. G. Bouchon, op. cit., pp. 16-17; M. Dellon, *Relations d'un voyage des Indes Orientales*, Tome 1, Paris, MDCLXXXV, pp. 134-5.

CHAPTER 4

Conversion in Kannur and Malabar

The most popular belief related to the conversion of a Malabari ruler to Islam was the conversion of Cheraman Perumal, the ruler of the second Chera kingdom. Another story of conversion that is prevalent in north Malabar is the conversion of a Kolatiri king to Islam. I intend to check the veracity of these two conversion narratives by using in the first place the accounts of the foreign travellers to Malabar from ninth century onwards.

CONVERSION IN KANNUR

It is noteworthy that between Cosmas Indicopleustes of the sixth century and Marco Polo of the thirteenth century, most of the well known travellers to southern India were indeed Arabs or Persians. None of them including Atula, author of *Musakavamsakavya* had written a word about any conversion of a Malabar king or prince to Islam until then.

Nearly 60 years after Marco Polo's remarkable work, we have the travels of the famous Moroccan traveller Ibn Battuta, whose work is of immense interest and importance to Malabar in general and precisely to Cananore. Ibn Battuta arrived in India in the year AD 1333. He presented himself for employment in the Delhi Sultanate and was appointed to head a prestigious embassy to the court of the Mongol emperor of China. During 1340s, Battuta arrived on the Malabar Coast as the ambassador of the Delhi Sultan Muhammad bin Tughlaq (r. 1325-51), and travelled through several cities and towns in Malabar, keenly observing and studying whatever he saw or experienced.

Ibn Battuta left a detailed description about his travels in Malabar. He arrived on the Malabar Coast first at Manjarur (Mangalore), which he said was situated upon a large estuary of the sea called the 'Estuary of the Wolf'. Manjarur was a large town, where he found several Arabs and Persian merchants from Fars and Yemen. The ruler of Mangalore was a certain Ram Deo. He observed about 40,000 Muslim merchants inhabiting the area and noted the frequent frictions between the Muslims and the inhabitants of the city.

After Mangalore, Ibn Battuta sailed to Mount Delli (Ezhimala), a promontory about 855 feet, or 259 metres high with a mosque at the summit, which attracted Muslim devotees on certain auspicious days. It appears that the Siva temple of Nannan's Ezhilkunram had given way to the mosque at some point of time. He described Ezhimala as an imposing city situated on a large bay in which ships from China and other countries entered.

From Ezhimala, Battuta went to Jurkannan/Jurfattan and then to Dadkannan/Dahfattan, and next to Budfattan/Badafattan. He had observed that the Sultan of these places were known as Kuwayl, and was the most powerful ruler of Mulaybar. The Kuwayl mentioned in his *Rehla* seems to be none other than the Kolatiri king. The Kolatiris seem to have succeeded the Mushika kings sometime before or after the end of the thirteenth century. We do not have any other historical reference to attest this transition from the Mushikas to the Kolatiris. Besides, there is no reference to any other intervening dynasty or king when this transition took place. Nevertheless, if we are to follow the accounts of Ibn Battuta, the aforementioned Kuwayl, or Kolatiri King was based in Cananore (Jurfattan).[1]

It is worth noting at this juncture, that there were three different translations of the original Arabic work of Ibn Battuta (1342-7) *Rehla* into English by European scholars, which I had located in the Bibliothèque Nationale de France (National

Library of Paris). All the three translations were not identical. It is for this reason that I am bringing out certain features related to Malabar in the three translations of *Rehla*. The first translation was by a British scholar named Revd. Samuel Lee. He translated from the original Arabic manuscripts of *Rehla* found in Cambridge. It was published as early as in 1829. It seems to be an exhaustive and complete translation from the Arabic original. Therefore, its contents are more reliable.[2]

According to this translation, Ibn Battuta sailed from the extreme northern part of Malabar, first to Mont Deli (Elimala), and then to Jurkannan. Now, the name Jurkannan appears to be derived from Kannan, which was the name of Lord Krishna, and Jur, which is nothing but Ur, meaning town or a place of dwelling. So the place name Jurkannan is derived from the word Kannan Ur, which in the course of time became Kannur, the original name of Cananore.

It is quite interesting to note that there is an old temple called Kadalayi Ambalam, which is a Kannan or Sri Krishna temple near Cananore town even today. Besides in Cananore town itself, we have what is called the Kanathur Kavu, which is also a small temple. Some claim that Cananore owed its origin to Kanathur or the Kannan temple at Kadalayi. Furthermore, in ancient Tamil *kanna* meant pepper. Hence, Cananore could also mean 'pepper town'. At the present juncture, we do not know which of these three derivations is the correct one, though we think that the last one might be the most appropriate as Cananore was actually a 'pepper town'.[3]

After Jurkannan, Ibn Battuta visited Dadkannan, according to Lee. This could be identified with Dharmapattanam (Dharmadam). It is believed that Dharmadam, meaning 'city of piety' was a sacred place and was the seat of Kolatiri kings during their earlier days. After Dadkannan, Battuta visited Fattan which has been identified with Baliapatam or Valapattanam. At this juncture, it is important to note that the Arabs used the word *fattan* to mean town. *Fattan* is the Arabic form of Sanskrit *Pattana* or the Tamil *pattanam*, meaning town or port.[4]

Samuel Lee claimed that in Jurkannan, there was a king, who was the greatest on the Malabar Coast, and the place Dadkannan was within his domains. Jurkannan was a large city abounding with gardens and situated upon a mouth of the sea. Outside the city, there was a large pond for retaining water surrounded by gardens. Lee further remarked that the Kuwyil was an 'infidel', who followed his own religion. It seems that the grandfather of the Kuwyil became a Muslim. It was he who built a mosque and made the pond at Dadkannan.

The reason for Kuwyil's grandfather receiving Islamic-faith was a miraculous tree or The Tree of Testimony (*darakhti shahadat*). One of the exceptional tales of miracle that convinced him to convert to Islam was his witnessing the fall of leaves from this miraculous tree. It seems that one of the fallen leaves contained the Islamic credo: 'There is no God but Allah, Muhammad is the Prophet of Allah'. Thus, the Kuwyil who had heard about the miracles of Prophet Muhammad from the multitude of sailors who touched upon his kingdom was persuaded to convert to Islam. At the time of his death, he appointed his son who was a 'violent infidel' as the king. It seems that the son tried to destroy the tree by uprooting it, but he did not succeed as the tree grew all over again. This violent 'infidel' Kuwyil died shortly, but the miraculous tree continued to exist. Ibn Battuta himself witnessed the tree. But he did not witness the miraculous writings on the leaf of the tree.[4] It should be noted that in the translation of Revd. Samuel Lee, the aforesaid King or Kuwyil mentioned by Ibn Battuta was none other than the Kolatiri king, as explained earlier. So, it is clear that during the first half of the thirteenth century itself, the Kolatiri kings had come into existence in Malabar and they were quite independent of their southern neighbours of Malabar politically speaking.

In the year 1859, we have a second translation of *Rehla*, this time in French by C. Defremery and B.R. Sanguinetti. In this work it is narrated that Ibn Battuta met at Djorfattan, a jurist from Baghdad called Sarsar. The latter had a very rich brother who had children, and resided at Djorfattan. In the French translation, Djorfattan has been identified with Cananore where the horses coming from Persia got unloaded. It was the residence of the king called 'Coueil' who possessed numerous ships, which sailed to Oman, Fars, Yemen. Ibn Battuta, then, proceeded to Dehfattan (Dharmapatnam), where he described the huge pond or bathing tank with stoned steps, surrounded by three storied buildings, besides a mosque.

It seems that Jurist Husain told Battuta that it was the father of the Sultan 'Coueil', who constructed this great bath and mosque. Further opposite, there was a cathedral mosque with a basin, where the faithful performed their obligatory ablution. The Jurist Husain seems to have affirmed to Battuta that the bath and mosque belonged to the ancestor of the Coueil, who converted to Islam because of his marvellous adventure with a tree (*derakht aché hadah*). He further divulged that the son of the Coueil returned to idol worship meaning returned to their ancestral faith after the death of his father and ordered the tree to be uprooted and demolished. The son who ordered for the destruction of the tree suddenly passed away, but the tree grew and regained its old growth.

It seems that the majority of the inhabitants of Boddfattan were Brahmins, who hated Muslims. Bodd-Fattan has been identified with Valapattanam. Ibn Battuta had also affirmed that Djorfattan, Dehfattan and Boddfattan were parts of the same kingdom and was ruled by 'Coueil'. The latter was none other than the Kuwyil, which denoted as the Kolatiri king, who had his seat in Cananore.[5]

We find, however, a serious contradiction in the French translation. At one place it is cited that the father of 'Coueil' converted to Islam, whereas in another place it is mentioned that the mosque was built by the ancestors of the present 'Coueil'. On the other hand, Samuel Lee had mentioned that it was the grandfather of the present King who converted to Islam.

The third translation of *Rehla* was in English done by H.A.R. Gibbs. It was published in 1929. Out of these three translations, the one by Gibbs seems to be the most popular and referred to by most of the Indian historians especially. According to him, the town of Hilli (Ezhimala/Elimala) was venerated by both Muslims and infidels on account of its cathedral mosque to which seafarers made offerings. He further mentioned about the towns of Jurfattan (Kannanur), Dahfattan and Boddfattan. He maintained on the basis of Ibn Battuta's accounts that the Kuwyil was the most powerful of the Mulaybar kings. The grandfather of Kuwyil converted to Islam at Dahfattan (Dharmadam). It was he who built the great bath (pond) and a cathedral mosque at Dahfattan. He also recounted that most of the inhabitants of Boddfattan were Brahmins, held in respect by the 'infidels' and hated the Muslims. That was the reason he gave for Muslims not inhabiting Boddfattan.

However, there are few omissions in this translation of Gibbs as compared to the other two. For example, Gibbs did not elaborate on the miraculous Tree of Testimony, which was the reason for the conversion of the Kolatiri king to Islam, according to Ibn Battuta. There is no denying the fact that all the two aforesaid translators (Gibbs, C. Defremery and B.R. Sanguinetti) were unanimous in identifying Jurkannan or Jurfattan with Cananore. Whereas Samuel Lee mentioned Jurkannan, which in native dialect meant Kannan Ur. Much before Ibn Battuta, al Idrisi had identified a very high mountain near Jirbattan covered with trees and villages, where cardamom was grown. This high mountain seems to be nothing but Ezhimala.[6]

Further, both the French translators and Gibbs mentioned the name of the king as Coueil and Kuwyil (Kuwayl). Al-Idrisi had noted the existence of Cananore as Jirbattan. It is quite possible that Jirbattan formed parts of the kingdom of Ezhimala in the eleventh and in the twelfth centuries, which was under the sway of the Mushika dynasty. Further, it should be noted that Colonel Yule had also identified Jurfattan with Cananore, whereas Nainar identified Jurfattan with Sreekandapuram due to the reason that there was a popular mosque. However, this mosque does not prove anything. According to Husayn Nainar, the kingdom of the Kolatiris extended from Kasaragod in the north to Korappula in the south. The eastern boundary was Kutakumala and the western boundary was the sea. The king had several residences spread throughout the country.[7]

It is significant to note here, that it was Ibn Battuta alone who had noted the conversion of a Kuwyil or Kolatiri prince of Cananore to Islam. None of the Arab or Persian or even Italian travellers either before him, or after him until the end of the fifteenth century had mentioned about this conversion of the Kolatiri prince or any other king or prince of Malabar to Islam. It appears then that this conversion had later got mixed up with the legend of the conversion of Cheraman Perumal to Islam and almost forgotten. But Ibn Battuta's records would not lie. The only conversion that happened on the Malabar Coast for which we have factual evidence is that of the conversion of a Kolatiri prince of Cananore.

Contrary to the factual evidence provided by Ibn Battuta in his accounts, the Arakkal family tradition claims that the origin of the Arakkals must be traced to the last Chera emperor. According to their version, after the Chera emperor Cheraman Perumal converted to Islam and before leaving for Mecca, he had asked his sister Sreedevi, who resided at Dharmadam to crown her son Mahabali who eventually converted to Islam and adopted the name Mohammad Ali, or Mamalli.[8] However, there is no literary or epigraphical evidence for such a glorious origin.

According to Arakkal tradition, in memory of the first ruler of Arakkal house who converted to Islam and as a symbol of his native ancestry, a *bhadra deepa* or an auspicious lamp is maintained in a southern room of the house even today. Near the lamp there is a bed spread over a cot, and that this lamp faced the Arabian sea in memory of the ancestor of the house who sailed to Mecca. This lamp is also called Tamburatti Vilakku, and is kept under a majestic throne-like big wooden arm chair facing the Arabian sea. It is believed that it was Cheraman Perumal's sister Sreedevi and her son Mamalli, who lit up the lamp in order to commemorate the return of Cheraman Perumal from Mecca. It is also believed that a saint from Arabia visited the Arakkal Palace every night, occupied the stately chair and then goes to sleep in the longish bed.

Another local tradition holds that the lamp was given by the neighbouring king of Chirakkal to the princess when she married a Muslim youth. That is why it was known as Tamburatti Vilakku. This lamp is considered as a symbol of religious fraternity between Arakkal and Chirakkal family. William Logan attributed another version, i.e. the first chieftain of this house (Arakkal) was one Aryan Kulangara Nair, one of the ministers of Kolatiri who lived during the eleventh or the beginning of the twelfth century AD, who embraced Islam and adopted the name Mohammed or Mohammed Ali.[9] However, no authentic documents corresponding to the period concerned are found to substantiate these traditional accounts of the origin of Arakkal family related above.

Arakkals had maintained the Keralite custom of matrilineal succession which was contradictory to the Shariat rules. It is believed that this custom of succession was later sanctioned by the Caliph in Turkey as the 'custom of the land in one of his letters'. Though initially it was the male members who became rulers of Arakkal, later on female succession became common and they came to be addressed as 'Beewi'.[10] However, the matrilineal succession custom of the Arakkal family proves beyond any doubt that they had a Malayali religious ancestry.

Leaving aside the traditional accounts related to the birth of the Arakkal family, we can affirm with certainity on the basis of the accounts of Ibn Battuta that the grandfather or an ancestor of the king of Cananore had converted to Islam in the thirteenth century or much earlier. The precise date or year of the conversion is not known. In any case, there is no other recorded event of conversion during this period and much later until the arrival of the Portuguese on the Malabar Coast. The Arakkals can be rightly traced to this conversion of a Kolatiri prince or king as noted by Battuta.

CONVERSION LEGEND OF CHERAMAN PERUMAL

We cannot end this chapter without taking a look at the various legends of conversion of the Cheraman Perumal to Islam in the Malabar, which had actually cropped up with the arrival of the Portuguese on the Malabar Coast in the early sixteenth century. Everything seems to have started with the Portuguese factors and officials like Duarte Barbosa and Tomé Pires.

Duarte Barbosa was a Portuguese factor who worked at the Malabar port of Cananore from 1500 to 1517. He recounted that the last Cheraman Perumal, the ruling king of Malabar converted to the Mohammaden religion and went to Mecca. But he died on the way to Mecca, or in Mecca itself. But before proceeding to Mecca, he is said to have divided his kingdom among his principal family members, i.e. the ruler Zourochi, known as Conelava-dyri, the King of Coulam (Quilon) known as Benate-diry, and the King of Cananore called as Coletri (Kolatiri). Thus, the legitimate kings of Malabar according to Barbosa after the division were the Zamorin of Calicut, the King of Quilon and the King of Cananore. All the rulers were related to each other. Zamorin of Calicut was actually the nephew of Cheraman Perumal. It seems that the Zamorin was given a sword and a chandelier (golden lamp) by Cheraman Perumal which he carried with him for state affairs. Appropriate instructions were also given to all the rulers and lords to whom he had given his lands that they should obey and honour him, save only the rulers of Coulam (Quilon) and Cananore whom he made independent. Barbosa asserted that the conversion of Cheraman Perumal took place in the ninth century.

Barbosa was also the first person to reveal the name of Cananore. He pointed out that, 'on the seacoast near the Kingdom of Calicut, towards the South was a city called Cananore in which there are many Moors and Gentiles of many kind who were all merchants and possessed many large and small ships'.[11]

Tomé Pires, who followed Barbosa, related in his accounts that there used to be a king who ruled over the whole country of Malabar who was persuaded by the Moors, to become a Muslim and go to Mecca. But before he could reach the mouth of the Strait, he died in the Kingdom of Dhofar. He added that the king was already out of his mind when he left Malabar and had divided up the whole country and distributed it to his relatives. But after the partition, a relative of his who arrived late for the function, asked for his share and he was given the land of the city of Calicut.[12] This last account regarding Calicut completely contradicts with that of Barbosa.

It is rather perplexing to know how Duarte Barbosa and Tomé Pires got all these details, because most certainly it appears that they based their narrations obtained from local sources. Besides, they were recounting something which had occurred perhaps five or six centuries earlier, for which there was no concrete literary or epigraphical evidences. The story recounted by Duarte Barbosa and Tomé Pires was the beginning without any end as the story caught the interest of the later travellers, Portuguese as well as other Europeans, who lost no time in embellishing it with their own theories, with some variations.

Joao de Barros, the official Portuguese historian of the sixteenth century, without ever setting his foot in Malabar recounted that a king, called Sarama Perumal reigned 612 years before with his headquarters at Choulam (Kollam), a place greatly frequented by the Arabs. According to him, the Moors who were fanatics, converted many of the Malabaris to Islam, and even succeeded in converting the very king Sarama Perumal also to Islam. He, then, went and lived in Calicut as it was the centre of pepper growth and Moorish population. The Moors, then, convinced him to go to Mecca to save his soul and die there. He accepted their advice, and before leaving he divided his kingdom among his nearest relatives. Camoens who wrote the greater part of his Lusiad during 1553-9 AD in India, narrated that Cheraman Perumal, who was the ruler of Malabar converted to Islam and went to Arabia to die there as a saint. As he had no heir, he divided his kingdom between his loyal servants and left for Mecca.

During the same period, we have Manuel de Faria e Sousa, a pirate, who had given a thoroughly different version of this legend. According to him, Xarao Perumal (Cheraman Perumal) of Cranganore (Kodungallur) was the most famous of all the Perumals. He was very favourably disposed towards St. Thomas and he is said to have converted to Christianity. In his old age heeding to the advice of the Christians, he went away to Mylapore on the Cholamandalam coast, where St. Thomas, was believed to be buried. In his turn, Muhammad Husayn Nainar claimed that Cheraman went away to Bethlehem after abdication.[13]

As we proceed further, this legend gets mired deeper and deeper into controversies and contradictions. Sheikh Zain uddin al-Malabari, a Muslim from Malabar of Arab descent, recorded a variation of this legend in 1583 in his account of Islam in Malabar. According to him, a group of Muslim pilgrims on a pilgrimage to Adam's peak in Ceylon, visited the Perumal at Kodungallur. They discussed with him about the tenets of Islam and narrated to him the miracle of the division of moon, which he himself had experienced. The king was thoroughly convinced and the 'heart of the King became warmed by a holy affection towards Muhammad'. As a result, he requested them to return to Cranganore after their visit to Adam's peak as he desired to accompany them on their voyage back to Mecca. However, before leaving for Mecca, he divided his kingdom amongst his officers. But on the way to Mecca he fell ill and died and was buried in Zofar. Sheikh Zainuddin did not know the exact date or period of this conversion. But he did not support the theory of the conversion taking place during the lifetime of the Prophet. In his opinion, it took place 200 years after *Hijra* perhaps during the ninth century.[14]

Indeed, there are literary evidences of a Chera king, bearing the title Cheraman Perumal who lived during the eighth or ninth century, and who ruled from Kodungallur (Makotai) during the second Chera period. If the so called conversion really took place during the ninth century it becomes important to turn back and go through the writings of the travellers who visited Malabar around the ninth and tenth centuries.

None of the Arab or Persian travellers right from Sulaiman al-Tajir and al-Masudi to Sulaiman al-Mahri, at the turn of the fifteenth century, had mentioned in their works about this conversion. Even since early days, Chinese travellers and traders had visited Malabar Coast. We find Kollam mentioned in the records of the Tang dynasty (AD 618-907) of China. However, there is no reference in the Chinese records related to the conversion during this period.[15]

Nevertheless, some Muslims of Malabar differed from the above narratives and presented their own version in which the conversion to Islamic faith of the Cheraman ruler is believed to have taken place during the time of Islamic Prophet. This has been recorded by William Logan too in his century account. It is believed according to this version that king Perumal was deeply impressed after hearing about the teachings of the Prophet from the pilgrims who visited Malabar and wanted to meet him and accept the new religion. With this intention, he is said to have visited the Prophet and having been blessed with an interview with him accepted Islam at his hands and returned to the coast of Arabia, where he is believed to have fallen ill and died. However, such a visit of the Prophet by the Cheraman king would have been definitely mentioned in the vast early Islamic literature. In the absence of such evidence, it is difficult to conclude that a Malabar King ever visited the Prophet and accepted Islam at his hands.[16]

We have definite epigraphic evidence of the existence of the Chera kingdom during AD 800-1122. The last Perumal, Rama Kulasekhara disappeared under strange circumstances, making it impossible to provide for accession to the throne. As a result, the kingdom fragmented, and the Perumal dynasty came to an abrupt end. Narayanan had endorsed the subsequent legend of the partition of Malabar and the conversion of the last Cheraman Perumal Rama Kulasekhara to Islam during the year (AD 1122-4). He supported this conversion with an inscription supposed to be in existence in the Madayi mosque since 518 AH (AD 1124). This mosque was supposed to have been built by Malik bin Dinar, the companion of Cheraman Perumal, during his sojourn in Arabia and who was deputed by the Perumal to propagate the new religion in Malabar. According to J.B.P. More, who had visited the Madayi mosque, there is hardly any evidence that the Madayi mosque was built by Malik bin Dinar, neither inscriptional nor epigraphical.[17]

Even the Italian travellers like Marco Polo who came to Malabar in the late thirteenth century and Nicolo Conti who was in Malabar in the fifteenth century had not mentioned a word about this conversion in their accounts. It is worth noting also that Ludovico de Varthema of Bologna (1503-8) came to Cananore in early sixteenth century. He too did not mention about the conversion of Cheraman Perumal. In his words, 'Cananore was a fine and large city in which the King of Portugal has a strong Castle (St. Angelo)'. He further mentioned that the Malabar rulers were very friendly towards the Portuguese. According to him, the King of Cananore had 50,000 Naeri (Nairs), who fought with swords, shields, lances and bows. According to him, Cananore was the port at which horses which come from Persia disembark, and that for every horse twenty-five ducats was paid as custom duty, before they proceeded on the mainland towards Narsingha territory. Other European travellers and writers right from the Dutchman Van Linschoten in the later part of the sixteenth century up to Francis Buchanan, Colonel McKenzie and A. Galetti have given their own versions or variations of the conversion of Cheraman Perumal to Islam, without providing the slightest factual evidence.[18]

As far as Malayalam literature is concerned, it was *Keralolpatti*, which seems to be the first local attempt to trace the history of Malabar from the early days. Sewell had asserted that this work was authored by Thunjathu Ramanuja Ezhuthachhan. It is also believed that it was translated from an original untraceable Sanskrit version. According to Sewell and More, *Keralolpatti* is an account chiefly from the Vedic Brahmanical point of view of the origin and history of Kerala. It is rather a recollection of oral stories, traditions and legends, which might contain some historical truth which is extremely difficult to identify. It was a product of the eighteenth century, as there is a reference to the coronation of Zamorin at Trikkavil Palace in Ponnani and his wars and conquests, and also to the foreign powers, such as the Portuguese, the Dutch and the English.

Keralolpatti referred to the legend of Kulasekhara Perumal, who was brought in from the Tamil country to rule Chera country. He was the last Cheraman Perumal. He is said to have given up his throne, embraced Islam and went on a pilgrimage to Mecca. It seems that he died in Zophar in 831 AD, where his tomb was still to be seen in the name of Abdul Rahman Samiri. He is said to have divided his kingdom into 18 divisions and having given his sword to the ancestor of the Zamorin of Calicut, he sailed from Dharmapatnam towards Arabia. After residing at Jeddah, he passed away. But before that, he persuaded the Arab chiefs to go to Malabar with a number of followers to establish colonies and convert the inhabitants to Islam. In accordance with this order, they built eleven mosques along the coast.[19] Mackenzie had given two versions of the conversion. The first one is related to the conversion of Cheraman Perumal to Islam. The second one dealt with his conversion to Buddhism. Another version of the *Keralolpatti* mentioned that among the Perumals, who were brought in from Tamilakam there was one Bana Perumal, who converted to Buddhism after losing out to the Brahmins in a debate. He was banished and excommunicated, and he went to Mecca after reigning for four years. Pachu Muthathu, a Sanskrit scholar and court physician of Travancore, who authored the *Tiruvithamkur Charitram* in 1867, had in his work called *Kerala Visista Mahatmaya* repeated that Bana Perumal, who was a Chera converted to Buddhism by the Buddhist monks from China and eventually followed them to China after reigning for four years. It is believed that before his departure, he divided the kingdom into 18 divisions.[20]

A translated work from the original Persian work of

Muhammad Qasim Ferishta by John Briggs (published in 1829) recounts that during the reign of a prince called Samiry, some vessels from Arabia having Mohammedans on board, going on a pilgrimage to the footsteps of Adam on the island of Selandep (Ceylon) which is also called Lunka (Lanka) were driven into the port of Cranganore, where the Samiry Raja resided. 'This Prince received the strangers with hospitality and was so pleased with the society of some holymen, who were among the pilgrims that after interacting with them, he converted to the Mohammedan faith, left his kingdom and departed to Mecca', and died in one of the ports of the Red Sea. Before his death he wrote to his representatives in Malabar to receive the Mohammadans in future with hospitality and permit them to settle and build *masjids*. This communication was written in the language of Malabar, whose ruler henceforth assumed the title of Samiry.[21]

Another view asserted that Cheraman Perumal became a Jain. But ancient Tamil literary works like *Periya Puranam*, *Tiruvilaiydal Puranam* and *Halasya Mahatyam* state that the Perumal was a devout Shaivite all his life and died in the celebrated temple at Thiruvanchikulam (Kodungallur). Logan had reported that Hindus actually believed that he was taken to heaven and still continue to expect his descent on which account they assemble at Kodungallur, and keep ready their wooden shoes and water and on a certain night of the year burn lamps as a kind of festival in honour of his memories.[22]

But by the beginning of the nineteenth century the story that Cheraman Perumal converted to Islam found its place in the court chronicles of Calicut and Cochin. During the same century, British administrators like William Taylor, Edgar Thurston, along with Logan, Sewell, etc. had recorded their own versions of the legend of Cheraman Perumal. There is no unanimity between them regarding the conversion or the events leading to the conversion or the events that took place after the conversion. Besides we find nothing about this conversion of a Malabar king in the Early Islamic. Otherwise his name would have appeared as an *Assahabi*, i.e. the companions of the Prophet. As far as Hind was concerned, the ruler of Kannauj named Sarbatak and Baba Ratan Haji were believed to be companion of the Prophet, but none from Malabar Coast.[23] Therefore, in the absence of evidence, the meeting of Cheraman Perumal with the Prophet and accepted Islam at his hands seems to be more a figment of imagination of its authors.

Further, to buttress the claim that the ancestor of Zamorin did not convert to Islam, we have the narration of Abdur Razzak in the year 1442. Abdur Razzak came to Calicut as ambassador of Shah Rukh Bahadur, the Timurid Sultan of Persia, with the deliberate intention of convincing and converting the Zamorin of Calicut to Islam as per the order received from the Sultan. Unfortunately, he failed in his mission to convert the Zamorin to Islam. He is said to have stayed in Malabar for six months.[24]

The question that arises in my mind is that if Abdur Razzak came to convert the Zamorin, he would have definitely heard about the previous conversion of the last Cheraman Perumal to Islam, who left for Mecca to meet the Prophet. Surprisingly, Abdur Razzak did not hear a word about the so called conversion in any of its versions. Besides, we do not know how the Zamorin could be converted afresh if his ancestors had already converted to Islam. This gives the lie to the version that claimed that the Zamorin or Samiry had converted and his tomb is in Zophar.

It is quite unfortunate that the historians hitherto, have completely neglected or ignored the conversion narration of a Kolatiri ruler or the prince of Kannur by Ibn Battuta. Nobody has ever consulted or given importance to the translation of Revd. Samuel Lee of Ibn Battuta's work where 'Jur Kannan' and 'Dadkannan' had been identified with Cananore and Dharmapatnam respectively, and the 'infidel' King was no one else but the Kolatiri king himself.[25]

Hence, the only conversion to Islam that took place during the thirteenth century or before was the conversion of the prince of Cananore mentioned by Ibn Battuta. Al-Idrisi had referred to Jirbattan (Kannur) in the eleventh century. But he had not mentioned any conversion of the Cananore king or prince to Islam in his accounts. Therefore, we can safely conclude that the conversion of the Kolatiri king or Prince, based in Cananore took place during the twelfth or thirteenth century. This conversion got mixed up with the legend of the conversion of the Cheraman Perumal after the arrival of the Portuguese and never before. The latter legend might have been concocted by the Muslims of Cananore, or the Arakkal House in order to attribute to them a prestigious ancestry. Barbosa was the first one to hear it and note it. Others followed their suit. Therefore, it is more judicious to accept that the conversion of a Kolatiri prince to Islam, noted by Battuta in the fourteenth century had given rise to the Arakkal principality, or the chiefdom of Ali Raja in later centuries.

NOTES

1. Samuel Lee (tr.). *The Travels of Ibn Battuta*, London, 1829, pp. 1, 169-70; Mahdi Husain (tr. & ed.), *The Rehla of Ibn Battuta*, Baroda, pp. liv, lv, 177-80; H.A.R. Gibb (tr.), *Travels in Asia and Africa 1325-54*, London, 1957, pp. 234-5; A. Schimmel, *Islamic Literatures of India*, Wiesbaden, 1973, p. 7; Ross E. Dunn, *The Adventurers of Ibn Battuta, A Muslim Traveller of the 14th Century*, Berkeley, Los Angeles, 1986, pp. 1-3, 183-6 , 193-4, 213-14; C. Defremery and B.R. Sanguinette (trs.), *Ibn Battuta. Voyages Inde, Extrême Orient, Espagne et Soudan*, vol. III, Paris, 1982, p. 106 (French); J.B.P. More, *Origin and Early History of the Muslims of Keralam AD 700 -AD 1600*, Calicut, 2011, pp. 69, 73-5.
2. *Tamil Lexicon*, II, 693, 1194, 1195; Samuel Lee, op. cit., p.170; A. Sreedhara Menon, *Kerala District Gazetteers*, Trivandrum, 1972, p. 1.
3. Samuel Lee, op. cit., p. 171.
4. Revd. Samuel Lee, op. cit., pp. 170-1; K.P. Padmanabha Menon, *History of Kerala*, vol. I, pp. 438-9.
5. C. Defremery and B.R. Sanguinette (trs.), op. cit., 1982, pp. 203-4 (French); Mahdi Husain (tr. & ed.), op. cit., pp.187-8; J.B.P. More, op. cit., p. 76.

6. S. Maqbul Ahmad (tr.), *India and the Neighbouring Territories in the Kitab Nuzhat al-Mushtaq fi ikhtiraq Al-Afaq*, Leiden, 1960, pp. 56, 63, 68; H.A.R. Gibbs, op. cit., 234-5.
7. Syed Muhammad Husayn Nainar, *Arab Geographer's Knowledge of Southern India*, Calicut, 1942, 2011, pp. 36, 45.
8. K.K.N. Kurup, *The Ali Rajas of Cannanore*, Calicut, 2002, p. 16.
9. William Logan, *Malabar*, vol. 1, Madras, 1951, p. 147; J.B.P. More, op. cit., p. 122.
10. K.K.N. Kurup, op. cit., p. 16.
11. H.E.J. Stanley (tr.), *Duarte Barbosa, A Description of the Coast of Africa and Malabar*, London, 1866, pp. 101-3, 149; M.L. Dames (tr.), *The Books of Duarte Barbosa*, vol. II, London, 1621, pp. 1 & 6, 20; J.B.P. More, op. cit., pp. 102-3.
12. Tomé Pires, *Sumo Oriental of Tomé Pires, 1512-15 and the Book of Francisco Rodriguez*, vol. 1, New Delhi, 1990 (rpt.), pp. 78-9.
13. Muhammad Husayn Nainar (tr. & ed.), *Tuhfat al-Mujahideen of Shaikh Zainuddin Makhdum*, Calicut, 2006, p. 101; J.B.P. More, op. cit., p. 102; J.B. Harrison 'Five Portuguese Historians' in C.H. Philips (ed.), *Historians of India, Pakistan and Ceylon*, London, 1961, pp. 156, 159; Joao de Barros, *Decada*, Book IX, Chapter III, Lisbao, 1778, p. 324; Luiz de Camoena, *Os Lusiades*, Canto 7, stanzas, 33-4; George Birdwood, *Report on the Old Records of the India Office*, Calcutta, 1891, p. 180.
14. Syed Muhammad Husayn Nainar, op. cit., pp. 29-32; E.J. Brill, *First Encyclopaedia of Islam*, 1913-36, vol. V, Leiden, 1987, p. 204; M.J. Rowlandson, (tr.), *Tohfat-ul-Mujahideen*, London, 1833, pp. 5, 50, 51-7, 59; Cf. also, J.B.P. More (ed.), *Offerings to the Muslim Warriors of Malabar*, Chennai, 2015.
15. Syed Muhammad Husayn Nainar, op. cit., Calicut, 2009, p. 94; J.B.P. More, op. cit., p. 46; R.H. Major, *India in the 15th Century*, London, MDCCCLVII, pp. xxv, xxvii, xxxiii-xxxiv; G.R. Tibbetts, *A Study of Arabic texts Containing Material of South East Asia*, London, 1979, p.75; Tan Ta Sen, *Cheng Ho and Islam in South East Asia*, Singapore, 2009, p. 144; J.J.L. Duyvendak, *Ma Huan Reexamined*, Amsterdam, 1933, pp. 1-2, 5; W.W. Rockhill, 'Notes on the relations and trade of China with the Eastern Archipelago and the coast of Indian ocean during the fourteenth century', in T'oung Po, vol. 16, 1914, p. 82; J.V.G. Mills (ed.), *Ma Huan Ying Yai Sheng Ian, The Overall Survey of the Ocean Shores*, 1433, Thailand, 1977, p. 35.

16. William Logan, op. cit., vol. 1, Madras, 1989, pp. 191-5; Abdul Rahim, 'Islam in Negapatnam', *Bulletin of the Institute of Traditional Cultures*, Madras University, July-December 1974, p. 85; K.M. Bahauddin, *Kerala Muslims: The Long Struggle*, Trivandrum, 1992, pp. 21-2; J.B.P. More, op. cit., p. 110.
17. A.P. Ibrahim Kunju, 'Origin and Spread of Islam in Kerala', in Asghar Ali Engineer (ed.), *Kerala Muslims. A Historical Perspective*, Delhi, 1995, pp. 19, 21; J.B.P. More, op. cit., pp. 124-32; M.G.S. Narayanan, *Perumals of Kerala*, Calicut, 1996, p. 65.
18. A.C. Moule and Paul Pelliot, *Marco Polo, Description of the World*, Vol. I, London, MCMXXXVIII, p. 416; G. Bouchon, *Regent of the Sea*, Delhi, 1988, p. 3; R.H. Major, *India in the 15th Century*, London, MDCCCLVII, pp. 17-19; John Winter Jones (tr.), *The Itinerary of Ludovico Di Varthema of Bologna from 1502 to 1508* (from the original Italian edition of 1510), Madras, 1997, pp. Iiii, 50; A.C. Burnell and P.A. Tiele (eds.), *The Voyage of John Huygen Von Linschoten to the East Indies*, vol. I, London, 1885, pp. 71-3; Francis Buchanan, *A Journey from Madras through Mysore, Canara and Malabar*, vol. II, London, 1807, p. 349; A. Galletti, *Dutch in Malabar*, Madras, 1911, p. 199. H.H. Wilson, *A Description of the Catalogues of the Oriental Manuscripts and Other Articles by Lieut. Col. Colin Mackenzie*, vol. I, Calcutta, 1828; Maqbul Ahmed, op. cit., pp. 56, 63, 68.
19. G. Bouchon, *L'Asie du Sud à l'époque des Grandes Découvertes*, London, 1987, vol. II, p. 22; William Logan, op. cit., vol. I, Madras, 1951, ch. III; Robert Sewell (compiler), *A Sketch of the Dynasties of Southern India*, Madras, 1883, p. 57; H. Gundert, *Keralolpatti: The Origin of Malabar*, Mangalore, 1961, pp. 121, 129; J.B.P. More, op. cit., p. 105.
20. M.G.S. Narayanan, op. cit., pp. 182-3; Cf. M.G.S. Narayanan, *Kozhikode Charithrattilninnu Chila Edukal*, Kozhikode, 2011, p. 17; Col. Mackenzie (compiler), op. cit., vol. II, p. 91; Robert Sewell, op. cit., pp. 55-6.
21. John Briggs (tr.), *History of the Rise of Mahomedan Power in India till the year* AD *1612, from the Original Persian of Mahomed Kasim Ferishta*, vol. IV, London, 1829, p. 531.
22. William Logan, *Malabar Manual*, vol. I, Madras, 1951, pp. 29-32, 221-31.
23. William Logan, op. cit., vol. I, Madras, 1989, p. 191, A. P. Ibrahim Kunju, op. cit., p. 19; Shaukat Ali Khan, 'Indo-Arab Relations before

Muhammad bin Qasim', in P.M. Joshi (ed.), *Studies in the Foreign Relations of India*, Hyderabad, 1975, p. 142.

24. O.K. Nambiar, *The Kunjali Admirals of Calicut*, Bombay, 1963, p. 14; T.W. Arnold, *The Preaching of Islam*, Lahore, 1961, pp. 266-7; David Morgan, *Medieval Persia* 1040-1797, London, 1988, pp. 94-5.
25. J.B.P. More, op. cit., p. 75.

CHAPTER 5

Early Portuguese and the Kolatiri Raja, 1498-1524

The Portuguese King Joao II (1481-95), the son of Prince Henry the Navigator, ascended the throne in 1481. His men were unable to reach the eastern lands and India through the land route, which was lying in the hands of the Arabs and Turks. So, in the year 1487 to 1488, he sent one of his ablest navigators, Bartolomeu Dias, to find out if the Atlantic Ocean was connected to the Indian Ocean. He hoped to establish a direct sea route around Africa to the Indian subcontinent, for purposes of trade. Bartolomeu Dias rounded the tip of southern Africa and returned to Lisbon in the year 1488.

The monarch further dispatched two persons, Pedro de Covilham and Alfonso de Pavya, both Arabic speakers by the usual land route to India via Egypt. Covilham is said to have sailed in an Arab vessel from Aden to Cananore and Calicut and returned to Cairo. He was the first Portuguese ever to set foot in Malabar and Cananore. He sent an exhaustive account of his travels in Malabar and invoked the name of the Zamorin and his Muslim allies who assisted him in the administration.[1]

In reality, it was the Portuguese who first revealed the name of 'Kannanur'. The only known mention of its existence is found in Ibn Majid's log book, which was compiled ten years before Vasco da Gama's first voyage and was used exclusively by the pilots. From 1495 to 1499, King Manuel I succeeded to the throne. The stories of Malabar country and Cananore's reputation and its immense production in spices, its flourishing seafaring trade, besides the stories of its notorious pirates, had already caught his imagination.[2]

On 8 July 1497, a Portuguese fleet under Vasco da Gama left Portugal to look for 'Spices and Christians'. They rounded the Cape following Dias and reached the port of Melindi. Vasco da Gama was wary and suspicious of the Africans. He did not disembark. But the Sultan of Melindi embarked on board his ship. Both sides exchanged gifts. At Melindi harbour, Vasco da Gama sighted four vessels belonging to Malabar 'Syrian Christians'. It is believed that at Melindi, Vasco da Gama sought the help of the famous Arab Navigator Ahmad ibn Majid to cross the Arabian Sea to reach the Malabar Coast. Sanjay Subrahmanyam concurs with this assumption.

Unfortunately, there is no reference of Vasco da Gama meeting Ibn Majid in any accounts by the Arab chroniclers. But Portuguese chroniclers like Castanheda and de Gois had mentioned that a Gujarati Muslim pilot called Canaqua guided Vasco da Gama, while Joao de Barros mentioned a certain Cana of Indian origin helped Gama to reach Malabar. It seems reasonable to admit that a stranded Gujarati pilot by the name of Molemo Canaqua, or Malemo Cana must have helped Vasco da Gama and his men to cross Arabian Sea. But Gabriel Ferrand identified Malemo Canaqua (master pilot astronomer) with Ibn Majid, the best Arab pilot and author of guide books during those days. According to More, Gama's reaching Malabar was not an exploit of the highest order as he was only following the footsteps of his predecessors like Dias, and the Arab or Indian pilots.[3]

VASCO DA GAMA ON THE MALABAR COAST, 1498-1500

The Portuguese crossed the Indian Ocean within 23 days. Vasco da Gama's pilot had foretold that the first land to be sighted would be a great mountain on the coast of India in the kingdom of Cananore. This mountain was nothing, but the historical Ezhilkunram or Ezhimala. After a hazardous voyage lasting ten months, Vasco da Gama finally anchored off Kappad village about 19 kilometres north of Calicut at the mouth of Elattur river on 20 May 1498.[4]

Vasco da Gama waited for several days offshore before actually setting foot in Calicut. Joao Nunes, Vasco da Gama's emissary, managed to obtain an audience with Zamorin of Calicut. After being convinced of his safety, Vasco da Gama went ashore to meet the Zamorin along with thirteen men on 28 May 1498. However, contrary to his apprehension, he and his men were given a rousing welcome by the Malabaris of Calicut. He introduced himself as the ambassador of the King Manuel of Portugal.[5]

The first meeting between Vasco da Gama and the Zamorin went on well. Unfortunately, the meeting on the following day did not end well as the presents offered to the Zamorin was so trivial, comprising 13 pieces of lamtel striped cloth, four scarlet hoods, six hats, four strings of coral, a case containing six basins for hand wash, a case of sugar, two casks of oil, and two of honey, that it was scorned by one and all who had gathered there. They jeered at the paltry gift. A Moorish officer laughed at the gifts and refused to forward them to the Zamorin commenting that this was not fit to be offered to Zamorin who will never accept such trash, as even the poorest merchant from Mecca or from any part of India presented more gifts. The displeasure of Zamorin to the insignificant presents compelled Vasco da Gama to admit that he was on a voyage of discovery, and that these were his personal gift and not that of the King. He also admitted that he did not bring any gold, and if he was given another chance to visit Malabar by his King, he will bring forth richer presents. According to More, the trivial gifts were probably suitable for the Hotentots and the Bantus but not for the Zamorin, the most powerful king of the Malabar Coast at that time.[6]

Muslim traders of Calicut who enjoyed undisputed monopoly in the overseas trade of Calicut resented the presence of Portuguese as the competitor on their soil. They soon began to resort to intrigues to turn the Zamorin against the Portuguese. Vasco da Gama, in his turn, was irked by the influence wielded by the Muslims of Calicut over the Malabar trade circles and over Zamorin himself. He tried unsuccessfully to turn Zamorin against the Muslim traders. But a naked truth dawned that he could never establish trade relationships with the Zamorin unless the Muslim traders were cast aside. Gama's reluctance to pay the custom duties further strained his relationship with the Zamorin. He sailed away from Calicut to Lisbon, where he also took some local people along with him, but enroute, he sailed to Cananore, land of the Kolatiri king. It so happened that at that time the Kolatiri was an independent king or chieftain, not subject to the Calicut ruler. In fact, he was an arch enemy of Zamorin at that time.[7]

Although the port of Cananore came into prominence with the arrival of Portuguese, the kingdom of Cananore had been known to the world since at least the time of Ptolemy. Cananore was part of the Nannan chiefdom and the famous Mount Eli/Mushika kingdom, which was ruled by the Mushika Kings. The Portuguese ships of Vasco Da Gama anchored on the western side of the harbour of Cananore. Gama had been briefed about the kingdom of Cananore before he embarked on his expedition, even though the prime objective of his voyage was to meet the king of Calicut. But once in Calicut, Vasco da Gama was disillusioned not only with its king, but also with its Muslim merchants.

When the Portuguese were in Calicut, the Kolatiri had sent his people to obtain information about what was happening there. The Moor merchants of Cananore tried to influence the Kolatiri against the Portuguese. But the Kolatiri did not pay heed to them.

While in Malabar, Gama realized that Kolatiri and Raja of Cochin did not get along well with the Zamorin. Taking advantage of this situation, the Portuguese wanted to befriend the Kolatiri Raja. Incidentally, he received an invitation from a messenger of Kolatiri asking him and his brother to disembark at Cananore on their return voyage to Portugal as Kolatiri was indeed interested in meeting Gama's brothers to eventually establish trade relations, contrary to the wishes of the Zamorin. While Gama anchored offshore at Cananore, the messenger of Kolatiri brought alongwith him the customary gifts, boats loaded with fowl, coconuts, desicated fish, coconut oil, butter and barrels of drinking water.

Ceremonial gun shots were fired from the ship to welcome da Gama. But da Gama did not go ashore as they were not authorized by their king to disembark at Cananore. As a customary, in return for the goods received from Kolatiri, Gama reciprocated the gesture by sending back the boats loaded with valuable items like pearls, mercury, plates made of copper and brass besides bundles of green silk cloth, velvet cloth, red table cloths, 30 red caps, besides 15 metres of black silk cloth, and two knives with cases. Unlike the Zamorin, the Kolatiri Raja was very delighted with the presents of Vasco da Gama.

Kolatiri Raja, who was observing the scenario from the observatory tower, facilitated his meeting with Gama by ordering a wooden bridge to be constructed which entered a good way into the water, reaching up to the ship of Vasco da Gama. The bridge was constructed wide enough for one person to walk on; a cabin was built at one end. Seats were also built inside the cabin. The Gama brothers were received with respect and honour by the minister of Kolatiri and escorted to the meeting venue. Kolatiri came up to the door to receive him and embraced him. Together, they entered the room of the audience where two chairs were placed, contrary to the local custom.[8]

Thus, the Portuguese succeeded in conducting a meeting without breaking King Manuel's order, thanks to the ingeniosity of the Kolatiri who was aware of the bad experience which Vasco da Gama had with Zamorin in Calicut. The latter informed the Kolatiri Raja that he would be pleased if they could enter into trade contracts. He also promised to take up the matter further with the King of Portugal. In return gesture, Gama handed over a gold sword in a velvet case to the Kolatiri Raja by reciting a pledge. It was the ancient Portuguese tradition that once the sword was given, the promise should not be broken. Kolatiri Raja made a written agreement in a charter made of gold and signed the charter. In reciprocation, Kolatiri Raja presented Vasco da Gama and his brother Paulo da Gama with a golden chain embedded with precious stones and pearls valued at about ten thousand *panam* (money), ten bundles of golden silk, six gold rings besides 20 white muslin. Elated with the gifts, Gama took leave of the Kolatiri Raja from Cananore promising to return soon. Hence, Vasco da Gama's first trade venture kick started from the Kolatiri Kingdom of Cananore.

SUBSEQUENT EXPEDITIONS, 1500-1503

The tedious return journey back to Lisbon was very painful as Paulo da Gama, the brother of Vasco da Gama, fell ill and died in the Terceira Island, along with 120 men of the crew. But they had returned home with the 'black gold', i.e. pepper and spices which was in high demand. Eventually, they were able to make plenty of profits. Moreover, the spices brought back home, became such a rage in Portugal that it was consumed not only in Portugal, but even in all the other provinces of Europe. The King of Portugal realized the value of pepper and spices in the international market and endeavoured to monopolize the spice trade. He thus, decided to send a second expedition to Malabar in the year AD 1500 under the leadership of Pedro Alvares Cabral. The observations of Vasco da Gama at Cananore coupled with the informations obtained from his crew helped Cabral in exploring this kingdom. This time they sailed off with 13 ships having on board 1,500 soldiers and manned by a crew totalling to 15,000. They had enough artillery on board to deal with potential aggressors. Besides, they carried merchandise and gifts specially earmarked for the sovereigns of Malabar. The members of the crew received clear instructions that their primary objectives were to affirm their position in the spice trade and to propagate Christianity in Indian Ocean.[9]

They reached Calicut on 13 September 1500. Meanwhile, a new monarch ascended the throne of Calicut. Cabral demanded permission from the Zamorin to establish trading posts under the threat of war and to allow five Franciscan fathers to preach the Gospel. He also tried to persuade the Zamorin to shut his ports against the traders from Arabia. A clash ensued. Cabral bombarded Calicut for one whole day. The Portuguese soon sailed off to Cochin, another rival to Calicut, for safety. From Cochin, Cabral sailed and anchored at Cananore on 15 January 1501, heeding to the invitation of the Kolatiri king and the instructions from back home.

The Kolatiri king actually sent his ambassadors to Cabral offering him trade, port and friendship. Arriving in Cananore, Cabral befriended the Kolatiri Raja. The Kolatiri made known his intention to help the Portuguese, if they waged war on Calicut. He did not make much headway with the Kolatiri, as his stay in Cananore was just for a day. When Cabral departed for Portugal, the Kolatiri delegated an ambassador from Cananore to call on the King of Portugal. Finally on 31 July 1501, the expedition of Cabral returned to Lisbon, with the ambassador of Kolatiri.[10]

Cabral's expedition was followed by a third expedition under the leadership of Joao da Nova, who being informed of the violence taking place at Calicut headed straight for Cochin. From Cochin, he soon sailed to Cananore where they were received with full honour by the Kolatiri Raja of Cananore. Nova, however, failed to sell his goods at the port of Cananore. Regardless the Kolatiri allowed the Portuguese to safely stock their unsold goods in Cananore and for this purpose, he even constructed a godown of redstone rocks near the harbour and a trench surrounding the godown. He even appointed six Nair warriors to safeguard the godown and its goods from the sea pirates. Joao da Nova left Goncalo Gomes Ferriera in Cananore as his representative along with two officials to take care of the trade and to maintain accounts. One of the official was Barbosa, who was in the service of Portuguese crown in India from AD 1500 till AD 1517. He stayed in Cananore for 16 years. He was fluent in Malayalam and gained knowledge of the local customs around Cananore.[11]

It should be noted that constructing a godown or factory in Cananore was the forerunner of a permanent fort being built in the same place in the year 1505. Both Cabral and Joao da Nova were received and treated with utmost consideration by the inhabitants of Cananore. The next Portuguese expedition was that of Vasco da Gama, who came to India a second time in 1502 with a fleet of 20 ships accompanied by 800 specially trained armed soldiers fully equipped for war and fully determined to enforce their king's will. This time Vasco da Gama was instructed to convert all Indians into Christianity and to eliminate Muslims from India. It was also a voyage of conquest and control of the sea. When they reached the Indian coast and were continuing on the Konkan coast, Gama saw a group of 24 small vessels loaded with rice, he immediately attacked them.

When the expedition reached Ezhimala, their ship was hit by a cyclone breaking the mast and to repair the flag mast they anchored at Marahi (Madayi) in Kolatiri territory. While they were repairing the flag mast, they sighted a ship the 'Meri' belonging to Koja Kasim brothers. Koja Kasim was a famous trader of Calicut. The ship was returning from Hajj. His ship was looted and the 700 pilgrims, including women and children put to death under the orders of Gama. Gama continued with his barbarous cruelty and insisted on expulsion of all Muslim merchants. Gama cannonaded Calicut for three days, destroying several houses including the palace of the Zamorin and killing hundreds in the process. The Zamorin was isolated in his fight. He sent his ambassadors to Cairo for Egyptian help rather than seeking help from his immediate neighbours, i.e. the Raja of Cochin and Cananore. Help from Egypt did not materialize. Vasco da Gama, then, claimed suzerainty over the seas and demanded that no ship should sail without a pass (*cartaz*) from the Portuguese. Heavy fees were charged for the ships which did not carry the Portuguese pass. Restrictions were placed on Indian and Arab ships from calling on Calicut port and carrying certain commodities of value.[12]

The Raja of Cochin, who ruled over a small territory, then gave permission to build a fort in his territory to the Portuguese. The Portuguese, thus, found a precious ally in the Raja of Cochin. Their claims to build forts and a church at Cochin and exclusive right to purchase spices at a fixed price was accepted by the Raja of Cochin despite opposition from the members of the royal family and the Raja of Edappally. Besides, the Raja of Cochin was supported by the Kolatiri Raja of Cananore in his fight against the Zamorin of Calicut. Thus, both became allies of the Portuguese. It was under these circumstances, Vasco da Gama sailed for Cananore where he wanted to renew his acquaintance with the Kolatiri Raja. The two had already met each other during the first expedition. This time also Portuguese were given a ceremonious welcome by the Kolatiri Raja with 4,000 sword-bearing foot soldiers. He was accompanied by his nephew holding a sword and shield. The King gave Gama a necklace and two bracelets and rings for the Queen and other rich jewels for himself. The king was also accompanied by several of his courtiers and two elephants. Guns were shot from the land and cannons were shot from the ship. The atmosphere was reverberating with the sound of beating of drums, trumpets and gun shots. The Kolatiri did not fail to extend his condolence on hearing the belated news about the death of the brother of Vasco da Gama. A meeting was organized by the Kolatiri for thrashing out trade details with Gama. This meeting was presided by Muslim traders, who disagreed on prices to be fixed for trade. This infuriated Gama. He was once again enraged like in Calicut at the power wielded by the Muslim merchants during the meeting.

He sent out the Muslim traders who were present and issued a complaint letter stating that Kolatiri ruler had fooled him by inviting foolish traders for these important discussions. Infuriated, Gama devised a strategy to counter the Muslims. He divided his fleet into two groups and sent them in two different directions. One ship headed by Vincent Sadre was earmarked for trade and the other with explicit order to attack the ships belonging to the Zamorin and the Moors.

Meanwhile, Kolatiri intended to make use of Gama for settling personal scores. He was nursing a grievance against a famous businessman Coje Mame Marcar of Cairo, who owed money to the Kolatiri and was there in Cananore. To please Kolatiri, Gama immediately ordered Sadre to cruelly punish this trader. Coje was whipped and insulted. A piece of bacon was thrust into his mouth along with dirt and tied up. In return for this service, Kolatiri agreed to bear their daily expenses and decided to give Sadre a gratification of thousands *pardaos* of gold and sent a gold *pardao* each day to the Portuguese commandant.

Gama, in his turn, wanted to expand the trade in Cananore. For this, he obtained permission from the Kolatiri to build a wall and palisade. As part of this expansion programme, Gama buried all the weapons and cannons in the land on the northern side of Cananore fort and posted two hundred soldiers on duty there. Finally, Gama and his men left Cananore on 28 December 1502, and reached Lisbon on 1 September 1503.[13]

From the foregoing narration, it becomes very clear that Cananore figured in the agenda of the Portuguese right from the arrival of Vasco da Gama on the Malabar coast. But the Kolatiri had an axe to grind with the Zamorin who was prospering at his expense by trading with the Arabs and Chinese. He wanted to use the Portuguese to his advantage. The Nairs of this land were the military men and esteemed cavaliars, and the most honourable people of all the country and in Cananore province they were about two hundred thousands of these men. They were very loyal to their king and worshiped him, and rarely it has been found that a Nair has been guilty of treason. But when they go to war they wear a red colour turban. The Portuguese records further mentions about the port of Cananore being a hub of sea traffic. It was said that around 200 ships come there from various countries.[14]

ALBUQUERQUE, ALMEIDA AND VASCO DA GAMA, 1503-1524

In the month of August 1503, a Portuguese fleet under the leadership of Don Francisco de Albuquerque reached Cananore in six ships. This group met the Kolatiri Raja and interacted with him. They then sailed off for Cochin. After the completion of the Fort at Cochin, Francisco de Albuquerque returned to Cananore, collected loads of cloves, and cinnanmon and with the merchandise he left for Portugal on 31 January 1504. The Kolatiri Raja was accompanied by the principal Muslim merchant, the Mamale, along with the rulers of the land, many noble Moors and 5,000 Nairs armed with swords, and daggers when he met Afonso in a well furnished tent in Cananore, outside the Portuguese fort. Albuquerque impressed upon the Mamale and the Moors that the King of Portugal was the sovereign of the high seas and not the Mamale or the Moors. It is noteworthy that both the Rajas of Cochin and Cannaore did not want Albuquerque to construct a fort or settlement in Calicut, as the Zamorin was their enemy.[15]

During the year 1504, Lopo Soares de Menus and his group commanding a fleet of 14 ships arrived in Cananore where he was received by Kolatiri Raja with three elephants and 5,000 warriors. The Portuguese fleet created havoc by attacking the Moors fleet, killing around 2,000 on board. They captured 17 ships and destroyed the rest before proceeding to Cochin. In Kodungallur, the Portuguese had attacked and destroyed the oldest mosque known as Cheraman Juma Masjid. Several people were wounded and rushed to a medical centre in Cananore. In the documents signed in Cananore by Lopo Soares de Menus was a *mandado* dated 5 January where he admitted that he had set ships on fire at Capocote (Kappat) near Calicut. Another document referred to his brief visit on 6 January to Cananore, where he collected provisions, medicinal drugs, ginger, etc. But before leaving Cananore, he made arrangements to build a hospital to treat soldiers who were wounded in the battle. Perhaps, this was a reference to the origin of the Cananore hospital. Pyrard de Laval, a French missionary too had alluded to this hospital at Cananore.[16] Thus, Cananore and the Kolatiri king played their role in helping the Portuguese against the Zamorin. At no point of time, since the arrival of the Portuguese on the Malabar Coast, it has been recorded that the Kolatiri king was subjected to the Zamorin of Calicut. The Kolatiris were always an independent entity of north Malabar since Nannan's time.

Under the order from the King of Portugal an expedition led by Don Francisco de Almeida left for India on 25 March 1505. Almeida sailed with 28 ships. He reached Cochin with 1,500 soldiers and eight ships. Very soon, he sailed to Cananore and reached Cananore around September 1505. Almeida was received warmly by the Kolatiri Raja. He took stock of the situation in Cananore. He was aware of the enmity existing between the Kolatiri king and the Zamorin. He convinced Kolatiri about the necessity to maintain an army in Cananore as the Zamorin's army and the Moors (Muslim merchants of Calicut) were their opponents in trade. He requested the Kolatiri Raja to allot some land and to give him permission to construct a fort in Cananore.[17]

The Kolatiri Raja acceded to this request readily, as he wanted to cut down the Zamorin's power. The Kolatiri king needed protection from the attacks of the Zamorin. That was the principal reason for him to allow the Portuguese to erect a fort in his territory. He also intended to divert the Calicut trade to Cananore as much as he could. As a result, he made use of the Portuguese to further his ends. But he never seems to have realized at that juncture, that the Portuguese might make use of their dominant presence in the high seas to undermine his own interests.

Barbosa was entrusted with the responsibility of building the fort. He selected the triangular land reaching out to the sea due to its strategic position. As the land was surrounded by water on all three sides and was 40 feet above sea level, the lower layer of the land was red rock, he felt this location was safe to build a fort. Kolatiri, thus, gave permission to build a fort in Cananore on condition that the key of the main entrance of the fort must remain in his custody. On 23 October 1505, foundation was laid and the work on the fort commenced. Almeida delegated all his workers and officers for this construction work.

The Kolatiri Raja also provided his country workers. The construction work was carried out under the guidance and supervision of an experienced engineer, Thomas Fernandes, who had earlier constructed the fort at Cochin. The construction of the fort began, using redstones which were locally available, and at times it was carted from nearby villages to the site by bullock carts or in boats. These stones of different dimensions were bound together with lime and calcium chloride and used for the construction of roofs and arches. They used a mixture of egg white and jaggery called *Surki* for binding, which was supposed to be stronger than the cement. While the construction was going on, a Portuguese commandant Lorenzo Britto arrived at Cananore, who was entrusted with the security of the fort. The fort was completed by the year AD 1507. It was named as Fort St. Angelo.[18]

It is interesting to note at this juncture that once the fort was constructed and Portuguese men were stationed there, it seems that in the course of time, there was some interaction between those men and the local society, apart from the relationship that they had with Kolatiri's men. In fact, some Portuguese men were attracted by Malabari women and had relationships with them. These women generally belonged to the Thiyya and Mukkuwa castes. As the Pope had lifted the ban on dealing with non-Catholics, such relationships became more and more frequent, though it was still very much an offence to frequent heathen girls. The fear of mortal sin was soon superseded by the attractions of the Malabar woman, who would prowl around the fortress and would sometimes succeed in setting up home with the soldiers of the garrison, for personal gain. The Viceroy had no other option, but to have the most beautiful ones baptized and to allow them to cohabit with their men. Gasper Correa, who recounts these facts, adds with a somewhat naive self-satisfaction that there was a sudden plethora of proselytization, that mother would offer their daughters, and that the Muslim women would defy their husbands in order to be converted into Christianity and share the life of the Portuguese. The unions do not appear to have been sanctified by marriage, as was the case later, but they saw the origin of the Luso-Malabari village which soon appeared round the fortess. The changes they brought about in the lower castes had a harmful effect on the interest of the Nairs who found themselves deprived of the duties and services that the Thiyyas and Mukkuvans could no longer guarantee once they entered the Christian community. It is interesting to note that the Kolatiri himself was aware of this situation. He even complained to King D. Manuel regarding the problems that such a situation was causing in terms of social hierarchy.[19]

During the 1506, Almeida left for Cochin as he was promoted to the rank of Viceroy by the King of Portugal. Before leaving he entrusted the security of the fort comprising of 150 soldiers and two ships to the Commandant Lorenzo de Britto. Presently, there was a Portuguese settlement in the Fort. From Cochin, Almeida closely monitored the developments in Cananore. He received a clandestine information that the Zamorin was preparing for a major attack on the Cananore fort. The Zamorin was never happy about the construction of the fort in Cananore, with the permission of the Kolatiri king. Probably, the Zamorin thought that by vanquishing the Portuguese he could bring the Kolatiri king to toe his line.

Almeida deployed his son Lourenzo de Almeida to Cananore with eleven ships and 800 Portuguese soldiers fully equipped for an eventual war. On the other side, Zamorin's Nair warriors and the Moor traders from Kozhikode joined hands. They were helped by the Turks, Arabs, and Moors from Ponnani, Pantalayini, Kappad, Kollam and Dharmapatam. This allied troops along with 210 cargo vessels, both small and big ships and boats and with 4,000 soldiers moved towards Cananore to wreak vengeance on an army comprising of 150 Portuguese soldiers guarding the Fort St. Angelo. Lourenzo de Almeida led his ships. He fired at the enemy boats and ships with guns and cannons and destroyed several of them. Briefly the allied forces retreated to Dharmadam, and after a while resumed the attack. In the savage attack that ensued, the Portuguese routed the allied force with their superior gun power. It is believed that the allied force lost 3,000 soldiers whereas the Portuguese lost only six soldiers. This was a superb victory for the commander Lourenzo de Almeida. This victory helped the Portuguese to establish a virtual monopoly on the Malabar Coast. Lourenzo arrived at Cochin to inform his father Francisco Almeida about this victory. To celebrate this victory, Francisco Almeida sent twelve ships loaded with goods from Cochin to Portugal and gifted an elephant to the king. This was the first elephant to land in Portugal.

Almeida revived the former system of issuing passes to all ships coming to Kerala Coast to trade. This pass (*Cartzes*) contained all the information regarding the route of the ship, its destination and details of its crew. This pass was issued by the commandants of Cananore and Cochin Fort. In Cananore, it was a Portuguese employee of the Fort, Ludwig, who issued this pass as he was well-versed in Malayalam. The Portuguese began patrolling the sea near Cananore to enforce this order. They waylaid a ship sailing with goods from Calicut to Cananore without a pass. The ship belonged to a well-known businessman of Cananore known as Mammali Marakkar, who was a relative of the Muslim chief of Cananore. The allegation proved to be false, as they did carry a pass issued by the commandant of Cananore Fort. Unfortunately, the Portuguese believed it to be a forged document and as a punishment, they caught the captain along with a crew member of the ship, sewed them up in a cloth and threw them overboard after plundering and wrecking the ship. The Malabaris were furious at this barbaric act perpetrated by the Portuguese, especially when they saw the dead carcass cast ashore and recognized the body. One body was that of Aboobacker Ali, the nephew of Mammali Marakkar. Almeida realized that things were getting out of control. He tried to calm down the subjects of Kolatiri by putting the blame on Captain Gonsalves for the goof up of the pass. But the Moors cried for revenge. Unfortunately, when this incident happened the old Kolatiri king, who was instrumental in inviting the Portuguese, was on very friendly terms with them had passed away and his nephew became the new Raja. It happened that he was an ally of the Zamorin and an enemy of the Portuguese.[20]

The Moors carried the dead bodies to Valarpatanam fort, informed the Kolatiri ruler of the incident and requested him to take revenge for this heinous act. Kolatiri Raja then, called for a meeting and discussed the matter with his ministers and naval commanders. They realized quite belatedly that the Portuguese were trying to establish control of the sea and sea trade and becoming belligerent. After taking stock of the situation, the Kolatiri Raja decided to attack Fort St. Angelo. He even sought help from the Zamorin. When such things were happening, Cananore Fort, the commandant Britto sent a message to Almeida at Cochin apprising him of the situation. Within a few days, reinforcement came with arms and ammunition from Cochin. In addition, one thousand Portuguese soldiers were already camped inside the fort.

Kolatiri Raja gathered 40,000 warriors. The reinforcement came from Zamorin with 20,000 to 50,000 warriors, 23 pieces of artillery, and 200 small boats. The Malabari warriors systematically went about cutting off access to the fort. They dug a trench around it. The fort was surrounded by water on three sides and it was isolated. Ludovico Varthema (1504-7), who served under the Viceroy Dom Francisco de Almeida, observed that on 27 April 1507, the allied army of Kolatiri and Zamorin attacked the fort. They soon sensed that they were no match to the superior fire power emitting from the cannons of the Portuguese. Kolatiri realized the futility of continuing the war and he ordered to stop the hostilities. But after a brief respite, they tried to block the provision and water supply to the fort. The Portuguese did not have any well inside the fort, but one well was situated outside their fort. So to draw water the Portuguese had to come out of the fort. Whenever they came out to get water, the 'Moors' attacked them.

When the situation looked bleak, the Portuguese commandant Britto asked Thomas Fernandes who had supervised the construction of the fort to find a solution. He dug an underground tunnel upto the well outside the fort. Thus, they succeeded in getting water, but their provisions were getting depleted.

There was a food shortage and due to starvation, the Portuguese soldiers became physically weak. This blockade continued for four months and in the month of August, the army of Kolatiri once again began their onslaught. Many perished inside the fort. Even so, commandant Britto continued to fire cannons at the Cananore town. They even destroyed a mosque, where the Muslims used to assemble for their Friday prayers. This antagonized the Muslim community, who joined the Kolatiri army and unleashed a bloody attack. Both sides suffered casualties. At least 600 men died in this encounter. Britto realized that he had to surrender as his soldiers were too weak to fight.

On 27 March 1507, an unexpected arrival of Portuguese expedition comprising of sixteen fleets under the leadership of Tristo de Cunha saved the situation. His fleet had only 300 soldiers, but his ship carried cannons, guns and other powerful artillery. The allied forces boats and catamarans were no match to the superior military might of the Portuguese. Thus, the Portuguese who were on the brink of surrender, succeeded in reversing the situation by their military might which prompted Varthema to remark that after the siege an Ambassador named Mammali Marakkar who was the richest man in the country came to demand peace. It is interesting to note that the Marakkars were the sea captains of the Zamorins during that period.

Tristo de Cunha's army ravaged the Cananore market and set fire to it. Commandant Britto, then, called for a meeting to end this fight, outside the Cananore fort. Kolatiri and his ministers attended this peace meeting. A treaty was signed under which terms, the trade rights in Cananore were ceded completely to the Portuguese. A church was built in Cananore during this period which was christened as St. Antony's Church. Kolatiri was forced to sign this treaty though it did not serve his interests. Meanwhile elsewhere Lorenzo Almeida's (the son of Viceroy Don Francisco de Almeida) was shot and killed by the Zamorins fleet along with everyone on board. Viceroy Almeida wreaked vengeance for the death of his son in the most savage manner.[21]

Meanwhile Alfonso de Albuquerque came with the King's order to replace Almeida. The latter was reluctant to hand over the charge of viceroyship to Albuquerque. He took control over the army of Albuquerque along with his fleet and forcibly imprisoned Albuquerque at Cochin and returned to Cananore on February 1509. Later, he headed for Gujarat intending to attack ships belonging to Zamorin and Moors.

After plundering Egyptian ships and boats, he returned to Cananore with the plundered wealth and the captives were sent to the dungeon in the Cananore Fort. Some of them were hanged, or blown with cannons. They cut the dead bodies into pieces and threw them in the localities where the Moors were living to instil warning and fear in them. On March 1509, Almeida and his army sailed for Cochin again. While in Cochin, Albuquerque once again requested Almeida to hand over the charge of Viceroy to him. He was finally taken as a captive to Cananore fort, imprisoned and thrown into the infamous Cananore dungeon without light or water. Subsequently, Almeida returned to Cochin leaving Albuquerque to the charge of Britto. Before long in October 1509 a contingent under the command of Marshal John Fernado Coutinho with 15 ships and 1,600 soldiers anchored in the Arabian Sea on the western side of Cananore Fort. The news of the enmity and ill-treatment meted out to Albuquerque had reached Coutinho and his mission was to save him.

On landing on the shore, Coutinho and his group went straight to the fort seeking Albuquerque. He met commandant Britto, who informed him that he was a prisoner inside the fort and that Almeida had declined to relinquish the post of

Viceroy and was still in-charge. Sensing trouble, the very night, Britto secretly left for Cochin and apprised Almeida of the situation in Cananore. Almeida knew his game was up and anticipating problems, he immediately resigned from the post of Viceroy and along with Britto and few close friends got into a ship and sailed for Europe. Albuquerque was finally released from prison and installed as Viceroy in October 1509 by Marshal John Fernado Coutinho with great celebration in the fort of Cananore. The army parade was inspected by Albuquerque who took the guard of honour. Albuquerque had the full support of the Kolatiri king.

Albuquerque governed for six years. He captured Goa on 25 February 1510 AD. He alongwith his crew embarked for Cananore on 15 September 1510. While in Cananore, he held a meeting in a tent outside Fort St. Angelo with Kolatiri, his minister Chenacheri Kurup and his Muslim naval commander Mammali Marakkar. Later, he left for Goa on 15 October 1510. Albuquerque shifted their administrative office from Cochin to Goa. He had even requested the Raja of Cochin to convert to Christianity. He took Malacca in July 1511, and the fortess of Ormus and rendered the King of Maldives Islands tributary to the Portuguese. Albuquerque, contrary to his predecessors, entered into peaceful arrangements with the Zamorin. The Kings of Cananore and Cochin and their Moors disliked this, as it was detrimental to their trade and political interests.[22]

In 1524, Vasco da Gama was nominated as the Viceroy of Portugeuse possessions in India. He visited the Kolatiri Raja at Cananore. The king welcomed Gama with great pomp and honour. He was particularly pleased that Gama had wreaked vengeance on the Zamorin. He gave him a rich jewelled neck-chain and the Viceroy sent him a rich present consisting of pieces of silk from Portugal. Gama stayed in Cananore only for three days. Gama died on 24 December 1524.

Thus, by the second half of the sixteenth century, the Portuguese had established themselves as a trading body in Malabar largely at the expense of the Muslim traders and by plotting and scheming with one Malabar king against another with the sole aim of seizing absolute control over Malabar pepper trade. Their domination in Malabar lasted for over a period of 150 years. They established settlements at Cochin, Quilon, Cranganore and Cananore. They garrisoned and fortified Fort Manuel at Cochin and Fort St. Angelo at Cananore. In Attingal, which is situated south of Malabar, they possessed a college the Jesuits and a number of Christian churches. [23]

However, the Portuguese, in spite of their superior military and naval power were unable to make any headway into the interior lands of Malabar and colonize it. They were successfully restricted to their coastal settlements and forts by the Malabar kings and their Nair militia and Muslim seamen. Even that they could do so only by exploiting the rivalry that existed between the Kolatiri/Cochin and the Zamorin kings. It would not be an exaggeration to conclude that the Nair militia and Malayali Muslim seamen had successfully resisted the first wave of colonization of Malabar and India by the Europeans. They saw to it that the colonization of India did not take place from the western coast.

From the above, it is quite clear that almost all the Portuguese navigators and officers from Vasco da Gama upto Albuquerque and others, who led expeditions to Malabar were officially welcomed by the Kolatiri ruler of north Malabar and his Moorish ministers. Besides, in the early Portuguese writings and records, there was hardly any reference to any Muslim king or chieftain who ruled over Cananore. It is true there was a strong Muslim presence in the court of the Kolatiri as there was a close bond between the latter and his powerful Muslim merchants of Cananore; on whom he depended for trade purposes, especially to sell the products of Malabar in foreign markets.

Nevertheless, it should be noted that until the arrival of Vasco da Gama in Malabar, the Muslims of Malabar, whether an Arab or a Malayali, were trading more or less peacefully with the Chinese and other parts of India. One cannot deny that the Indian Ocean, which hitherto was a zone of free trade, until then became an arena of conflict and tension since the arrival of Portuguese, which had a telling effect on the trade in the region. The violence unleashed by the Portuguese against the Malayalis was something new to this region. The Portuguese were the inaugurators of this unprecedented violence in the Indian Ocean region.

It is also quite clear that right from the arrival of the Portuguese on the Malabar Coast, the Kolatiri ruler was an enemy of the Zamorin of Calicut. All the Portuguese accounts of sixteenth century establish him as an independent king. Even before the arrival of the Portuguese, we do not find any reference to the Kolatiri king as being subject to the Zamorin, or even the Cheraman Perumal in the accounts of the Arabs, Persians and Italians, right from Marco Polo upto Abdur Razzak. This being the case, it is simply far-fetched and fanciful to contend that the Kolatiri was subject to the Zamorin in any way at any point of time. In the light of this, the story that the Zamorin had precedence over the other Malabar kings especially the Kolatiri must be admitted as mere legends, concocted to glorify the Zamorin. It does not stand on any rational grounds. Right from the time of Nannan down to the Kolatiri, north Malabar had largely maintained through thick and thin, a separate political existence, though they might have had marital relationships with the other Malabar kings. Besides, the Malayali Moorish traders and their chiefs in the court of the Kolatiri king worked during this period and even before in the shadows of Kolatiri Raja without nursing any ambition to break away from his hold.

NOTES

1. Sir George Birdwood, *Report on the Old Records of the India Office*, Calcutta, 1891, p. 164; C.R. Boxer, *The Portuguese Seaborne Empire*, 1415-1815, London, 1969, p. 25; E.G. Ravenstein, 'The Voyages of Diogo Cao and Bartholomeu Dias, 1482-8, in *The Geographical Journal*, vol. xvi, 1900, pp. 625-55; J.B.P. More, *Origin and Early*

History of the Muslims of Keralam, 700 AD-1600 AD, Calicut, 2011, pp. 145-6.

2. G. Bouchon, *Regent of the Sea, Cannanore's Response to Portuguese Expansion 1507-28*, Delhi, 1988, p. 1; Jose Paul, ' Vasco da Gama's discovery of a maritime route to India—The Myth and Realities, Paper presented in the International Seminar on Maritime Malabar and the Europeans (1500-1962) held at Tellicherry, Canannore, from 14-18 January 2002, p. 5; Jean Cassou, *La Decouverte du Nouveau Monde vu d'ensemble*, Paris, 1966, p. 325.
3. Sir George Birdwood, op. cit, pp. 161-2; E.G. Ravenstein, op. cit., pp. 1, 44, 173-4, 178-9; F.C. Danvers, *The Portuguese in India - I*, London, 1894, pp. 48, 50; Sanjay Subrahmanyam, *The Career and Legend of Vasco da Gama*, Cambridge, 1997, pp. 79, 152-3; G. Bouchon, op. cit., pp. 103, 107; G.R. Tibbets, *Arab Navigation in the Indian Ocean before the Coming of the Portuguese*, London, 1981, pp. 9-11, Léopold de Saussure, 'Commentaire des instructions Nautiques de Ibn Majid et Suleyman al-Mahri', in Gabriel Ferrand (ed.), *Introduction à l'Astronomie Nautique Arabe*, Paris, 1928, p. 195; J.B.P. More, *Origin and Early History of the Muslims of Keralam 700 AD 1600 AD*, Calicut, 2011, p. 151.
4. Joao de Barros, *Da Asia*, Decad, 1, Lisbon, 1973, p. 438; K.P. Padmanabha Menon, *History of Kerala*, vol. I, New Delhi, 1989, p. 14; William Logan, Malabar, vol. 1, Madras, 1989, p. 282.
5. Sanjay Subrahmanyam, op. cit., pp. 128-31; J.B.P. More, op. cit., pp. 155-6; Stephen Neill, *A History of Christianity in India, The Beginnings to AD 1707*, Cambridge, 1984, p. 87; H.E.J. Stantley (tr.), *A Description of the Coasts of East Africa and Malabar in the Beginning of the 16th Century*, New Delhi, 1995, pp. 162-5, 221; E.G. Ravenstein, op. cit., pp. 58, 60, 62-3.
6. E.G. Ravenstein, op. cit., pp. 58, 60, 62-3; J.B.P. More, op. cit., p. 156; G. Bouchon, op. cit., p. 66.
7. J.B.P. More, op. cit., p. 160; P.A. Saythu Muhammed, *Kerala Muslim Charithram*, Calicut, 1951, 2010, p. 82; O.K. Nambiar, *An Illustrated Maritime History of the Indian Ocean*, New Delhi, 2013, p. 32; Stephen Dale, *Islamic Society on the South Asian Frontier*, Oxford, 1980, p. 35.
8. Thomas Astley, *A New General Collection of Voyages and Travels*, vol. 1, London, MDCCXLV, p. 52; P.A. Saythu Muhammed, op. cit., Calicut, 1951, 2010, p. 82; A. Sreedhara Menon, *Kerala District Gazetteers*, Trivandrum, 1972, pp. 62-3; Henry Stanley (tr.), *The Three*

Voyages of Vasco Da Gama and his Viceroyalty (from the Lendas da India of Gaspar Correa), New York, 1963, pp. 224, 228, 230.

9. K.R. Singh, 'Some pattern of political and maritime intraction between Indians, Arabs and Europeans in the Arabian sea region in the first half of the sixteenth century', in K.S. Mathew (ed.), *Indian Ocean and Cultural Interaction (d. 1400-1800)*, Pondicherry, 1996, p. 181; J.B.P. More, *Offerings to the Muslim Warriors of Malabar*, Chennai, 2015, pp.13, 96; Sir George Birdwood, op. cit., p. 165; Glenn J. Ames – *Nome De Deus: The Journal of the First Voyage of Vasco da Gama to India, 1497-9*, Leiden, 2009, p. 163; Jean Cassou, op. cit., p. 325.
10. Philip Baldaeus, *A Description of East India Coasts of Malabar and Coromandel and also of the isle of Ceylon with their adjacent kingdoms and Provinces and of the idolatry of the Pagans in the East Indies*, Amsterdam, 1671, London, 1703, p. 623; Grunlee (ed.), *The Voyage of Pedro Alvarez Cabral*, 1938, pp. 46, 50, 176; Nicolas Bon Fons, *Histoire de Portugal contenant des enterprises navigations, gestes memorable des Portugallois Tant en la conquete des Indes Orientales par eux decouvertes*, Paris, MDLXXXVII, pp. 54, 56; Robert Sewell, *Archaeological Survey of Southern India, Lists of the Antiquarian remains in the Presidency of Madras*, vol. 1, Madras, 1882, p. 241.
11. John Winter Jones (tr.), *The Travels of Ludovico di Varthema in Egypt, Syria, Arabia Deserta and Arab Felix in Persia, India and Ethiopia, AD 1503-1508*, London, MDCCCLXIII, New York, 1963, New Delhi, 1997, p. 123; Duarte Barbosa, *The Book of Duarte Barbosa*, tr. M.L. Dames, vol. II, London, 1921, pp. 75-6, 93, 97.
12. O.K. Nambiar, op. cit., p. 34; Stanley, op. cit., New York, 1963, pp. 322-5; Nicolas Bon Fons, op. cit., p. 57; O.K. Nambiar, *An Illustrated Maritime History of the Indian Ocean*, Delhi, 2013, p. 34; O.K. Nambiar, *Our Seafaring in the Indian Ocean*, Bangalore, 1975, p. 51; Peter Padfield, *Tide of the Empire, Decisive Naval Compaigns in the Rise of the West, 1481-1654*, vol. 1, London, 1979, p. 22; J.B.P. More, op. cit., p. 164.
13. John Winter Jones, op. cit., 1997, p. liii; Stanley, op. cit., New York, 1963, pp. 324, 326; K.S. Mathew, *Portuguese Trade with India in the 16th Century*, Delhi, 1983, pp. 100-3, 175, 210-11; M.L. Dames (tr. & ed.), op. cit., vol. I, London, 1989, pp. xliii-xliv, vol. II, p. 94; Leena More, *English East India Company and the local rulers in Kerala: A case study of Attingal and Travancore*, Tellicherry, 2003, p.11; Henry Stanley, op. cit., pp. 320, 322, 335.

14. John Winter Jones, op. cit., pp. 124; G. Bouchon, *Regent of the Sea, Cannanore's Response to the Portuguese Expansion*, Delhi, 1988, p. 24; Walter de Gray Birch (tr.), *The Commentaries of the Great Alfonso Dalbuquerque*, vol. II, London, MDCCCLXXVII, pp. 78-9.
15. G. Bouchon, *Albuquerque. Le Lion des Mers d'Asie*, Paris, 1992, pp. 213, 233-4, 236; Walter de Gray Birch (tr.), op. cit., pp. 104-5.
16. Mehrdad Shukoohy, *Muslim Architectures of South India, The Sultanate of Ma'Bar and the Traditions of the Maritime Settlers on the Malabar and Coromandel Coasts, Tamil Nadu, Kerala and Goa*, UK, 2003, p. 141; G. Bouchon, op. cit., 1988, pp. 66-7; Pierre Pyrard de Laval, *Voyage de Pyrard de Laval aux Indes Orientales, 1601-11*, Paris, 1998, p. 415.
17. A. Sreedhara Menon, *Kerala District Gazetteers*, Cannanore, Trivandrum, 1972, p. 3; Nicolas Bon Fons, op. cit., p. 106; John Winter Jones, op. cit., p. ixxix.
18. Philip Baldeus, op. cit., p. 623; *Satyan Edakkad, Vasco da Gama and the unknown facts of History*, Ramanattukara, 2010, pp. 64-5; K.R. Singh, 'Some pattern of political and maritime intraction between Indians, Arabs and Europeans in the Arabian sea region in the first half of the sixteenth century', ed., K.S. Mathew, *Indian Ocean and Cultural Interaction (AD 1400-1800)*, Pondicherry, 1996, p. 175; Innigo de Biervillas, *A la cote de Malabar, Goa, Batavia and autres lieux des Indes Orientales*, Premier partie, Paris, MDCCCXXXVI, p. 187.
19. K.R. Singh, op. cit., Philip Baldeus, op. cit., Innigo de Biervillas, op. cit., Genevieve Bouchon, op. cit., Delhi, 1988, pp. 86-7.
20. John Winter Jones, *The Itinerary of Ludovico de Varthema*, op. cit., p. lxxxi; Satyan Edakkad, op. cit., p. 68; Philip Baldaeus, op. cit., p. 623.
21. O.K. Nambiar, *An Illustrated Maritime History of the Indian Ocean*, op. cit., p. 39, 54; Sreedhara Menon, op. cit., p. 3; H.E.J. Stanley, op. cit., p. xxxvi; Satyan, op. cit., pp. 71, 74-5, 77; John Winter Jones, *The Itinerary of Ludovico di Varthema*, Madras, 1997, p. lxxxi, New York, 1963, pp. 280-2; Maffei, *L'Histoire des Indes Orientales et Occidentales*, Paris, 1665, pp. 123-5.
22. F.C. Danvers, *Report on the Portuguese Records*, New Delhi, 1991, p. 8; Walter de Gray Birch, op. cit., vol. I, London, MDCCCLXXV, p. xii; Leena More, op. cit., p. 11.

23. *Anjengo Factory Records 1704-1749*, Simon Cowse, *Anjengo to the Court of Directors*, June 1704, p. 5; TNA, H.E.J. Stanley, op. cit., pp. 399, 426; Jan Kieniewicz, 'The Portuguese Factory and Trade in Pepper in Malabar during the 16th Century', *Indian Economic and Social History Review*, vol. IV, no. I, March 1969, p. 63; James Forbes, *Oriental Memoirs*, London, 1813, 1834, vol. I, p. 187.

CHAPTER 6

The Rise of the Ali Rajas of Cananore

THE MAMALES

We gave discussed in the previous chapter that Ibn Battuta had recorded in his accounts about the conversion of a Cananore Kolatiri Prince to Islam during the twelfth or thirteenth century. It is quite possible that this prince had taken to trading and seafaring because that was the profession of the Arab or Muslim traders, who frequented the Malabar Coast.

Mamales as they were called, were believed to be native Muslims from Cananore. But during the year 1507, a French man Jerosme Osorius mentioned that in Cananore there was an Arab named Mamelas who was the richest person of all the nations who lived in Cananore. He also stated that it was the Mamale's nephew, a pilot of a ship who was killed in an encounter by the Portuguese, Gonsalve de Goez. This is a very important information alluding to Mamale's Arab ancestry as the generally accepted belief was that he was a Malabari Muslim.[1]

The emergence of Mamale in Cananore gave an added boost to the Muslim community who defended the Kolatiri king from Portuguese domination for several years. However, we do not know if these Mamales had some blood relationship with the Kolatiri prince or his descendants, who converted to Islam in the thirteenth century or before as noted by Ibn Battuta.

The Mamale possessing a powerful naval force gradually became the sole ruler of the high seas by obtaining rights and concessions from the ruling Kolatiri. As a trader, he not only controlled its economy, but also became a strong force to be reckoned with by the adversaries of Kolatiri. He wielded some power over a part of Cananore.[2]

The Mamale ruled over some islands off the Malabar Coast invested on him by the Kolatiri Raja. Initially, he worked within the inner circle of the Kolatiri Raja and gained his trust. Soon, he became a powerful and permanent entity. Kolatiri recognized his ability and capacity to deal with foreigners and his shrewdness in business negotiations and trade skills. As a result, his presence became indispensable in every meeting and in every discussion that took place with foreign dignitaries in Kolatiri's palace.[3] Mamales were originally seafarers and the captains and admirals of the naval fleet of Kolatiri Raja.[4]

The Portuguese factor at Cananore, Barbosa was the first to use the term 'Mapulere' to differentiate between the Malabar Muslims, and the 'Pardesi' or foreign Muslims.[5] Today, the term Mappila is applicable only to the Malabari Muslim community. Barbosa also remarked about the wealth of the Mappila shipowners of the town compelling him to pass a remark that, 'If the Portuguese had not discovered India, this country would now have a Moorish (Muslim) king'. He also added that the Muslim merchants were omnipresent in Calicut, Quilon, Cochin and Cananore.[6]

We have also Tomé Pires, who remarked about the increasing authority exercised by the Moors, which led him to say, 'If the power of your highness did not extend to this kingdom, it would have already been in the hands of the Moors, because a certain Mamale Mercar has become all powerful here.'[7]

Ludovico Varthema (1502-8) had described Cananore as a fine and large city in which the King of Portugal had a very strong castle and that the ruler of this city despite being a pagan, was a great friend of the King of Portugal. He made references to the presence of Moors, but specifically to one 'Mamale Maricar', a Muslim who was the richest man in the country at that time.[8] The King referred to as pagan by

Varthema was none other than the Kolatiri Raja. By the sixteenth century, the authority of the Mamale grew from strength to strength.

We have Portuguese writings of Barbosa which said that the city of Cananore was inhabited by many Moors and gentiles of many kinds who were merchants, and who possessed many large and small ships and traded in different types of goods with the Kingdom of Cambay and Hormuz, Colan, Dabul Banda, Goa, Ceylon and Maldive islands. He further gave insights into how this 'Reino de Cananore' (Muslim chieftain) effectively used Mount Eli's location as a harbour for foreign ships. He also remarked that the King of Cananore had a fortress in Balapatnam, where he constantly resided.[9] An important point to be noted here is that during the tenure of Barbosa in Cananore, he frequently referred to the Muslim chieftain, but he never referred to him as Ali Raja. This clearly demonstrated that the transition from Mamale to Ali Raja had not taken place yet.

Thus, it is clear that Ali Raja did not exist as a ruler even when Vasco da Gama or Varthema arrived in Cananore or else they would have definitely alluded to him. But there was a powerful Muslim, i.e. the Mamale, who was always present in the Kolatiri durbar.

EMERGENCE OF THE ALI RAJAS

Sheikh Zainuddin, the author of *Tuhfat-ul-Mujahideen* written in Arabic in AD 1580 indicated in his work about a powerful Muslim, who was styled as the 'Great warrior, Alee Azraja, the Chief of Cananore', who fought the Portuguese in defence of the Muslims, and that the islands of Maldives and Laccadives belonged to him. Undoubtedly, Alee Azraja was the Ali Raja, or Azhi (Sea) Raja or Adi (First) Raja of Cananore himself. For a long time, these chiefs were subordinate and dependant on the Kolatiri Raja.[10]

It appears that in 1559, Alee, or Ali Raja led a coalition against the Portuguese during which his authority became so strong while the Kolatiris were gradually losing power in the region. In 1564, the Portuguese were at war with the Kolatiri of Cananore. They displayed great brutality by capturing ships and killing the sailors whom they had made prisoners. Very much weakened by the Portuguese attacks, the King almost left Cananore to the Ali Raja. The French missionary, Pyrard de Laval, who was then in Malabar referred to the Ali Raja as being an usurper and not really the rightful King but who became the Prince of Cananore by force.[11]

The Frenchman Pyrard de Laval, who visited Cananore in the early part of the seventeenth century, described Cananore as a pretty beautiful city located on the sea side possessing a good port. He made a sensational revelation that the King of Cananore (obviously Kolatiri), no longer wielded unmistakable power and was beginning to lose his grip over the people when there arose another parallel personality who was powerful, rich and had retinue of followers. He was known as Ali Raja, who was a Mohammedan and who was an extremely wealthy trader. His army comprised of the best soldiers of the country, both on land and on the sea and carried out exercises with their arms just as the Malabar Nairs. They controlled the entire navigation and sea traffic of the country. He was not only powerful, but he possessed several ships and seafarers and controlled the island of Divandruou (Laccadive) and Maldives. He was handsome, courteous, and flashy, who loved foreigners. However, the other Kings of Malabar did not address him as the King of Cananore, as he was not a lawful King.[12] He also explained as to how Ali Raja, a Muslim by religion in course of time clashed with the Kolatiri, became independent, and finally became the sole ruler of Cananore.[13]

Captain Alexander Hamilton (1688) described Cananore as a 'pretty large town built in the bottom of the Bay', and as independent of the Dutch stationed at Fort St. Angelo, whose Government was in the hands of Mohammedan (Malabar Moors) under 'Adda Raja', who was addressed as a Malabari Prince. His dominions extended 10 miles southward of Cananore upto River Tellicherry, near which he had an harbour

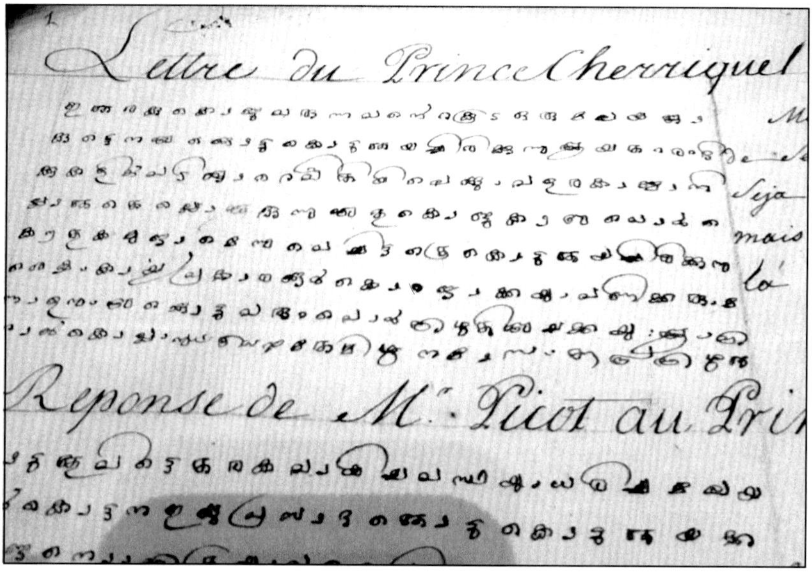

Figure 1: Letter in old Malayalam from Kolatiri Raja to Picot, Governor of Mahé, gifting him with a rare mountain squirrel, 16 June 1776, NAF 9108, BNF (Richelieu), Paris.

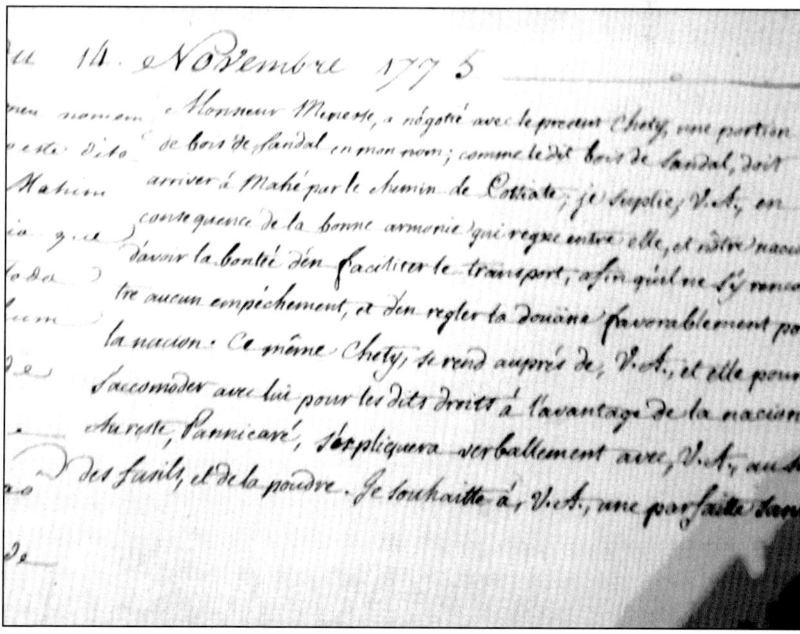

Figure 2: Letter (translation) in French from Governor Picot to Prince of Chirakkal, 14 November 1775 regarding purchase of sandalwood, BNF (Richelieu), Paris.

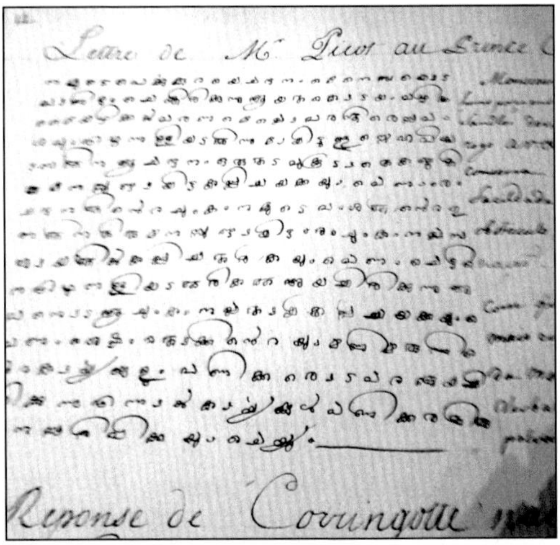

Lettre de Mr Picot au Prince

Reponse de Corringotte

Figure 3: Letter in Malayalam from Governor Picot to Prince of Chirakkal, 14 November 1775 regarding purchase of sandalwood, BNF (Richelieu), Paris.

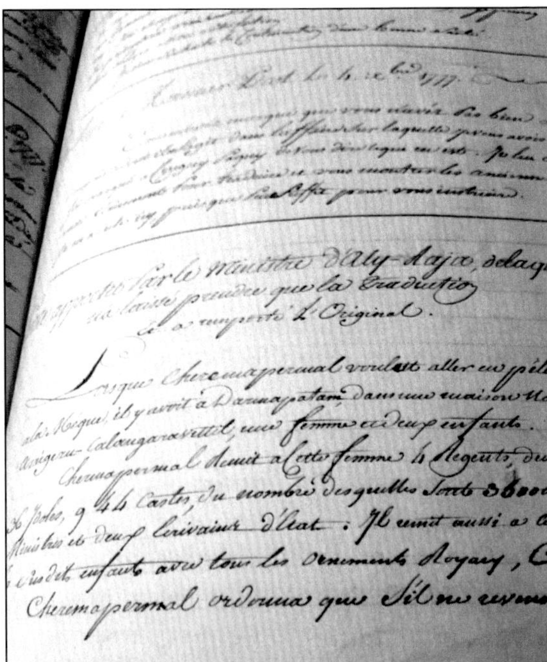

Figure 4: Narration given by Ali Raja's Minister in 1777, regarding the ancestry of Ali Raja's family, where the famly house is mentioned as Arrigeru Calanngaravittil (line 3)—NAF 9113, Translation of the letter sent or received by Ali Raja from 1769, BNF (Richelieu), Paris.

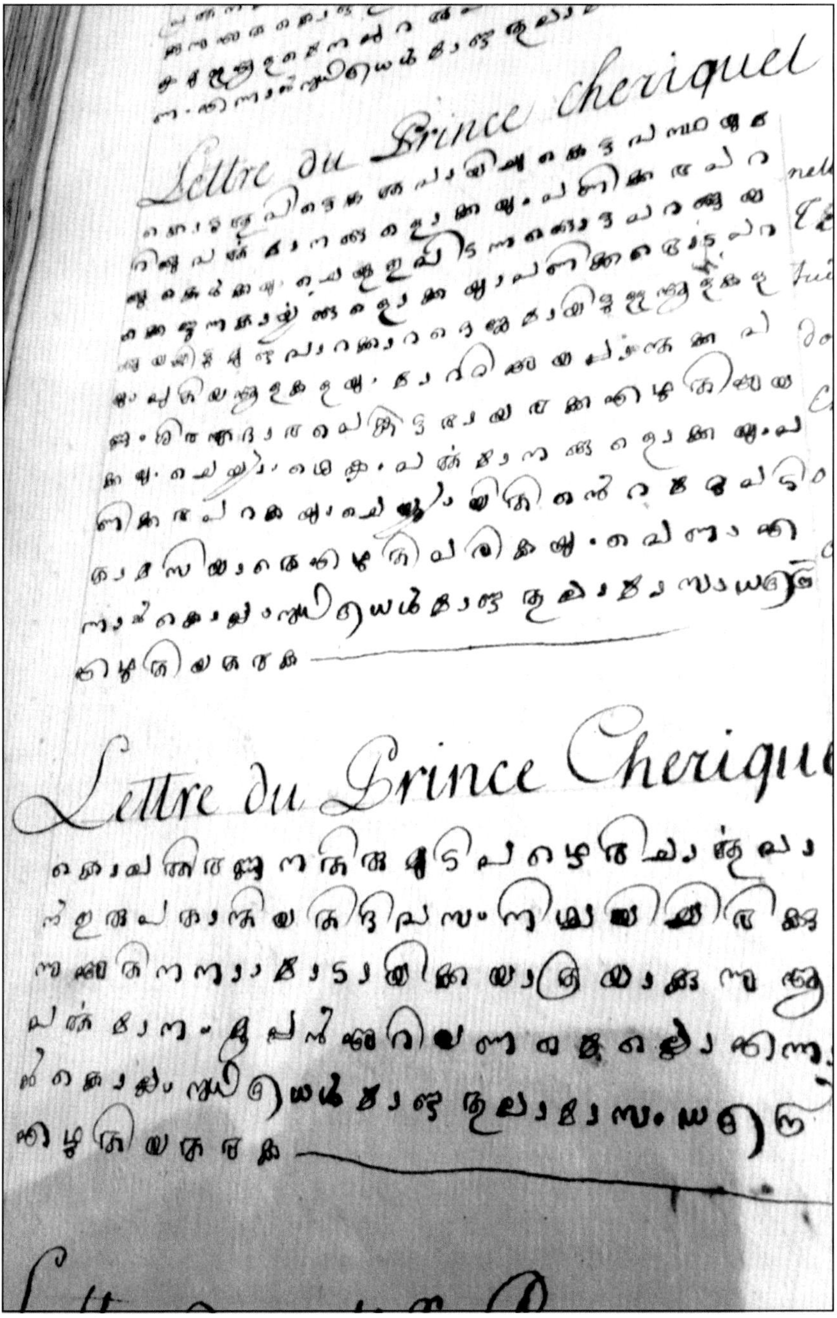

Figure 5: Letter written by the Prince of Chirakkal to Picot, Mahé informing him about the coronation ceremony of Kolatiri Raja to be celebrated on 20 December 1778 at Madayi—NAF 9109, Letter from Prince Chirakkal to Picot, 30 October 1778, BNF (Richelieu), Paris.

Figure 6: Letter from Ali Raja to Picot inviting him to attend the grand ceremony of depositing the treasure inside the Fort—NAF 9113, Letter from Ali Raja to Picot, 11 April 1771, BNF.

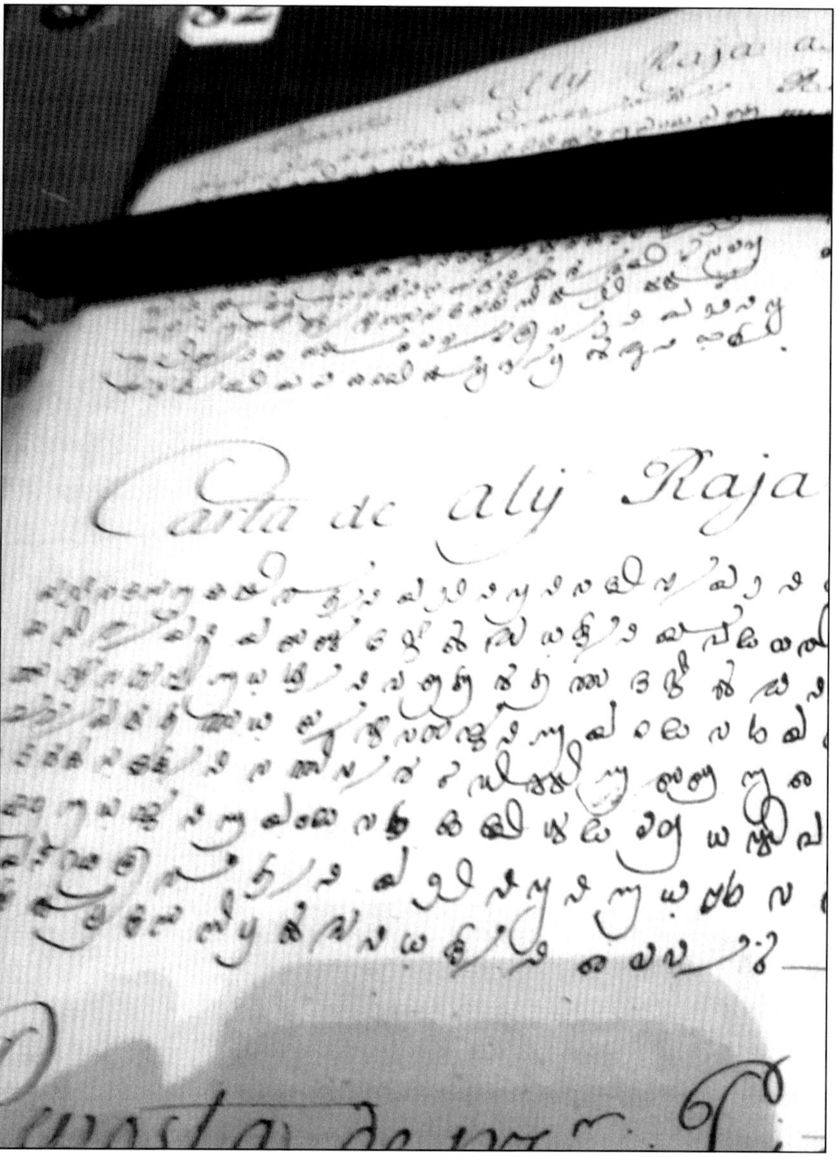

Carta de aly Raja

Figure 7: Letter from Ali Raja to Picot, Mahé, 4 September 1769 requesting for 25 Candics of iron assuring him of immediate payment, NAF 9113, BNF (Richelieu), Paris.

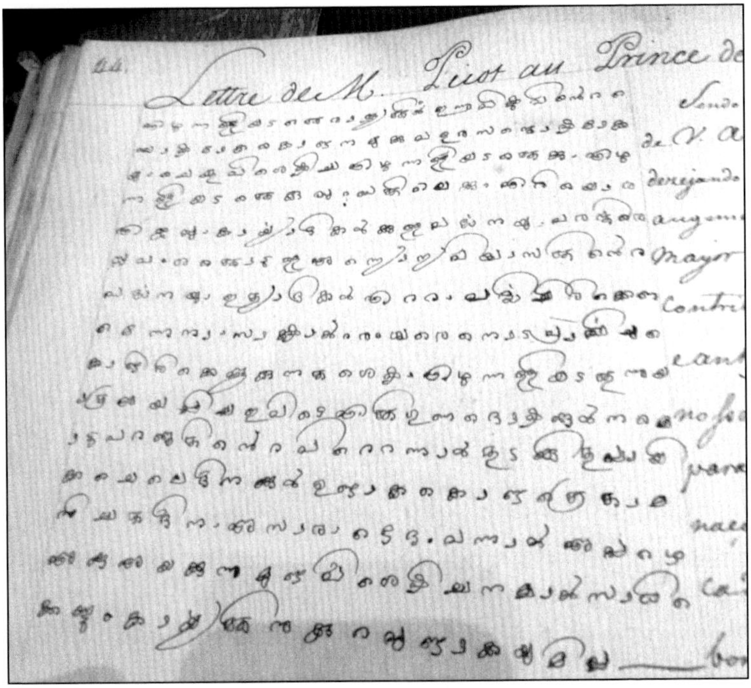

Lettre de M. Picot au Prince de

Figure 8: On the occasion of the grand celebration of Vishu in Malabar, Picot extends warm wishes and good health to the Prince of Chirakkal and his family—NAF 1907, Letter from Picot to Prince Chirakkal, 9 April 1776, BNF (Richelieu), Paris.

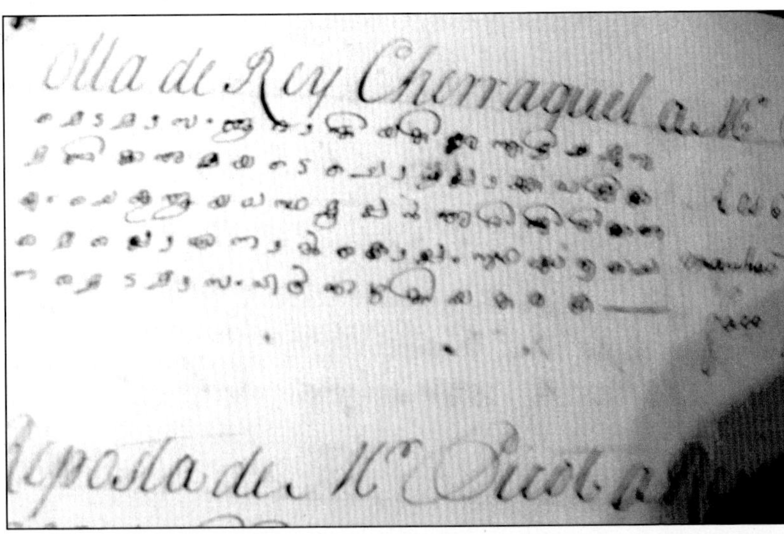

Figure 9: Letter from Chirakkal to Picot, 18 April 1772, informing him about the demise of his mother—NAF.

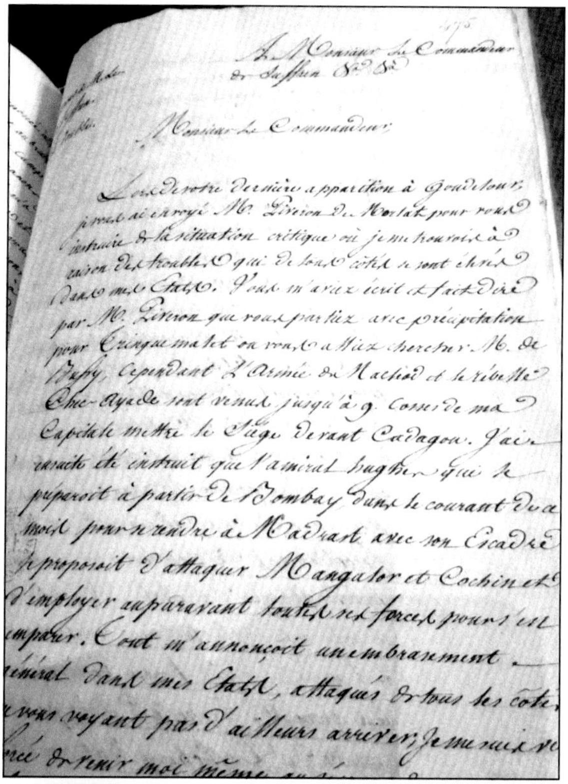

475

A Monsieur le Commandeur de Suffren &c. &c.

Monsieur le Commandeur,

Lors de votre dernière apparition à Goudelour, j'avois envoyé M. Piveron de Morlat pour vous instruire de la situation critique où je me trouvois à raison des troubles qui de tous côtés se sont élevés dans mes Etats. Vous m'avez écrit et fait dire par M. Piveron que vous partiez avec précipitation pour Trinquemalet où vous alliez chercher M. de Bussy, cependant l'armée du Nabab et le rebelle Chec-Ayaze sont venus jusqu'à 9 cosses de ma Capitale mettre le Siège devant Cadagou. J'ai ensuite été instruit que l'amiral hughes qui se préparoit à partir de Bombay dans le courant du mois pour se rendre à Madras avec son Escadre se proposoit d'attaquer Mangalor et Cochin et d'employer auparavant toutes ses forces pour s'en emparer. Tout m'annonçoit un embrasement général dans mes Etats, attaqués de tous les côtés, ne vous voyant pas d'ailleurs arriver, je me suis vu forcé de venir moi même ...

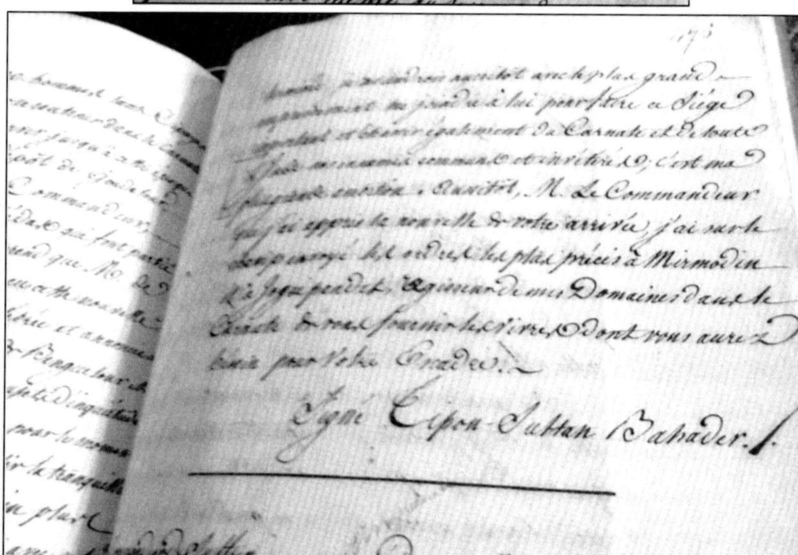

473

... avec la plus grande ... pour faire ce Siège ... Carnate et de toute ... c'est ma plus grande ... Aussitôt, M. le Commandeur que j'ai appris la nouvelle de votre arrivée, j'ai sur le champ envoyé les ordres les plus précis à Mirmodin ... de mes Domaines dans le ... de vous fournir les vivres dont vous aurez besoin pour votre Escadre.

Signé Tipou-Sultan Bahader.

Figure 10: Letter (translation) of Tipoo Sultan Bahadur in French written to Suffren, the commander of the French forces, NAF 9347, BNF (Richelieu), Paris.

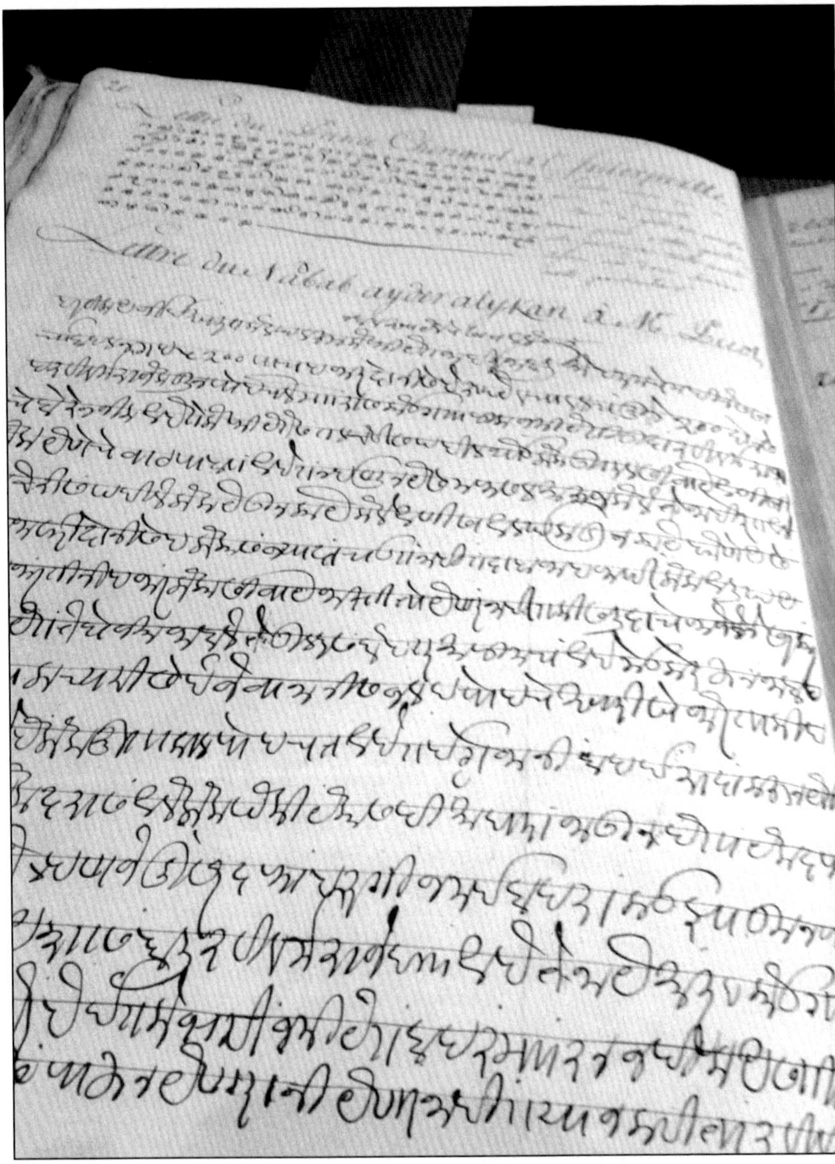

Lettre du Nabab ayder alykan à M. Pico

Figure 11: Letter written by Nabob Ayder Alikan (Haider Ali Khan) to Picot, Mahé, March 1770, BNF (Richelieu) Paris.

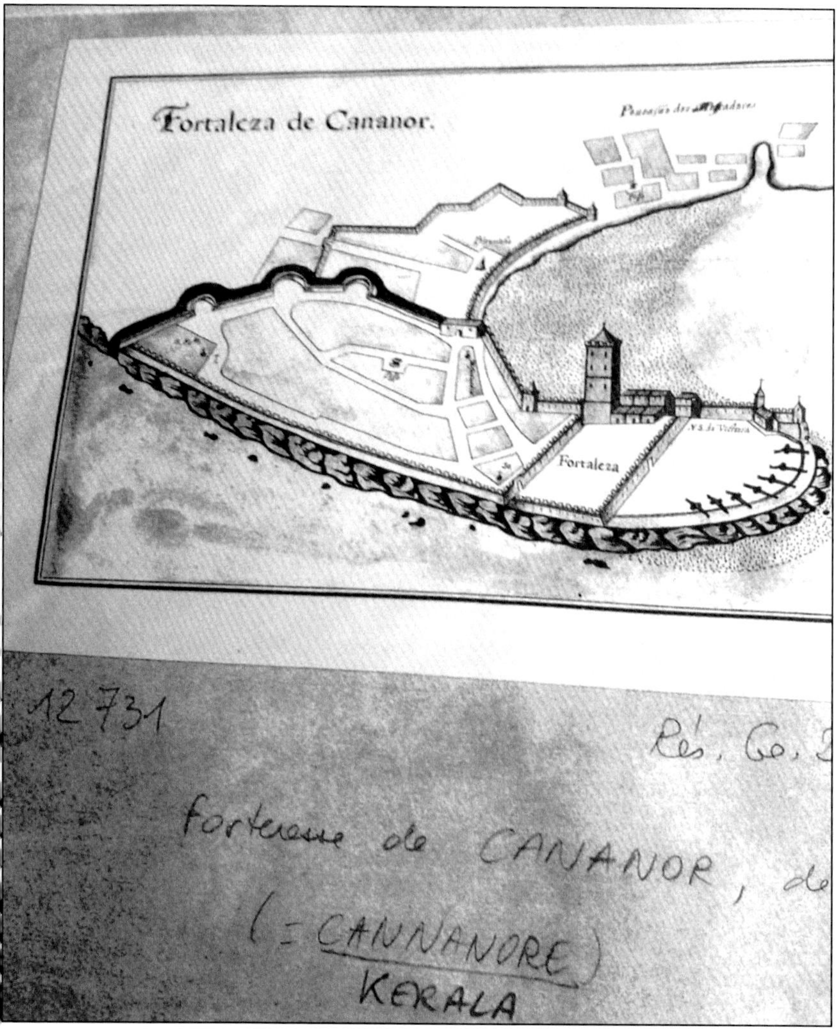

Figure 12: Fortress of Cananore, BNF (Richelieu), Paris.

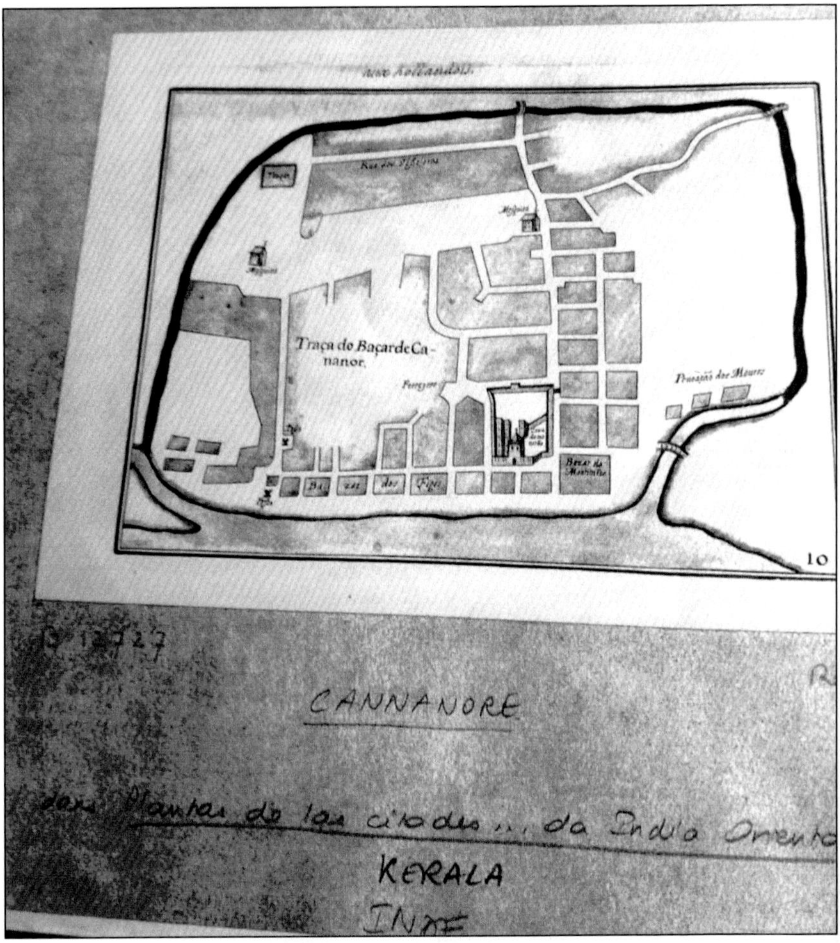

Figure 13: Plan of Cananore, BNF (Richelieu), Paris.

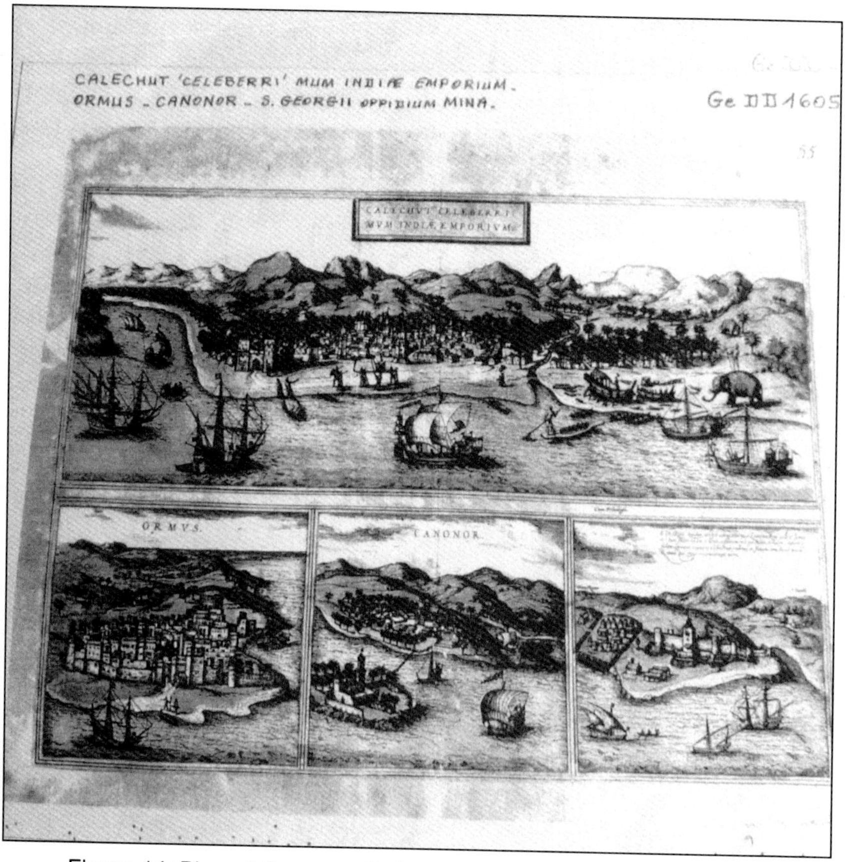

Figure 14: Plan of Cananor, Calicut, Ormuz BNF (Richelieu), Paris.

Figure 15: Tipoo Sultan Bahadur BNF (Richelieu), Paris.

called Dormapatanam (Dharmadam). It also has an island against its mouth called Cacca Diva about half-a-league from the shore. Besides, Adda Raja also held dominion over Laccadiva islands which was about 40 leagues of the Malabar Coast. He further mentioned that 'Adda Raja, in times of need could bring 20,000 men into the field'.[14]

According to the Dutch records, the Ali Raja family was of Collastry or Kolatiri extraction. Their origin was traced to a rich princess of this dynasty who on account of having had to do with a person of lower caste standing had lost her caste or nobility, and in order to cover up the disgrace, she was given in wedlock to a rich Arabian Moor on whom was conferred the title of prince, and the general name of Adi Raja or Ali Raja, which meant Lord of the Seas. He obtained for his maintenance the Lekkerdiva (Laccadive) islands and some estate round about Cananore from the Kolatiri king. He was known as the Sultan of the Lekkardiva islands. Ali Raja held higher position in the government and exerted great influence in the affairs of the kingdom of Kolatiri. He carried on extensive sea and land trade by plying his vessels and transporting the native products and bringing back plenty of saleable goods.[15]

During 1727, the Dutchman, Jacob Canter Visscher attributed a slightly different variation to the Ali Raja story. He claimed that one of his ancestors was a princess of the royal family, who marrying a Muslim received Cananore as a dowry on the condition that the descendants from the wedlock while remaining faithful to Islam and should adopt the laws of *marumakkatayam*. Later, James Forbes in his trip to India in 1765 had confirmed that Cananore was a large seaport town, which belonged to a Mahomedan Prince called Ally Rajah who was also sovereign of Maldives Island.

In the year 1771, a French cavalry officer passed by Cananore. According to tradition, any foreigner who came to Cananore had to call upon the Ali Raja. In the accounts left by this officer, it is mentioned that they were called Ali Rajas, as they originally belonged to the sect of Ali. At that time, he was generally known as 'Mappelet Ali' (Mappila Ali). His subjects were mostly Mappilas, who numbered about 9,000, armed with guns, but undisciplined. There were also Nairs in his territory.

Ali Raja had informers in his territory, who apprised him of all those who left his territory. For instance in the year 1776, a Cananore Thiyya woman, who had converted to Islam had left for Mahé to get herself reconverted on her own to Christianity there, along with two of her brothers. Ali Raja was not happy with this event and intervened with the French in Mahé to get her back as nobody had the right to convert his subjects. The French governor, Picot replied that the case of the woman was examined in the presence of Canddette Assem Kutty, a subject of Ali Raja and it was concluded that her conversion to Christianity was genuine. Picot added that the lady was under the jurisdiction of the vicar of Cananore, and nobody should molest her, as she would remain obedient to the Ali Raja. In another instance, one merchant Panoly Cunhi Amoden, a subject who owed money to the French governor Picot. Since he was unable to repay the debt, Kurungotte Nair, a chieftain near Mahé arrested Panoly's mother, wife and children and put them under house arrest on behalf of Picot. Ali Raja was unhappy with this incident. He admonished Picot for arresting the women and children for the non-payment of debt by Panoly and asked to release them forthwith, as it was not a worthy act of somebody belonging to the French nation. He told that such a heinous act was not in vogue in Malabar or anywhere in the world. Picot replied that the family was being held in a comfortable house with furniture and slaves and once the debt was settled, they will be set free. Ali Raja finally convinced Panoly to repay the debt and the matter was settled.

The French Cavalry officer who met Ali Raja gave a detailed description of his meeting with Ali Raja. According to him, he was dressed like any ordinary Muslim, except for the fact he wore a turban, which was very white. He was about 40-year-old with a brownish complexion and pot bellied. He was not tall. Instead, he was well-built, but nervous. He came down a flight of steps holding on to the shoulder of his minister in order to meet the French officer. Ali Raja was inquisitive about his whereabouts and discussed with the Frenchman in Portuguese language. All the while, he held on to the shoulder of his minister as he was unsteady on his feet. Ali Raja conveyed his compliments to Governor Picot of Mahé. According to the French officer, Ali Raja spoke Portuguese, the Mappila dialect, Canarese (Kannada), Malabari and, he knew some English and French.[16]

From the preceding accounts and narrations, it is quite clear that Ali Raja came to prominence as a ruler in Cananore only during the sixteenth century. Though we have numerous accounts of the travellers who had visited Cananore from very early days, before the arrival of the Portuguese, no one ever mentioned about the existence of Ali Raja before the sixteenth century. It was only during the sixteenth century that many accounts, especially that of Sheikh Zainuddin, had remarked about the powerful Muslim merchants who controlled the seafaring activity and trade of the Kolatiris. The Raja's dependence on the Muslim merchants and their chieftain grew to such an extent, that the latter's presence was inevitable and unavoidable in every important meeting held in his court. An important point to be noted is that the 'Ali Raja' or 'Ada Raja' or 'Adi Raja' was the title of the ruler, but and not their actual name. We do not know the exact year when he acquired or was conferred that title, though it is certain that he got it only in the course of the sixteenth century, and not before, unless proofs to the contrary are forthcoming. However, it is quite obvious that the name Ali Raja came about because he originally belonged to the sect of Ali as noted by the French officer in 1771. It was certainly not a derivation from any other word, as it was popularly thought.

TRADITIONAL ACCOUNTS RELATED TO ARAKKAL

According to the *Keralolpatti*, the traditional legendary account of Kerala, written from the Brahmanical or the Nair/Nambutiri point of view, it is revealed that Cheraman Perumal invited a Mohammedan and his wife, i.e. a *Jonaka* (Moplah) male and a female from the land of Aryapuram and installed them at Cananore. The male was bestowed with the title of 'Azhi Raja', or the Lord of the Sea, and endowed with all authority befitting such a position.

According to a note by a minister of Ali Raja in 1777, addressed to Picot, the French governor of Mahé, which I recently located in Bibliothèque Nationale de France (Richelieu), Paris. The version of the origin of Arakkal family is given as follows:

> When Cheraman Perumal wanted to go on pilgrimage to Mecca, he lived in Darmapatam in a house called 'Arrigeru Calangaravettil', with a woman and two children.
>
> Cheraman Perumal gave this woman 4 (*sic*), two governors, 36 idols, 944 castes which includes 3,50,000 Nairs, two Ministers and two writers of the State. He also handed over the lady and the said children, all the royal ornaments and crown.
>
> Cheraman Perumal ordered that in case he did not return from Mecca within 12 years, the above people of the country must obey the lady and children. After issuing the order, Cheraman Perumal departed for Mecca.
>
> The reason for giving the name of Pallikulam is because of a dispute between the persons about the place. The said lady and children were given the place of the mosque of Madayi to construct a palace. It is called Pallikulam since then.
>
> These are the old things. You will learn about them when you have the above information with the persons (*sic*).[17]

According to the preceding two accounts, it is clear that the Arakkal family traces its lineage to Cheraman Perumal. But the problem with these accounts is that the second Chera dynasty had ceased to exist in about the twelfth century itself. Therefore, the account was most probably a concocted floating legend until it was recorded by *Keralolpatti* and the Minister of Ali Raja. What is however interesting in the minister's account is that he had mentioned the house of Arrigeru Calangaravettil in Dharmadam, as being the original abode of the Arakkals. There may be some truth in this contention because Arakkal is just a shortened form of Arrigeru Calang-aravettil, Arakkal being a diminutive of *Arri* in Arrigeru and 'Cal' in Calangara resulting in *Arr* + *Cal*, or Arakkal in course of time.

Late ninteteenth and twentieth century scholars and writers mostly based their versions or derived their versions from the preceding two accounts or its variations. William Logan mentioned that one of the ministers of Kolatiri, who lived around the end of the eleventh century or the beginning of the twelfth century, converted to Islam and adopted the name of Muhammad, or Muhammad Ali. Observing his skill and ability, the Kolatiri retained him as his minister after his conversion and his successors were known as *Mamalli Kidavu*. They were the hereditary ministers of Kolatiri. Tradition also says that Mamalli, or Mamad Ali and his successors were admitted to all the important counsels of the Kolatiri and that they used to stand on such occasions with a sword point resting on a box signifying they were involved in the finances of the Kingdom.[18]

According to Padmanabha Menon, one of the Kolatiri princess, had a misalliance with a Muhammadan, and the Kolatiri Raja yielded to her wish and allotted the territory as a provision for the issue of the prince. Sreedhara Menon, citing Arakkal records mentioned that the seat of the family earlier was at Dharmadam (Dharmapatanam) from where Sreedevi, sister of Cheraman Perumal converted.[19] Her son Mahabali who converted to Islam and took the new name Muhammad Ali was supposed to be the Ali Raja, the founder of the Arakkal dynasty, who was the Lord of the Cananore bazaar.[20]

Roland Miller, on the basis of the Arakkal family archives preserved in the Calicut University, held that the Arakkal house traced its origin to the earliest days of the Mappilas and to the legend of the conversion of Cherman Perumal to Islam. However, as a symbol of this combination of Hindu and Muslim traditions, a *bhadra deepa*, or an auspicious lamp was kept alight on the first floor facing the seaside in the Arakkal *kottaram* or palace, found in the Muslim locality of Cananore town. This lamp was also known as '*Tamburatti Vilakku*'. It is believed that this lamp was lit in memory of the departure of Cheraman Perumal to Mecca as we have already discussed this in greater detail on Chapter 4. Close to a throne like wooden chair is a longish cot of about four metres covered with white cotton sheet. It is believed that a saint from Arabia visits the Arakkal Palace every night occupies the stately chair and goes to sleep.

All the above versions somehow connect the origin of the Arakkal family to Cheraman Perumal, who had ceased to exist in the twelfth century. Besides, Kolatiris did not come into existence before the fourteenth century as we have seen. Therefore, it may be deemed that these versions were at the most concocted or imagined.

Both Logan and Arakkal ancestral records gives different genealogical details of 29 Ali Rajas of Cananore. Details of the Arakkal dynasty are also displayed on a board in the Arakkal Museum. However, there are some discrepancies in Arakkal compilation pertaining to certain names and the years of their reign when compared to the compilation made by Logan. For instance, Logan in his compilation mentioned Valiya Mammale (1364-5), while Arakkal records cited Muhammad Ali (1365-1452).[21]

While going through the compilations one can observe that the period of reign of the first four chieftains were unknown. But the fifth one, Ali Musa is believed to have conquered Maldive islands in 1183-4 for the Kolatiri. Laccadive Islands had probably been colonized earlier. The Kolatiri is said to have arranged for a payment of 18,000 fanams for the islands and additional money to be paid in case of need. Apart from this, the port of Cananore, and the *desams* of Kanattur and Kannottanchala were also assigned to him by the Kolatiri as a reward for his service. However, it is noteworthy that the Kolatiri dynasty had not come into existence in the twelfth century. Therefore, the preceding accounts were either concocted or false.

Another tradition, which appears to be closer to reality, reveals that the *Tamburatti Vilakku* was given by the neighbouring Raja of Chirakkal (Kolatiri) to the Princess when she married the Muslim youth. That is why this lamp is known as *Tamburatti* lamp, or lamp of the Princess. This lamp is a symbol of religious fraternity between Arakkal (Malabar Muslim) and Chirakkal (Malabar) families. The Arakkal house strictly maintained the Hindu custom of matrilineal succession, which was not in accordance to the *Shariat* rules. It seems that this Hindu custom of succession had been later sanctioned by the Caliph as the 'custom of the land' in one of his letters. Later on female succession became common to this house.[22]

If we are to believe the accounts and stories of a traditional character related above, then it could be supposed that after several years since the conversion of a Kolatiri prince of Cananore, there must have been another conversion of a Kolatiri damsel in distress by a certain Muhammad Ali, or Mammali who plunged into the river water and saved her from drowning. He might have been an Arabian Moor merchant of the Kolatiri court or some other Muslim of mixed descent. The Kolatiri, in order to avoid a scandal of ostracization, converted her to Islam and married her off to Muhammad Ali. This conversion and marriage seems to be the closest to reality, as it has been confirmed by the letter of Ali Raja's minister that a lady (probably Sreedevi as mentioned by Sreedhara Menon above) with two children belonging to the 'Arrigeru Calangaravittel' family of Dharmadam, of Kolatiri extraction, who converted to Islam to marry a Moor.

As the lady belonged to the 'Arrigeru Calangara' family, her family dynasty after her marriage with the Muslim came to be known as the Arakkal house. The combination of *Arri* and *Cal* gave birth in the course of time to Arakkal. This lady seems to have been allotted a territory by the Kolatiri Raja in Cananore and her descendants became the Ali Raja. They followed the *marumakkatayam* system, because the lady of

Nayar extraction was a convert to Islam and related to the Kolatiri, and not to Cheraman Perumal, which is without any foundation. That is why we find the *Tamburatti Vilakku* at the Arakkal Museum even today, which was given by Chirakkal to Arakkal. In the light of the preceding, it is quite clear that Arakkal and Chirakkal were related to one another through the conversion of the Nair lady.

In the beginning, since Vasco da Gama came to Cananore upto Afonso de Albuquerque (1509), it was the Kolatiri Raja who welcomed and received them and entered into trade negotiations with them in Cananore, assisted by a chief of the Muslim traders who played an important role in regulating the trade, i.e. fixing the rates of spices, setting aside Kolatiri's share and above all regulating the maritime traffic and trade. There was an instance when Vasco da Gama became furious and stormed out of the meeting place as he disliked having to interact with Muslim officials, who according to him were not a responsible lot. Nevertheless, it was observed that this Muslim Captain or his predecessors were always besides Kolatiri Raja during important meetings scheduled with the Portuguese. Actually, it was the Kolatiri Raja who received the Portuguese emissaries as head of the State and not any Muslim chief. During this period, the Muslim merchant/chief had not become powerful enough for his name to figure on equal footing with the Kolatiri Raja. He had not yet become a parallel power to the Kolatiri. It must be recalled that the Kolatiri Raja even employed a Muslim scribe to write all his diplomatic and commercial correspondence in Arabic. Therefore, the latter was aware of all the happenings in the Kolatiri court. Thus, Muslim traders and captains, Muslim officials and scribes were an essential part of Kolatiri adminstrative set up during the early period of the Portuguese in Malabar, whereas the Nair constituted the ruling establishment and the local militia. The Kolatiris had a prime minister of Kolathunadu, finance minister commander of the army, and in-charge of the administration, who were mostly Nambiar officers in-charge of negotiations, translators, and interpreters.

Arakkal house too, though their rule did not extend for a long period, yet had a fairly well organized administration, where the *karyakar* had the overall responsibility of the chiefdom. Arakkal Rajas had his own ministers who managed the administrative departments. The mosques were put in-charge of a minister, weavers and fishermen had their own chiefs. Defence was entrusted to the *gurukals*. Besides, he had translators, interpreters, informers and a spy network. [23]

ARAKKAL *vs.* KOLATIRI

None of the pre-fifteenth century foreign travellers who had left ample records about Malabar, and mentioned about the Mamale. It was only after the arrival of the Portuguese that the Mamales gained prominence. The matter was referred by the Portuguese as *regedor* meaning regent, a hereditary role which was passed from brother to brother and uncle to nephew in keeping with the *marumakkatayam* custom. This regent had the right of justice over his co-religionists and represented them before the king, who invited him to attend certain Durbars. Nevertheless, credit must be given to Barbosa and Pires, who foresaw with accuracy, the numerical importance of the Muslims in Cananore and Malabar.

Despite their differences, Portuguese maintained cordial relations with the Muslim merchants of Cananore. Muslim merchants supplied commodities to the Portuguese on credit. Khoja Shamsuddin, who had his base in Cananore, had given a huge loan of 7,50,000 pardaos of gold to the Portuguese Governor, who went personally to the house of this Khoja to receive the loan. In the 1540s, the Portuguese were offended by the Arakkal Raja who refused to give the compulsory loan which they had asked for. As a result, they launched in the year 1545, an unexpected attack on the Arakkal palace situated near Fort St. Angelo and killed Pokkar Ali Koya, the Arakkal Raja, his father Aboobacker Ali and his uncle Kunhi Sooppi Ali.

After the death of Albuquerque, a new Viceroy Lopos Suvaris alias Lopo Soares was appointed on 2 September 1515 as the

Governor of the Portuguese territories in India. After taking charge from Goa, he concluded a treaty with the King of Quilon. He, then, proceeded to Cananore and handed over the gifts sent by the King of Portugal to Kolatiri.[24] Thus, the relationship of the Kolatiri with the Portuguese was renewed and strengthened.

Vasco da Gama was appointed as the Viceroy in 1524 at the age of 62. Earlier, when he headed the naval expedition, it was in the capacity of a commander. This time, he was formally appointed as Viceroy to India on 11 September 1524. His two sons, De Estevao and De Paulo, accompanied him in this voyage. Immediately after assumption of the post, he left for Cananore to meet Kolatiri Raja whose ancestor had welcomed him earlier. This shows once again the importance of Cananore and the Kolatiri for the Portuguese.

In Cananore, Gama held discussions with the Kolatiri Raja. He took a note of the changing scenario on the Malabar coast. He also observed that there were several guerilla sea fighters who were hounding the Portuguese fleets. Famous guerilla sea leaders of that period were Kutti Ali brothers of Calicut, Captain Balia Hassan, and Ali Haji of Dharmadam, Pattu Marakkar, Atikal of Purakkad. Among them, Pattu Marakkar and Balia Hassan were the most notorious. At that time, Arakkal Raja was still under the control of the Kolatiri.

Balia Hassan was actually Arakkal Raja's naval chief and his relative. He was an expert in sea guerilla tactics. He was wrecking havoc on the Portuguese ships and was becoming such a nuisance to the latter that Vasco da Gama decided to put an end to this. Balia Hassan put himself under the protection of the Kolatiri. Gama personally asked the Kolatiri Raja to hand over Balia Hassan to him. Kolatiri gave in and on 25 September 1524, handed over Balia Hassan to Gama. He was tortured and locked up in the dungeon in Cananore fort. After this incident, Vasco da Gama left for Cochin, where he fell seriously sick ill and passed away on 24 December 1524.[25]

This incident proves two things: First, the fact that the

Kolatiri Raja was not in a position to antagonize the Portuguese. Secondly, Kolatiri himself might have found that the Arakkal Raja was becoming more assertive, due to his seafaring activities and his control over the trade. That would have pushed him to get rid off Arakkal's naval chief, Balia Hassan, hoping that by doing so the Arakkal Raja would be weakened.

Don Henrique de Menezes succeeded Gama. Arakkal Raja tried in vain to negotiate for the release of Balia Hassan in return for a large amount of money. He even asked Kolatiri to intervene in this affair. But the new Viceroy did not relent. All efforts by the Arakkal Raja to obtain his release failed. Finally, on the Portuguese Viceroy's orders, Balia Hassan was hanged to death at the Fort of Cananore. Naturally, the Arakkal Raja was extremely unhappy with the incident, as Balia Hassan was not only his sea captain, but also his relative. He felt that the Kolatiri had let him down, listening to the Portuguese. Kolatiri would have probably thought then that he had weakened the hand of the Arakkal Raja by allowing the execution of Balia Hassan.

This incident shook the Malabaris and the Muslims alike. The hanging of Balia Hassan and Kolatiri's silence or helplessness to save Balia Hassan provoked the Muslims to turn against the Kolatiri. They marched to the fort to avenge the death of Balia Hassan. But the Portuguese, who had become an ally of the Kolatiri managed to drive them away and routed them upto Dharmadam, where they burnt their huts and property. Soon the Muslim warriors of Arakkal, realized the futility of depending on Kolatiri and decided to slowly steer away from him. This was the beginning of the decline of the Kolatiris and the rise of the Arakkals, with a specific identity of their own.

Meanwhile, in 1526, the Portuguese under the command of Henrique de Menezes attacked Arakkal and in the ensuing clash he was injured. Later, there was another clash near Mahe in which the Viceroy was injured again. He was brought to Fort St. Angelo for treatment. But he did not survive and died of the wound on 2 February 1526.[26] He was buried at the Cananore's church graveyard.

Henrique de Menezes successor, Lopo Vaz da Sampayo came to Cananore on receiving secret news of an impending attack on Cananore fort by the Turks. He fortified the fort, and constructed ramparts on the western side. Meanwhile, in the year 1526, Mascaranjo sailed from Malacca for India to replace Lopo Vaz. Lopo Vaz refused to hand over the charge and imprisoned Mascaranjo and took him in chains to the Cananore fort, where he was locked up in the dungeon. He met the same fate as Albuquerque. When there were such dissensions amongst the Portuguese, Kolatiri Raja himself came to Cananore fort to intervene in this dispute. A decision was taken by a 13-member commitee, who accepted Lopo Vaz as Viceroy.[27]

On 21 December 1527 dejected Mascaranjo returned to Lisbon. Meanwhile, the Kolatiri Raja passed away. The Mamale also died in the same year by the end of 1527. On 18 November 1529, Nano de Cunha reached Cananore to take charge as the Viceroy of India. He had come with the instruction from the King of Portugal to punish Lopo Vaz for insulting Mascaranjo. Lopo Vaz was chained and imprisoned in Cananore fort. In 1530, he was taken to Portugal for punishment.

From the year 1540 to 1542, Vasco da Gama's son Estevo was the Portuguese Governor to India. By 1540, there was practically no opposition to the Portuguese except from Kunjali Marakkar's fleet, who was the army commander of Zamorin. In fact, four Kunjalis fought against the Portuguese. But the greatest challenge the Portuguese faced was from the Kunjali IV.

The Portugeuse confronted the Moors right from Cananore up to Ponnani during the 1550s and 1560s. During 1559-60, Captain Lewis de Mellow ravaged the Malabar Coast. Moorish ships were confiscated. In 1564, Don Paya de Noronha destroyed 40,000 coconut trees in Cananore to teach the natives a lesson.[28]

The atrocities committed by Captain Mesquito were without bounds. He got the captives beheaded. He sewed them up in sacks with their teeth broken so that they cannot bite the sack and escape and thrown overboard. Mesquito killed more than 2,000 persons in this manner. Some of the bodies were washed ashore at Cananore in 1564. A young widow carried her husband's body and marched through the streets stirring the people. Both Hindu and Muslims joined together under Ali Raja and they attacked and destroyed thirty Portuguese ships. Thus, Ali Raja was leading the revolt against the Portuguese in Cananore and the north Malabar coast.[29]

Meanwhile, relations between the Kolatiri and Portuguese began to deteriorate as the Portuguese governor issued an order to plunder the Malabar temples on the Malabar Coast. Besides, the Portuguese used to harm the Muslim women living in the regions of the Cananore fort. Hence, Kolatiri and Arakkal jointly proclaimed war against the Portuguese. Simultaneously, Zamorin under the command of his admiral Kunjali Marakkar also declared war against the Portuguese. After the death of Arakkal Raja, his nephew Ali became the Raja of Arakkal. As per the family tree drawn up by Logan, Valiya Mamale who reigned over the Maldives was the predecessor of Pokar Ali Koya who was assassinated by the Portuguese in 1545. Diogo do Couto called him as 'Porcarrale Adeiraja'.

After the death of Pokar Ali, the *regedor* of Cananore, his nephew Ali Raja succeeded him. He gave his name to the dynasty of Muslim sovereigns at Cananore, who were to reign until the end of the eighteenth century.[30] The Portuguese gave the Mamale a historical identity and made it possible to trace the present Ali Raja's line back to the early sixteenth century.

Ali Raja became a considerable power following the footsteps of the Mamales. The only difference being that the Mamales were seafarers and traders interested only in commercial pursuits, whereas Ali Raja made a slow transition from the role of a trader to that of a political entity.

Around 1556, there was a fight in the Cananore bazaar. As a result, Ali Raja attacked the Portuguese fort with his troops.

His cousin Kutty Musa with the help of some Turkish sailors attacked Portuguese ships at sea and overran Maldives, where the Portuguese had earlier installed a Christian king.[31]

In 1559, Ali Raja led a coalition against the Portuguese proving his skill in warfare and broke away the shackles binding him to Kolatiri Raja. The Kolatiri was considerably weakened at that time. In 1564, Kolatiri Raja went to the extent of allying with his once upon a time enemy the Zamorin of Calicut and both of them attacked Cananore fort unsuccessfully.

The new Portuguese Viceroy who took charge did not consider the Kolatiri with respect, as they saw a parallel power personified by Ali Raja with whom frequent battles were waged. By the end of the century, Ali Raja brought about the weakening of the Kolatiri, who had no other option but to surrender Cananore to the power of the Ali Raja who was the sole ruler of the high seas. It was during this period that Ali Raja styled himself as a king, though he had no traditional right to attribute to himself such a title.[32]

The Portuguese, thenceforth, faced lots of problems from the Kunhali Marakkars who were the trusted army commanders of Zamorin. Kunhali III, or Pattu Marakkar Kunhali built a maritime fortress known as the Marakkar Kotta at Kottakal at the mouth of the Kotta river, with the consent of the Zamorin and continued his battle against the Portuguese. From this fortress, he began to wage war on the Portuguese plundering the Portuguese ships.

After constructing the Kotta, Kunhali III died in the year 1595. He was succeeded by his nephew Kunhali Marakkar IV, whose name was Mohammed Kunhali. He was the new naval commander of Zamorin. The sea power of Kunhali Marakkar increased greatly and this success went to his head. He dared to defy both the Zamorin and the Portuguese. This pushed Zamorin to ally with the Portuguese against Kunhali. Several battles were waged by the Portuguese against Kunhali. When Kunhali Marakkar surrendered to Zamorin, he was arrested by the Portuguese treacherously and executed mercilessly in Goa.[33]

Kunhali Marakkar's body was dismembered and exhibited in public on the seashore of Bardez and Panchim. Later, his head was salted, dried and brought back to Fort St. Angelo of Cananore, where it was spiked on a bamboo post and kept on top of the fort for exhibition, to create terror and fear amongst the Moors of Cananore. The Portuguese danced and celebrated the victory. The Malabaris of Cananore watched this horrible scene.

Kunhali Marakkar's episode was a significant example of a feudatory trying to defy his overlord, Zamorin and losing his life in the bargain. The supportive role played by Kolatiri Raja in Zamorin's war against Kunhali Marakkar eventually strained relations between Ali Raja and the Kolatiri. Kolatiri himself faced almost the same problem with the Ali Raja who was increasingly defiant against him. He who supported the Zamorin to prevent the Kunhali Marakkar from becoming an independent power, could not prevent the Ali Raja from becoming a power in Cananore, defying his authority.[34]

NOTES

1. A. Jerosme Osorius, *Histoire de Portugal Contenant les enterprises, navigations, et Gestes Memorables des Portugallois tant en la conqueste des Indes Orientales, par eux qu es guerres d'Afrique et autre exploitx depuis l'an mille quatre cents soixante six*, Paris, MDLXXXVII, p. 129.
2. G. Bouchon, *Regent of the Sea, Cannanore Response to the Portuguese Expansion*, Delhi, 1988, pp. 174-5.
3. Francis Buchanan, *A Journey from Madras Through the Countries of Mysore, Canara and Malabar*, vol. II, London, 1807, p. 349.
4. Revd. H. Gundert, *A Malayalam and English Dictionary*, Germany, 1970, p. 80; K.P. Padmanabha Menon, *History of Kerala*, vol. II, New Delhi, 1983, p. 538.
5. Duarte Barbosa, *The Book of Duarte Barbosa*, tr. M.L Dames, vol. II, London, 1921, pp. 75-6, 93, 97; Bouchon, op. cit., pp. xiv, 68.
6. Duarte Barbosa, op. cit.; Edgar Thurston, *Castes and Tribes of Southern India*, vol. IV, New Delhi, 1993, p. 460; Pierre Meile. *Les Yavanas dans l'Inde Tamoul* in *Melanges Asiatiques*, Paris, 1940-1, p. 101; J.B.P.

More, *Origin and Early History of the Muslims of Keralam 700 AD-1600 AD*, Calicut, 2011, pp. 33-4, 100, G. Bouchon, op. cit., p. 23.

7. Tomé Pires, *Sumo Oriental*, 1990, p. 77; G. Bouchon, op. cit., p. 24.
8. John Winter Jones, *The Itinerary of Ludovico Di Varthema of Bologna from 1502-1508*, Madras, 1997, p. 50.
9. Henry E.J. Stanley (tr.), *Duarte Barbosa. A Description of the Coasts of East Africa and Malabar in the Beginning of the Sixteenth Century*, Madras, 1995, pp. 149-51.
10. Sheikh Zainuddin, *Tohfat-ul-Mujahedeen* (Offerings to the Muslim Warriors of Malabar (ed.) J.B.P. More, Chennai, 2015, p. 143; K.P. Padmanabha Menon, *History of Kerala Written in the Form of Notes on Visscher's letter from Malabar*, New Delhi, 1983, vol. II, pp. 540-1; Colonel Yule, *The Book of Sir Marco Polo*, II, 1903, pp. 386-7.
11. R. Sewell and S.K. Iyengar, *The Historical Inscriptions of Southern India*, Madras, 1932, p. 257; Cf. Pyrard de Laval, *Voyage de Pyrard de Laval aux Inde Orientales, 1601-1611*, Paris, 1998; G. Bouchon, op. cit., p. 173.
12. Pierre Pyrard de Laval, op. cit., pp. 409-10.
13. Ibid., Philip Baldaeus, *A True and Exact Description of the Most Celebrated East India Coasts of Malabar and Coromandel and also of the Isle of Ceylon*, translated from the High Dutch, Amsterdam, 1672, pp. 622-3.
14. William Logan, *Malabar*, vol. I, Madras, 1989, pp. 358-9; Alexander Hamilton, *A New Account of the East Indies from 1688 to 1723*, Edinburg, MDCCXXVII, New York, 2001, pp. 293-4.
15. A. Galletti, *The Dutch in Malabar*, Madras, 1911, p. 142; M.K. Noushad and Muhammed Shihad, 'The Mappila Raja: The Rise of Arakkal Dynasty in Malabar, Kerala', in *Kannur Muslim Heritage Congress*, 2019, Kozhikode, 2019, pp. 410-11.
16. James Forbes, *Oriental Memoirs*, vol. 1, London, 1813, pp. 315, 318; G. Bouchon, op. cit., p. 25; NAF 9368, *Notes extrait des lettres d'un officier de cavalier qui a voyagé aux Indes Orientales 1771*, pp. 164-6, BNF, Paris; NAF 9113, *Lettre d'Ali Rajah à M. Picot*, Mahé, 12 Avril 1776, p. 56; *Lettre de Picot à Ali Rajah*, 12 Avril 1776, p. 56; *Lettre d'Ali Rajah à Picot*, 17 Avril 1776, p. 58; *Lettre de Picot à Ali Rajah*, 18 Avril 1776, p. 59; *Lettre de Picot à Ali Rajah*, 22 Avril 1776, p. 60, BNF, Paris; NAF 9113, *Lettre d'Ali Rajah to Picot*, Mahé, 21 Mai 1777, p. 68; *Lettre de Picot à Ali Rajah*, 22 Mai 1777, p. 69; *Lettre d' Ali Rajah to Picot*, 26 Mai 1777, p. 70, BNF, Paris.

17. NAF, 9113. *Copie et traduction des lettres écrites et reçues d'Aly Raja et d'autres Mapelese de la côte Malabar depuis*, 3 Janvier 1769 jusqu'au 1778—Note written by the Minister of Aly Raja to Picot, governor of Mahé, 1777, p. 83, BNF (Richelieu), Paris; cf. H. Gundert (ed.), *Keralolpatti*, Mangalore, 43, Trivandrum, 1961.
18. K.K.N. Kurup, *The Ali Raja's of Cananore*, Calicut, 2002, p. 15; William Logan, *Malabar*, vol. I, Madras, 1989, pp. 236-7, 357-8; G. Bouchon, op. cit., pp. 25-6, K.P. Padmanabha Menon, *A History of Kerala Written in the Form of Notes on Visscher's letter from Malabar*, vol. II, New York, 1983, p. 539.
19. K.P. Padmanabha Menon, op. cit., p. 539; A. Sreedhara Menon, (compiler), *Kerala District Gazetteer, Canannore*, Trivandrum, 1972, pp. 90-1.
20. Ibid.; Sreedhara Menon, op. cit., p. 93; K.K.N. Kurup, op. cit., p. 3.
21. William Logan, *Malabar*, vol. 1, Madras, 1989, p. 358. Details of the Arakkal dynasty displayed on a board in the Arakkal Museum is as follows: (1) Mohammad Ali, (2) Husain Ali, (3) Ali Musa, (4) Kunhi Musa, (5) Ali Musa–1184-1205, (6) Ali Bappan–1205-84, (7) Issa Aboobacker–1284-1365, (8) Muhammed Ali–1365-1452, (9) Aboobacker Ali–1452-1545, (10) Ali–1545-91, (11) Aboobacker–1591-1607, (12) Aboobacker–1607-10, (13) Mohammed Ali–1610-47, (14) Mohammed Ali–1647-55, (15) Kamal Adi Raja–1655-56, (16) Mohammed Ali–1656-91, (17) Ali–1691-1704, (18) Kunhi Hamsa–1704-20, (19) Mohammed Ali–1720-8, (20) Harabichi Kadavu Bi Adi Raja Beewi–1728-12, (21) Junumma Bi–1732-45, (22) Kunhi Hamsa–1745-77, and (23) Junumma Bi–1777-1819; see also K.K.N. Kurup, *The Ali Rajas of Canannore*, Calicut, 2002, pp. 103-4.
22. William Logan, op. cit., K.K.N. Kurup, op. cit., p. 16; J.B.P. More, op. cit., p. 122; Roland Miller, *Mappila Muslims of Kerala: A Study in Islamic Trends*, Madras, 1976, p. 57.
23. Vanidas Elayavoor, *Lore and Legends of North Malabar*, Ashvin Kumar (tr.), Kottayam, 2019, p. 501.
24. F.C. Danvers, *Report to the Secretary of State for India*, London, 1892, pp. 8-10; G. Bouchon, op. cit., pp. 24, 66-7; Leena More, *English East India Company and the Local Rulers in Kerala: A Case Study of Attingal and Travancore*, Tellicherry, 2003, p. 12; K.M. Bahauddin, *Kerala Muslims: The Long Struggle*, Trivandrum, 1992, pp. 47, 52; G. Bouchon, op. cit., p. 172.
25. O.K. Nambiar, *Our Seafaring in the Indian Ocean*, Bangalore, 1975, p. 55.

26. O.K. Nambiar, op. cit., pp. 55-6, 90-1.
27. K.M. Bahauddin, op. cit., p. 49.
28. Ibid., p. 53.
29. Ibid., Robert Sewell, *A Forgotten Empire*, New Delhi, 1962, p. 188.
30. G. Bouchon, op. cit., pp. 172-3; Roland Miller, op. cit., p. 68fn.; K.M. Bahauddin, op. cit., p. 52.
31. G. Bouchon, *L'Asie du Sud à l'époque des Grand Decouvertes*, London, 1987, p. 755.
32. G. Bouchon, op. cit., p. 757; G. Bouchon, op. cit., 1988, pp. 174-5; K.K.N. Kurup, op. cit., pp. 19-21.
33. M.G.S. Narayanan, *Kozhicodinte Katha* (Malayalam), Calicut, 2001, pp. 42-3; M.G.S. Narayanan, *Calicut*, Kozhikode, pp. 188-9; P.A. Saythu, Mohammed, *Kerala Muslim Charithram* (Malayalam), Calicut, 1951, 2010, pp. 118-19; cf. Pyrard de Laval, vol. I, 1998; O.K. Nambiar, *An Illustrated Maritime History of the Indian Ocean*, New Delhi, 2013, pp. 39-41, K.K.N., Kurup and E. Ismail, *The Saga of Iringal (Historical Tradition of Kadathanad)*, Vatakara, 2011, pp. 31-2, 54-60; William Forster (ed.), *Early Travels in India, 1583-1619*, New Delhi, 1985, p. 45.
34. Francois Pyrard de Laval, 'History of the Kunhalis, the Great Malabar Corsair', in Albert Gray (tr. & ed.), *The Voyages of Francois Pyrard de Laval to the East Indies, the Maldives, the Moluccas and Brazil*, vol. 2, part II, London, 1887-9, pp. 509-27; Kenneth Latourette, *The History of the Expansion of Christianity*, vol. III, New York, 1971, pp. 249-55; Sir George Birdwood, *Report on the Old Records of the India Office*, Calcutta, 1891, p. 113; K.K.N. Kurup and E. Ismail, op. cit., pp. 54-60.

CHAPTER 7

Towards Revolt and Secession of Ali Rajas

By the second half of the seventeenth century, the European powers were in stiff competition with one another to obtain a monopoly of the spice trade on the Malabar Coast. The Portuguese had an edge over the other European nations as they had already established fortresses, factories and settlements at various points especially on the Malabar Coast much before the others. They had succeeded in establishing their naval supremacy also along the southwest coast. They even succeeded in imposing a monopoly over the spice trade of Malabar Coast.[1]

From the ample materials left by the Portuguese, an interesting fact surfaced about their attitude towards the Malabaris. They were particularly prejudiced against the Muslim Malabari traders and seafarers right from the beginning and their attitudes towards the indigenous Malabaris were nothing better. The latter were referred to as belonging to the 'cult of the devil', though there were exceptions in the writings of some Portuguese like Duarte Barbosa.[2]

ENTRY OF OTHER EUROPEAN POWERS INTO MALABAR

When the Portuguese fortunes were dipping low after the execution of Kunhali Marakkar, they faced acute resistance not only from the rulers of Calicut, Cananore, and Cochin, but also from the ferocious Muslim seafarers. It was during this turbulent period, that the English and the Dutch organized themselves and found their way to India. They were soon followed by the Danes and French.

The Danes founded their East India Company in 1616, and four years later in 1620, they acquired their first trading settlement at Tarangambadi (Tranquebar) on the Coromandel Coast and further extended to Bengal. The Danes also obtained pepper from the Malabar. At that time, Cananore was still the seat of the Kolatiris. It had an inlet and a harbour within, capable of small vessels. In due course, another important West European power, the French established a factory at Surat in 1668 and in 1674, they acquired Pondicherry on the Cholamandalam Coast. They also established a settlement at Mahé in 1721 in the country of Badagara, a vassal of the Kolatiri. Mahé was situated at about 20 km. south of Cananore on the coast.[3]

The real contact of the English with the Malabar Coast began with the arrival of Captain Keeling at Calicut with three ships on his way from Surat. They founded a settlement in Madras in 1639. On the Malabar Coast, the English built a fort at Tellicherry, in the country of Kunji Nayar, a vassal of Kolatiri. They also obtained a grant to build a fort at Anjengo in Attingal in 1694.[4]

By the end of the sixteenth century, Netherlands, a small country in Western Europe also entered the fray. The Dutch East India Company was, thus, founded by the Dutch merchants in 1602. On the Indian coasts, they had to contend with the Portuguese. Interestingly, the Dutch were conversant with the marketing of Malabar pepper, because initially when the Portuguese brought pepper and spices to Lisbon, it was the Dutch who distributed them to the European market. This was a major source of income for them. They understood that it could be more lucrative to avoid middlemen and establish direct trade relations with the places of production in Malabar. The Dutch East Indian Company's relations with Malabar Coast debuted, when they sent their fleet under the command of Admiral Steven Vander Hagen to Calicut on 11 November 1604.[5]

The Zamorin of Calicut, who was unhappy with the monopolistic tendencies of the Portuguese and their early alliance with his rivals, the Raja of Cochin as well as the Kolatiri, welcomed the Dutch to his territory with open arms. He entered into a treaty with the Dutch to expel the Portuguese from his territories and the rest of India. This is an important landmark in the history of the Dutch, as they received solid internal support and they eventually managed to wrest Cochin from the Portuguese. As a matter of fact, the Zamorin and the other Malabar rulers like the Kolatiri welcomed the Dutch to their territories in order to extricate themselves from the Portuguese.[6]

From Calicut, the Dutch went to Cananore. Curiously, they held a meeting with the Arakkal Raja of Cananore, who gave them a friendly reception. The Dutch, then, concluded a treaty with the Kolatiri Raja which gave them monopoly of exporting pepper and cinnamon and importing opium. Initially, the Dutch maintained their settlement mainly for pepper trade and were not interested in extending their dominion. They also noticed that the English bought Malabar pepper outside its production area elsewhere in Malabar and exported it not only to Europe, but to Persia where high prices were paid for the commodity. Apart from pepper, they bought cardamom, areca nut and other spices for exports to Persia. In due course, they also perceived the importance of cotton goods and Malabar sandalwood for the European and Chinese markets.[7]

Thus, by the latter half of the seventeenth century, the Dutch became more dominant in the Indian Ocean region. In Malabar, the conflict was mainly between the Dutch and Portuguese, and later the English. During the year 1623, the Dutch overthrew the English from the Spice Archipelago. After this humiliation, the English were now bent on securing an upper hand in the pepper trade of 'Malabar'. Around this time, the Englishman John Fryer visited Malabar and alluded to the existence of the Kingdom of Quilon, Calicut, Cochin, Porcad and Cananore.[8]

As far as history of Cananore is concerned, the role played by the Dutch in its history is very significant. They were responsible for defeating the Portuguese and becoming the masters of Fort St. Angelo. This was made possible due to the friendship they cultivated with the Ali Raja of Cananore. Pyrard de Laval (1601-11), who visited Malabar during this period had remarked about the declining power of King of Malabar (Kolatiri), who was losing his grip on his Kingdom. He also made an observation about the simultaneous rise of the Muslim chieftain named Ali Raja in Cananore in the kingdom of the Kolatiri.

Pyrard described Ali Raja as a handsome and stylish man, who liked foreigners. He was an extremely rich trader who possessed fleet of ships which plied the seas carrying merchandise all over the countries and brought back goods. He was very powerful in the sea and owned the islands of Laccadives and Maldives. Besides, he possessed several factories in different parts of the country. Pyrard mentioned that during this period, the Portuguese were at peace with Ali Raja. But the Portuguese held that the Ali Raja was a usurper and not the rightful king. The rightful king of the region was none other than the Kolatiri, if we go by the Portuguese accounts. The Ali Raja at that time must have been Mohammed Ali Adi Raja (1610-47) according to the list cited in the Arakkal records.[9]

Pyrard de Laval in his accounts made a distinction between the local Nairs and foreign Moors, who migrated from Arabia and settled on the Malabar Coast. The latter owed allegiance to their Nair King and paid the tax (tribute) on the land, where they resided (probably land tax). Their religion was Islam and that they were extremely wealthy traders who followed the laws of Mohammed and who lived in a predominantly Malabari society.

They were the best soldiers of the country both on land and sea and controlled the entire navigation and sea traffic of the country. They employed persons belonging to the fishermen and Thiyya community on salary basis who worked in their ships and on land carrying out miscellaneous mechanical work. They cultivated friendly relations with the Nairs and got along very well with them. They followed the culture, custom of the country and were highly superstitious. They respected the tradition of the country. Whenever they paid a visit to other's house, they would not sit down or touch the walls or furniture of the house, to avoid polluting the house.

Pyrard de Laval also cited about the way in which the Dutch tried to intimidate the Cananore people. Whenever they sailed past their fort, they fired cannons and the king reciprocated by sending lots of presents. He also pointed out as to how the Dutch often threatened to besiege their fort, but the king pleaded with them saying that he and his subjects wanted peace. Pyrard also remarked about the bustling market of Cananore called as Bazaars.[10] He further remarked that the Ali Raja was an opportunist. He narrated a story of how he took advantage of the state visit of Ranabaderi Takuram of Maldives in 1607, who was the contender to the throne in the event of the death of the then Sultan Ibrahim of Maldives. Ali Raja turned this visit in his favour as his family traditionally enjoyed certain rights over the Maldives.

Ali Raja did not get along well with the Portuguese, but when he sensed that bad blood was running between the Portuguese and the Kolatiri, he decided to befriend the Dutch to counter the Portuguese. He sought help from them to fight the Portuguese. Soon, the Dutch began to throw their weight around by signing agreements with the Malabar rulers as a counter to the Portuguese menace, knowing fully that the Portuguese were still a power in Cananore.

By 1645, the Dutch began to procure pepper and by 1653, they were carrying ship loads of cardamom from Cananore to Persia for sale where they made large profits. An astonishing fact was that the trade with the East which was till then the monopoly of the Portuguese, began to slowly slip away from their hands and went straight into the hands of the Dutch. By the year 1654, the Dutch had established themselves firmly in Jakarta. The princes of Malabar did not offer any resistance and entered into exclusive contracts with the Dutch by which all strangers were denied trade in pepper, cassia lignum, spice, timber and teak, which the Dutch called 'prohibitory goods'.[11]

ATTACK ON FORT ST. ANGELO

The Dutch, then, embarked on a naval expedition to subdue the Malabar Coast from Colombo. With their flagship, 'Semoos Kathboom' comprising of 1,800 foot soldiers and 100 sailors they attacked and captured Cochin from the Portuguese in the year 1662.

The Portuguese witnessed their settlements falling like a pack of cards one after another in front of the might of the Dutch. After the capture of Cochin, the next target of the Dutch was Cananore. They had an eye on the solid Fort St. Angelo. The Dutch naval fleet under the command of Jacob Hustaart, Peter Dippon and Henry Van Rheede along with a strong battalion of soldiers set out for Cananore. On reaching the shores of Cananore, with their army, they were joined by great number of Malabaris, who were weary of the tyranny of the Portuguese. On sighting the strong and well fortified Fort St. Angelo, they decided to launch attack principally on the land side as the side facing the sea was impregnable. The siege continued for several days. In the cannon attack, parts of the fort walls were shattered. The Portuguese commander of the fort, Antonio Cardosa escaped leaving the garrison to capitulate for themselves which they did the next day to save more bloodshed on 13 February 1663. Most of the Portuguese garrison returned to Goa. The commander Antonio Cardosa met with a tragic end at the hands of his own government. He was decapitated by the order of the Viceroy for capitulating the fortress without a reasonable cause and surrendering without a fight. Eventually, the Dutch captured literally all the Portuguese ports south of Goa, and also Sri Lanka.[12]

After their victory over the Portuguese, the Dutch renovated parts of the Cananore fort which were destroyed in cannon firing. Further, they added a large curtain with two royal bastions facing the land side of the fort. To obtain stones for the construction, they demolished Cananore town along with the buildings, and the stones thus obtained were used to build the defence of the fort. However, their garrison consisted of only 40 soldiers and a captain, who was the governor of the fort. Van Weerden became the chief commander of the Dutch in Cananore, and Daniel John Kijs was the head of the trade centre in Cananore. They affirmed authority in matters related to trade which was under the control of commandant of the Dutch East India Company. Thus, they occupied and consolidated their position in Fort St. Angelo together with its outpost at Elimala, which was a strategic point commanding the river navigation of north Malabar.[13]

Winning the battle in Cananore after a siege of few days made the Dutch very confident of their supremacy. They slowly tried to bring Zamorin within their fold. A pact was signed by the Dutch and the Zamorin on 7 March 1663 according to which the Zamorin should provide 2,000 Nairs soldiers to the Dutch, if need arose and must supply pepper to them at market value. Kolatiri Raja followed suit. He also entered into a treaty of peace and friendship with the Dutch. According to the trade pact made by the Dutch and Kolatiri Raja on 20 March 1663, Cananore town and its administration went to the Dutch on condition that 50 per cent of the tax and other income collected would be made over to the Kolatiri Raja. Since this was just an oral contract between the two, the Dutch did not abide by it.

CONFLICT BETWEEN ALI RAJA AND THE KOLATIRI

It has been reported that during this period, not far from the fort, there was a pretty large town built at the bottom of the Bay which was independent of the Dutch and under the rule of Adda Raja, or Ali Raja. According to Alexander Hamilton, Adda Raja's government was neither absolute nor hereditary. Dutch put a garrison of 300 men in the fort and entered into a commercial alliance with the King of Cananore (Kolatiri) on 22 July 1664 in which Adi Rajas name was included for the first time and free sea trade was once again accorded to him.[14]

This shows the growing importance of the Ali Raja in north Malabar and Cananore. It appears more probable that it was the Dutch, who officially gave formal recognition to the Ali Raja by including his name in the treaty. The Dutch knew that the Moors were the principal traders and seafarers of the kingdom. Hence, they would have included the name of Ali Raja, who was their representative in the treaty. The Kolatiri Raja by himself could not have done it, as the Ali Raja was his subordinate and not an independent chief.

It was specified in the treaty that the Dutch would be supplied with pepper, cloves and other commodities as per their demand. However, conditions were imposed on the imports and exports by Ali Raja by limiting the quantities of cardamom, opium and pepper to be imported by him within the Kolatiri territory. Moreover, the treaty also prohibited the Ali Raja from procuring pepper or cinnamon by sea or land from the Kingdom of Zamorin and the Raja of Cochin. But Ali Raja continued to trade clandestinely without the knowledge of the Dutch by secretly selling his produce to others who offered him more money which made the Dutch comment that 'he had been as unfaithful as all the other native Princes'.[15]

It is quite interesting to note that due to Dutch pressure in the 1660s, Ali Raja had tried to shift his trade operations to Mangalore. He tried to revive an old fort there as his central seat in 1666. But the Ikkeri Nayak of the Canara region did not agree to his entrenchment and expelled him from the fort. Thus, Ali Raja was at loggerheads with the Ikkeri Nayak of the Kannada country thenceforth.[16]

From the above statements, it is very clear that during this period, Ali Raja had not become totally independent of the Kolatiri, but being a vassal he had no other choice but to sign this agreement even though he did not abide by certain clauses of the treaty that was detrimental to his own welfare. Attempts of the Dutch, hence, to maintain a monopoly on trade back-fired as it was infringed by not only Ali Raja but also by other Malabar princes clandestinely. Ali Raja, unmindful of the internal quarrels and intrigues, strengthened himself and his bazaars and threw up various works round about it.[17]

On the political front, the Dutch tried to pursue an impartial approach towards the Kolatiri and the Ali Raja of Cananore. On account of this, they obtained from Kolatiri the monopoly of bringing opium to Kolathanadu. Simultaneously, they permitted Ali Raja to bring six candies of opium annually as a favour for the service that he rendered to the company's merchants in obtaining pepper from his territory. Opium was in high demand in Malabar. Its use was popular amongst 'the Nairos', who consumed the product to intoxicate their brain when they go to fight.

Soon, there arose a misunderstanding between Ali Raja and the Dutch. Ali Raja was aware of the support given to the Dutch by the Kolatiri. But knowing the strength of the Dutch, he kept a low profile. There was an instance when the Ali Raja had confiscated 24 pieces of iron cannon from a stranded Dutch ship in Maldives and audaciously refused to hand it back to the Dutch. Ultimately, the Dutch had to pay him money to obtain their own cannons. Despite this incident, the Dutch did not take any retaliatory measures against Ali Raja as they did not want to disturb the peaceful trade relations existing with him.[18]

Meanwhile, the English began to try their luck in the region. In the year 1668, Abbe Carré, a French missionary mentioned that while passing along the Malabar Coast he sighted English ships anchored at Dharmapatnam, near Tellicherry. Later, the English settled at Baliapatnam. The Kolatiri had allowed the English to occupy Catacombe (Cottacunu) in 1669, which meant 'Fort Hille' where there was an old Malabar fort. Cottacunnu was near River Baliapatam built on a hillock, one side having a beautiful view of a large river and its branches flowing through the pleasant meadows, while on the other side dense jungle full of trees and bushwood, home to great number of tigers, boars, leopards and wild beasts.[19]

Initially, the English factors had established friendly relations with Ali Raja, but very soon there arose a rift in their relation due to inland duty. The English were asked to give some *mosque* dues to the Muslims at Cananore which they declined. This resulted in friction in their smooth relations. In the year 1670, the French built a factory at Tellicherry to the south of Cananore near Mahè, with the help of the Kolatiri in spite of opposition from the Dutch.[20]

In 1668, Alexander Hamilton described an event which showed the cruel side of the prince of Cananore, i.e. the Ali Raja. The Prince paid a visit to the Dutch fort accompanied by 50 of his attendants to pay compliment to the captain of the fort. While the prince was in a discussion with the captain, the Malabaris, who nursed grievances against the Dutch managed to sneak inside the fort and killed the security guard on duty. But the alert Dutch soldiers intervened and foiled their attempt by killing 20 of the intruders. They drove out the rest and closed the gate of the fort without alerting the prince and the captain, who were unaware of this incident and were continuing their exchanges. But on being informed about the incident, the Prince was furious at the treachery of his men and immediately ordered for a search to be carried out to nab the ringleader of this attack. The ringleader was caught and sentenced to a cruel death by smearing his body in honey and fastening him to a coconut tree in the scorching sun till he died. The sentence was carried out the next day.

The coconut trees produced country liquor called toddy, which was very sweet and the smell that emanated from this toddy brought vast number of wasps and large red ants to drink the liquor. But when the sun became hot, these insects will leave the top of the tree and go down and burrow in the body smeared with honey. The bites of the ants and the sting of the wasps in the scorching sun would have been truly hell for the poor man. He died a slow and terrible death after three days of suffering. The Dutch captain seeing the suffering begged the Prince to pardon the man or at least give a minor punishment, if not a quicker death. But the prince was inexorable. This incident brought out the cruelty of the Cananore prince.[21]

Meanwhile, dissensions were taking place within the Kolatiri kingdom. In 1680, a shocking incident occurred in the kingdom. Some members of the royal family conspired to kill the Kolatiri Raja to usurp the kingdom. But this conspiracy was detected and all the conspirators were caught and beheaded at the altar built of stones about two miles from Cananore. Alexander Hamilton had seen the altar when he visited this place. This incident left a bad impression about the enmity churning within the royal kingdom. However, the Kolatiri Raja continued to wield power within his flourishing kingdom. Around 1684, Thévenot described Cananore as a place where you found everything necessary for livelihood. He further cited that the port of Cananore was big and its ruler was known as the King of Cananore, who did not reside there but held his court in a strait quite far away from the sea.[22]

When the situation was thus in Cananore, elsewhere in the country, the English were desperately looking for a place to establish trade. The growing rivalry between the Dutch and the English threatened the state of comparative peace in Malabar. The English managed to establish factories in north Malabar, first in Calicut, then at Tellicherry in 1684. Currently, they were on the lookout for a place abounding in pepper but out of Dutch influence to construct a factory in south Malabar. They chose to settle at Anjengo in the Attingal kingdom in 1694.[23] The Dutch were not happy with it.

During the same period, the Kolatiri Dynasty was divided principally into two divisions—Udayamangalam and Vadakankoor. The English, who were trading from Tellicherry in 1699 had established their trade centre in Tellicherry with the consent of Vadakankoor. This alliance of English with Vadakankoor was viewed with dislike by the Udayamangalam division. Thus, in 1704, the Udayamangalam division joined hands with Kurunotu Nair, the chief of Erumbahzi, a neighbouring state, and attacked and destroyed the godown in Tellicherry inflicting heavy loss to the English Company. The English requested the Vadakankoor to make security arrangements for their warehouse to ward off such attacks from the Udayamangalam group in future. In lieu of this, Vadakankoor gave permission to the English to build a fort in Tellicherry. It was the Vadakankoor Rajah, known as the Raja of Chirakkal, who laid the foundation stone of the fort of Tellicherry, which was completed on 20 August 1708. Thus, the Fort of Tellicherry became the first British settlement in North Malabar, whereas as early as 1699 Anjengo Fort was already established in the kingdom of Attingal in Travancore.[24]

A short time later the Kolatiri Raja died. There arose a fight between two contenders for the throne. One was the junior prince of Kolatiri and the other, the prince regent of Kolathanadu. Ali Raja and the Dutch supported the junior prince of Kolatiri, whereas the English supported the prince regent of Kolathanadu. Ultimate ascendancy of the minor prince to the throne was disliked by the English.

At the beginning of the eighteenth century, the Kolatiri and the English continued to be at loggerheads. However, in Cananore other events were unfolding. Ali Raja seemed to have become independent of Kolatiri at that time. Hamilton, who visited Cananore in the year 1703 has alluded to this transition. 'Town (Cananore) with the circumjacent (*sic.*) country is under the government of Adda Rajah a Mohametan Malabar Prince, who upon occasion can bring near 2,000 men into the field.'

Hamilton described the Ali Raja as a powerful Muslim ruler, who traded extensively via sea and land. His vessels transported the native products to other countries and brought back plenty of saleable goods. He was highly respected and played a prominent role in quelling several disturbances and dissensions in the country. Hamilton mentioned about how the finances of the country and its administration were managed by Ali Raja. Chests were specially made with holes on their lids. Gold coins were extensively used. Whatever money was received by the treasurer was put into the holes of the chest which had four locks and their keys were in the custody of the Raja, the commissioner of trade, the chief judge and the treasurer. Whenever there was necessity for withdrawing money from the chest, it could be removed only in the presence of the four officers or their deputies.

It is clear that at the end of the seventeenth century, the Ali Rajas had a watertight system of maintaining their treasury and the existence of the commissioner of trade, chief judge, treasurer points out to a well organized government. This system had existed even during the period of the affluent ancestors of Ali Raja, i.e. 'Lord of the Seas'. His ancestors were so rich that it is cited that their coins 'were all gold'. The situation in Cananore was becoming grim between Dutch and English. But Ali Raja carried out trade activities undeterred. His dominion extended 10 miles south of Cananore to River Tellicherry, near which he had a harbour called 'Dormepatam', its passage inward though deep was rocky.[25] This place was known as Dharmapatam (Dharmadam) a 'city of piety', which was a sacred place as it was the seat of Kolatiri kings in earlier days.

A number of small territories between Tellicherry and Kotta was also under Ali Raja's control. Almost enjoining the territory of Dharmapatam there was a small island against its mouth in the Arabian Sea called 'Caca Diva' about half-a-league from the shore full of rocks. It was also known as Grove Island. As large numbers of crows were nested in this island it was called *Kakkadvipa*, or island of crows. The possession of this strategic island of *Kakkadvipa* testified to the expansion of Ali Rajas dominion at the expense of Kolatiri Kingdom. Thus rivalry between the Arakkal kingdom and Kolatiri kingdom accentuated throughout the eighteenth century.[26]

By the beginning of the eighteenth century, Dharmapatam had a strong Muslim population. Once there was an incident when there were conflicts for the post of *Curtow* (Governor). One Conjee (Kunhi) Pocur was the *Curtow* of Dharmapatam. However, Kolatiri claimed his authority over this place. On the other hand, Ali Rajah also wanted to stake his authority as he nurtured ambition to become the *Curtow* (governor) of Dharmapatam. During this period, the Dutch at Cananore came with their ships and boats to Dharmapatam and entered into a business deal with Ali Raja and Kunhi Pocur, to exchange Dutch goods for 500 candies of pepper and cardamom annually, breaching the existing trade deal of the merchants not to sell any commodities to any other European nation. When the events were thus unfolding suddenly Kunhi Pocur, the *Curtow* died of poisoning and it was widely believed that Ali Raja was responsible for his death, as he was nurturing an ambition to become the *Curtow* of Dharmapatam, in addition to being the ruler of Cananore. But as destiny would have it, he failed in his design to become the governor of Dharmapatam, as he was driven out by the late *Curtow's* rightful successor in 1682.

This untimely death of Kunhi Pocur dealt a great blow to the English factory at Tellicherry as Pocur had helped them in the pepper investment and also owed money to them. But by 1683, Ali Raja regained some authority in Dharmapatam to the utter surprise of the English at Tellicherry who sent him a congratulatory letter. English were apprehensive of both the Dutch and Ali Raja. On the other hand, the Kolatiri Prince who was still in reckoning continued to extend protection to the factors of the warehouse at Tellicherry by delegating Nair soldiers to guard their factory against possible attacks by Ali Raja and other enemies. Ali Raja's notoriety was spreading far and wide. Knowing this, when Robert Adams took charge as the Chief of English Affairs in Malabar, he adopted a policy of appeasement towards the Ali Raja and established friendly relations with him and the Arakkal kingdom.[27]

Ali Raja also had his dominion in 'Laccadive islands', which was a cluster of 18 islands according to Hamilton, who had visited them. He recounted that these island were about 40 leagues off the Malabar Coast and were low and dangerous. The channel between them and the Maldives islands was called the eighth degree channel. The main products of these islands were coconuts and fish. Coconuts were used in cooking, and from coconut kernels, they extracted oil which were used for various purposes. The fibre of the coconut casks were also spun and made into cordage and cables which were used in the shipping industry and for several other purposes. Alongside, fish industry also flourished, fish was dried and exported to the continent. However, eclipsing all the above, the sea provided priceless objects. Sometimes, in the south-west monsoon Ambergris was sighted floating on the sea, which was invaluable and very expensive. These were supposed to come out from mouth of the whales (vomit of the whales), and used in producing perfume.

Ali Raja possessed one big piece of Ambergris valued at Rs. 10,000, which was a big show piece in his house. This was one of his prized possession. Ambergris was held at great esteem by the Malabaris, which was brought in from the Maldives, which was under Ali Raja's control. Philip Baldaeus commented that he had personally seen an ounce of it sold at Cananore for six *reals*. The fame of Ali Raja began to spread due to his dynamism and business acumen. He carried on an extensive trade with flourishing harbours like Surat, Goa, Cochin on the Indian coast, and also on the other side with the harbours of Arabia.

Ali Raja was becoming prominent in Kolathanadu. For defending his territory, he constructed a fort in Cananore in 1712. The site and remains of this fortress is still known by the term, 'Khajna Kotta' in Cananore. A contemporary French writer testified to Ali Raja's naval superiority from Mangalore to Calicut on the Malabar Coast. Even the King of Maldives recognized him as their sovereign. Over and above, the Moors of Malabar treated him as a symbol of their political unification. The title of 'Thangal', generally used by the Moplahs, who claimed direct descent from the Prophet was assumed by the Arakkal house. So, in political as well as in religious affairs, the Arakkal house began to play a dominant role. Thangals or chief leaders traced their origin to Ali and Fatima, the son-in-law and daughter of the Prophet respectively. Being of Arab ancestory claimed to be of more honourable birth than the Turkish Muslims from North India. In religious matters, Thangal was the head and his office was hereditary.

In Malabar, each mosque was presided by an imam or *mullah* appointed by a Thangal.[28]

The rising power of Ali Raja was also noted by Jacob Canter Visscher, the Dutch Chaplain at Cochin, who mentioned that the most powerful of all the Moors who were almost an independent prince resided in Cananore. He was the Ali Raja, who was also king of the islands especially Laccadive islands, which was ceded to him by Kolatiri and in return for this favour, it was agreed that new Ali Raja must always 'receive his crown from the reigning Raja of Colastre (Kolatiri).

The fact which emerged from the above was that the Arakkal Raja was not totally free from the yoke of the Kolatiri. Regardless, the ceremony of receiving the crown from the Kolatiri and paying the tribute for *jagir* of islands was gradually stopped. Visscher further stated, 'Ali Rajah has a large and handsome Bazaar where most of the Moors in his dominions reside'. He traded with the Dutch in turmeric, cardamom and ambergris. Ali Raja maintained good relations with the Dutch, and at times he even carried the Dutch pass in his foreign trade.

It should be noted at this juncture that though the Portuguese had ceased to be a naval power in the Arabian sea, they were not done yet. They remained active and even threatened Ali Raja's fleet in the sea. In 1720, the Portuguese attacked a ship of Ali Raja which was transporting horses from Mecca, under the pretext that no one has the right of importing horses. Taking this as an affront, Ali Raja immediately dispatched 20 well manned vessels to pursue the Portuguese as far as Cochin. Portuguese captain was so terrified that he requested the mediation of the Dutch. This was a standing testimony about the might of Ali Raja's naval power and his flourishing trade with Mecca and other parts of the world,[29]

Soon there arose friction in his relations with Kolatiri. In 1722, a war broke out between Kolatiri and Ali Raja. According to Visscher, a simple private dispute between them triggered into an open war. A group of Muslims killed some

Nairs of Kolatiri Raja and in act of revenge, Kolatiri wreaked vengeance by killing as many Muslims that they came across. Thus, the account was settled. But in a sudden counter flare up the Muslims insulted a Kolatiri prince at the famous Cananore Bazaar, which ignited further problems. Observing these developments, the English factor Robert Adams at Tellicherry stepped in to help Kolatiri to attack the famous Cananore Bazaar. The English wanted to capture Cananore town and Bazaar and expel the Muslims from that area. But prior to implementing the above, they sought permission from Kolatiri to construct a factory and fort in Cananore in the vicinity of the Dutch Fort to carry on trade. This move of the English infuriated the Dutch, who saw through their game. As a counter, they supplied arms and ammunitions to Ali Raja in his battle against Kolatiri. This incident brings to limelight, the methods followed by Europeans in Malabar of fishing in troubled waters to get some privilege for them. Whether Portuguese, Dutch, French or English their *modus operandi* was the same. In order to further their ambitions, they resorted to devious and unscrupulous methods. Henceforth, the animosity between the Ali Raja and the Kolatiri leading to violence became a regular feature of the history of Kolathanadu, or north Malabar. Ali Raja became more and more ferocious towards the Kolatiri. He forcefully seized the Kadalayi Fort and made himself master of this fort on 6 June 1727. This fort was erected by the prince regent, Kunhihoma (Kolatiri) purely as a barrier to his vast country, which produced great quantity of pepper. According to prince regent's report to the English, the Moors entered into Kolatiri country, broke down Nairs' dwellings, robbed their women and violated their pagodas and tanks. This was unacceptable to the Kolatiri, who sought help from the English. They immediately dispatched a garrison of soldiers, but Ali Raja refused them access to cross over his island at Dharmapatam.[30]

The English panicked. They knew that to reach their trading posts in Etakkat, they had to go through Dharmapatam.

They sought the help of Kottayam Raja to allow their soldiers to pass through his country. On the other hand, the Kolatiri Prince Regent colluded with the King of Kottayam at Dharmapatam and captured one of the forts of Ali Raja. He even succeeded in destroying his ships and captured two of his elephants and took total control of the island of Dharmapatam. But Kolatiri had to pay a price to Kottayam Raja for his help, as the King of Kottayam (Cotiota) demanded half of Dharmapatam for the service rendered by him. At this point, Kolatiri decided to completely annihilate Arakkal principality and continued with his oppressive measures against Ali Raja. Unfortunately amidst all the tension, Ali Raja went on a pilgrimage to Mecca. He sailed to Jeddah on 1728, where he is said to have died.[31]

Gauging from the year cited on the board exhibited at Arakkal Museum, this must have been Mohammed Ali Adi Raja (1720-8). After his death, his subjects continued their skirmishes against Kolatiri. They sought help from the Siddis (of Janjira), beyond the northern tip of Malabar, in order to counter Kolatiri. Siddis were an Islamized community hailing from different parts of Africa, mainly from Abyssinia (Ethiopia), who had been shipped to India originally as slaves during different periods of history and who settled at Gujarat, Maharashtra and Karnataka.

Some vessels of the Canarese reached as far as Valapatnam. On the other hand, the Kolatiri Prince was facing problems from the Kottayam Raja who threatened to withdraw his troops if his demand for half of Dharmapatam Island was not met with. Nevertheless, Kolatiri managed to appease the Kottayam Raja temporarily. When the situation was boiling between Kolatiri and Kottayam Raja, both the Dutch and the Canarese wanted to station their army at Dharmapatam. This was not acceptable to the English, who negotiated with the Kolatiri Prince Regent for the possession of the island of Kakkadvipa or Grove island near Dharmapatam.

At this juncture, Ali Raja realized the impossibility of subduing the Kolatiri prince. Hence, he sought help from the King of Canara, though peace prevailed between the Prince

Regent of Kolathanadu and the Canarese ruler. But on being solicited by Ali Raja for assistance, the King of Canara became ambitious and decided to expand his kingdom into Malabar under the pretext of helping Ali Raja. Thus, in the year 1730, his troops crossed the frontier and invaded Kolathanadu. The Canarese invasion of Kolathanadu had far-reaching consequences in the economic and political history of this region. The Prince Regent was in a fix as he found it difficult to fight internal as well as external enemies. He sued for peace with Ali Raja. One Kalliadan Nambiar mediated and through him Ali Raja obtained the favour of Kolatiri Prince Regent and even gave him hundred thousand *fanams*. Prince Regent even informed the English that he had obtained a respite for four months.[32]

We have seen earlier that the Kunhali Marakkars, who were at the service of the Zamorin had revolted against the latter and broke away from the control of the Zamorin and tried to establish a separate principality. This attempt was thwarted by the Zamorin with the help of the Portuguese. A point to be noted here is that Kunhali Marakkars were not related to the Zamorin family through matrimonial alliance in any way. They were simply seafarers and traders who were at the service of the Zamorin.

Similarly, in Cananore the Ali Raja and his ancestors were also at the service of the Kolatiri king. But unlike the Kunhali Marakkars, the Ali Rajas were blood relatives of the Kolatiri dynasty. They were most probably the descendants of a Prince of Cananore who had converted in the thirteenth century or even before, according to the travelogues of Ibn Battuta. The list of Arakkal Rajas maintained in the Arakkal Museum and records seems to stand testimony to this. However, later accounts have recorded that a princess of the Kolatiri dynasty had married a Muslim. As a result, the Kolatiri king had given them the territory of Cananore coast as their fiefdom. Whatever may be the truth, it is certain that the Arakkal family followed the *marumakkatayam* custom like the Nairs (and also Thiyyas) of north Malabar. As a result, we can conclude that they were related to the Kolatiri king.[33]

Like the Kunhali Marakkars, the Arakkal Rajas too were at the service of the Kolatiri king. They were the ones who were the merchants and seafarers of the Kolatiri. But in the course of time, they became sufficiently autonomous financially and militarily that they became increasingly defiant towards the Kolatiri. The Kolatiri could not rein them in. They allied with the Dutch and other local and European powers to trouble the Kolatiri. The Kolatiri was unable to subdue them, unlike the Zamorin who subdued the Kunhali Marakkars. As time went by, the Ali Rajas became more defiant and insubordinate and practically shook off their allegiance to the Kolatiri, whose power was fast diminishing in the region. This led the Ali Rajas to become practically independent of the Kolatiri. In other words, they seceded from the Kolatiri kingdom to establish their own principality, of which Ali Raja was the chief.

I would like to draw the attention to another important historical fact, which had crucial implications for the north Malabar region, which was till then safe more or less from foreign intruders. The Malabaris hitherto had successfully restricted the Europeans to their forts and settlements. But it was the Ali Raja, who in order to counter the Kolatiri invited the northern Canara forces into Malabar. This brought about a new dimension into Malabar politics. Thenceforth, Malabar was open to invasions from the Canara country, which as we are going to see in the next chapter had far-reaching consequences. Malabar or rather Kolathanadu, which had maintained its independence or separate political existence more or less from Nannan's time, some two thousand years ago, was presently open to aggression, coming from its northern and eastern frontiers, due to the short-sighted actions of the Ali Raja.

THE CANARESE INVASIONS OF KOLATHANADU

Around this period, the Canarese were planning to expand their kingdom. The Canarese army of Somasekhara Nayak

II decided to overrun the northern territory of Kolatiri, and to plunder the rich Taliparamba temple. The ruling Prince Regent met Zamorin who was one of the protectors of that place and sought his help for the defence of the place. He even raised an army of 40,000 men whose salary was to be paid out of the treasury of the temple. However, this army was not a match against the invaders. On 16 January 1732, the Canarese army attacked Kolathanadu and captured the region upto Ezhimala and proceeded to Valapatanam.[34] They received assistance from a Pirate Cutty Coilem, who reached Baliapatam with his fleet to help Canarese to fight against the Prince Regent. The English detachment immediately launched an attack against the pirate to safeguard their trade and Moplah navy from the atrocities of the enemy. Later, on 10 May 1732, Canarese captured the Matame (Mattul), a predominantly Muslim region near the mouth of Valapatanam.[35] This invasion by the Canarese was regarded as a threat to the English, who feared that eventually the Canarese could become the masters of the river and also the country as far as Tellicherry, as they faced no opposition from the Kolatiri and his subjects.

After a short break on 22 October 1732, the Canarese army once again crossed River Valapatanam and attacked the dominions of Kolatiri. The fortunes of the country fell into low ebb and eventually Kolatiri Raja Udayaverma and the Canarese General Raghunath came to an agreement, whereby the ruling Prince surrendred his kingdom to the north of Taliparamba to the Canarese ruler. To be precise, the region from the west of River Valapatanam upto Nileshwaram would belong to Kolatiri as a tenancy under the control of the Bednur ruler. The Bednur king could build three forts, at Madkaro (Madakara), Kavi (Kawayil), and Nileshwaram. At the same time, the region south of River Valapatanam would be under the direct control of Kolatiri. It was also agreed that they would assist the prince regent to suppress the rebellious Moplahs. The latter just became a mere tributary of Bednur, which he regretted later. After this agreement, the Canarese captain became so formidable that he undertook to root out the Moors of Adi Raja and Cotteate (Kottayam); 'for in the territory of Cotteate belonging to the Kingdom of Colastry there were many moors'.[36]

The irony is that it was Ali Raja who sought the help from the Canarese to invade the territory of Kolatiri Raja. But to his dismay, he found out that both Kolatiri and the Canarese General entered into an agreement to wipe out the Moors in his own territory. Ali Raja took counter measures to fortify his Fort at Kadalayi and requested help from the English. As the English did not want to antagonize both the Kolatiri and the Canarese, they refused to accede to the request. Meanwhile, in 1733, the joint armies of the Canarese and Kolatiri approached the neighbourhood of Cananore to reduce the Moors. The English seeing the danger to their trading interests, if Cananore fell to the enemies, clandestinely agreed to help the reigning heiress of Ali Raja of the Arakkal principality with arms.[37]

CONFRONTATION AT MADAKKARA

The Canarese rulers had built two forts, one in Madakkara at the mouth of River Valapatanam and the other in Kadalayi situated on a hilltop, two kilometres south of Cananore harbour, which was completed in 1734. Ali Raja confronted the Canarese army and captured the Madakkara fort. In retaliation, the Canarese captain recaptured the fort and devastated the enemy by killing nearly five thousand men and women of Muslim community. He undertook to root out the Moors of Adi Raja as well as the Moors of Kottayam (Cotteate), which was part of the kingdom of Collastry (Kolatiri).

However, this incident leading to immense loss of Muslim lives did not break the Muslims of Cananore. They managed to obtain reinforcement of 12,000 men from Calicut and Ponnani giving a religious twist to the whole affair by repeating that the Canarese had killed one of their highly revered priests. They tried unsuccessfully to capture the fort of

Madakkara. Meanwhile, Bednur faced problems in their home turf, the rivals of Bednur were encroaching on their territory. Chikly Khan with his army insisted that Bednur should raise the siege of Cananore. But this invasion hardly helped the Mappilas of Cananore.[38] Thus, the entire Kolathanadu was embroiled in endless wars, with each power fighting against another.

Meanwhile, in 1734, the English acquired Dharmapatnam in Kottayam Taluk, about two miles northwest of Tellicherry, where there was an old Arab mosque, which was demolished. Subsequently, they launched an attack on the Canarese fort at Madakkara and captured it on 17 March 1736. They wanted to destroy it but Kolatiri Raja had his own misgivings about the demolition of the fort as he believed that if the fort was destroyed, the Muslims of Valapatanam and Mattul might encroach on their region without any hindrance. He succeeded in convincing the English not to demolish the fort. However, they left a small garrison for its security. Seeing the garrison, Canarese army abandoned their fort at Madakkara and moved on to their second fort at Kadalayi, which was situated 12 kilometres from Madakkara.[39]

SUBJUGATION OF KADALAYI BY THE DUTCH AND THE ENGLISH

In March 1736, the English army from Tellicherry along with the Nair militia attacked the fort of Kadalayi, which was under the control of the Canarese. Initially, the Nair army and the English troops were badly injured and had to retreat. Meanwhile, when the battle was raging between the English and Canarese, the Dutch at Cananore who were closely monitoring the situation realized that the capitulation of the Kadalayi Fort posed a threat to their own existence because in case the English succeeded in capturing the fort, they were sure to make it their military base. Having an enemy base close to their fort was a matter of real concern which they wanted to avoid at any cost. Nevertheless, amidst all this, the Dutch in

1736 managed to make a contract with Ali Raja to supply them annually 500 catties about 1¼ lbs of cowries, which was brought from his Lekker Diva (Laccadives) islands.

Thus, the Dutch commandant Jacob met the English delegation headed by Stephen Lo and struck a deal with the English that in case the Kadalayi fort was captured, it should be totally demolished, which was agreed upon by the English. The Dutch assisted the English by dispatching 300 soldiers, including 180 Europeans. A pitched and bloody battle was fought to capture Kadalayi. The combined force of the English and Dutch lost only few soldiers whereas the Canarese incurred heavy casualty. They lost their chief Gopalji. Besides, hundreds of soldiers, and civilians including men and women perished in this battle. The Canarese army finally accepted defeat and surrendered. The English flag was hoisted on the flagstaff. As agreed Kadalayi fort was totally demolished.

In acknowledgement of the assistance given by the Nair militia, a contract was made with the Prince of Collastry in 1737, one of the condition of which was he must supply the company annually with 1,000 candies of pepper. Again, King of Canara invaded this country, the Dutch on their part tried to bring peace between the parties but all in vain, for the Canarese made preposterous demands to which Kolatiri refused to concede. But despite this setback, the Canarese refused to give up and invaded and captured the dominions of Kolatiri, north of River Taliparamba, except Madayi. The conquered territory remained in the possession of the King of Canara. The result was on 30 August 1737, the Kolatiri and the English commandant Linch met the Karnataka General Surappa at Madakkara and agreed to a temporary division of the region, i.e. the region from Madayi fort to Urpally in the south belonged to the King of Bednur and the area lying to the south of the above mentioned region would belong to Kolatiri. In a nutshell the result of division was, 'the best part of the kingdom came under the sway of the Canarese and the worst part remained in the possession of Kolastry'. The English however got in return for their mediation a beautiful piece of land called 'Mattume'.[40]

During this period, frictions were taking place in the Kolatiri family. Kolatiri Raja's nephew, Okku who was a rebel and the immediate successor to the throne turned hostile to the ruling Raja. With the support of Nair regiment, Okku and his followers rebelled against the Kolatiri and the English. He intended to go to Kadathanad in November 1739 to obtain assistance from the king there, but he was waylaid and imprisoned in Madakkara Fort by the English. Amidst all the confusion, the King of Canara passed away, but after s short respite, the turbulent princes and chiefs renewed their old quarrel, disturbances and dissension continued. In the year 1745, parties came to an agreement. The intrigues of Adi Raja as well as of the Princes of Collastry now with the Marathas then with the English and then, with the French continued to go on as before.[41]

SURRENDER OF DHARMAPATAM

It is known that it was Ali Raja who permitted the English to occupy Grove Island or Kakkadvip near Dharmapatam. In the year 1734, his successor, Januma Bi Adi Raja Beevi (1732-45) allowed the English to maintain a small garrison of 25 men along with the Nair force. In the midst the English negotiated and obtained the possession of Dharmapatam Island from the Beevi Adi Raja. They actually wanted to shift their Tellicherry factory to Dharmapatam. But after concluding the agreement, the Beevi had second thoughts and wanted to back out of the deal. She regretted having given up Dharmapatam and tried her best to regain this island. She requested the English for its restoration as, 'it was a place in great veneration by the Mahometans'. All her efforts went in vain as she could not recover Dharmapatam from the English as she was caught in a debt trap and was unable to reimburse the expenses incurred on it to the Company. It was obvious that the English did not have any intention of restoring Dharmapatam to the Beevi. They went ahead with their plan and made their intention clear by pointing out the drawback of their Tellicherry fort and demanded permission to erect a regular fortress at Dharmapatam, in order to make it their principal settlement and leave Tellicherry as a secondary one. Beevi was thoroughly disgusted as she realized that she was cheated and deceived by her own minister during the negotiations when she ceded Dharmapatam Island to the English. She even suspected that English had bribed one of her men a certain chief Krivan Mussan, for this deal. She punished him by taking his life.[42]

Friction continued unabated between the English and the Beevi. The English revived the Old Portuguese system of issuing passes for seafaring vessels. They denied passes to the ships of the Beevi bound for Surat. She was furious. She charted a new strategy to counter the English menace. Fully aware that the English were at loggerheads with the Canarese, to spite them she tried to render help to the Canarese with 200 Muslim soldiers. Her plan did not work as she was threatened by the English and had to abandon her plan. She realized her weak position and knew that in the event of a joint attack on her by the Prince Regent (Kolatiri) and the English, she would be squarely defeated. Finding no way out, she buckled under the pressure of the English, and on April 1737, her husband agreed to take an oath in the main mosque of Cananore declaring that they had never attempted anything against the English Company. This oath was taken by Beevi's husband 'Elaya' as a matter of political expediency and to heal the wound. In a return gesture, a vessel belonging to the Beevi seized by the English at Anjengo was restored to her.[43]

Beevi soon passed away and was succeeded by her very young son Adi Raja, who was devoted to the French, but hated the English. He made a reversal of the existing policy and extended whole hearted support to the French. This sudden love of Ali Raja for the French was looked down upon with disdain by the Dutch, who referred to him as a profligate young whelp who may become wiser as he grows in years. Under his support the French managed to enlist 1,500 Muslims in their army. Later, when the French fleet arrived in Mahè in

February 1747, Ali Raja paid a visit to them with a retinue of 500 men hoping to obtain their help against the English. But his expectations were dashed to the ground when the French fleet sailed away without attacking the English at Tellicherry.

ARAKKAL/KOLATIRI DEALINGS WITH EUROPEAN POWERS

Thoroughly disillusioned with the French, Ali Raja swallowed his pride and approached the English for friendship and even expressed willingness to settle an outstanding loan of his predecessors. Actual loan amount including interest was to the tune of 31,056 fanams. He offered to pay Rs. 15,000 and requested the remaining loan amount to be waived, which was accepted by the English. Thus, once again peace was established momentarily between the Arakkal house and the English.[44]

Contrastingly conflicts continued unabated between the Dutch and the English, which affected the pepper trade in 1739. The Dutch suddenly turned their attention towards the Travancore Kingdom, which had abundant supply of pepper. Travancore was ruled by Marthanda Varma, who ascended the throne at a young age of 23. He was well-versed in the art of warfare and statecraft. Marthanda Varma consolidated his power in the region. However, the Dutch were defeated by the Raja of Travancore in the battle of Colachel. The battle of Colachel had shattered Dutch hopes of conquering Travancore.[45]

Formal peace between the Dutch and the Raja of Travancore was concluded only in the year 1743. This was a humiliation for the Dutch who were compelled to recognize all the claims of the Raja of Travancore. They dropped all their schemes of territorial acquisition on the west coast of India for the moment.[46] This was a pointer to the dwindling ambition of the Dutch in Cananore.

As mentioned earlier in the year 1742, Ali Raja, who was very young and who succeeded to the throne, within a short span became a nuisance to the Dutch. The good relations that had existed between the Dutch and the Arakkal house became past history. Situation began to deteriorate between them. This Ali Raja mentioned as Kunhi Hamsa Adi Raja (1745-77) in the Arakkal Musuem, refused to abide by the contract and sold his products to others who offered him more money than the price stipulated by the Company. In retaliation to stop him from selling pepper to others and indulging in foul practices, the Dutch imposed restrictions on him by refusing passes for his vessels to trade. This seemed to have had the desired effect. In 1745, Ali Raja as appeasement entered into a new pepper contract with the Dutch Chief at Cananore and remained neutral in the dispute between the English and the Kolatiri. The following year, the Kolatiri prince clamped prohibition on all the estates of the Adi Raja, who was greatly distressed by this move and sought help from the Dutch. The Dutch intervened and settled their old disputes.[47]

Similarly, the Maratha pirates Angriyas were also posing a threat to the Dutch. In fact, the Dutch commander Van Gollenese found these pirates dangerous. Piracy was nothing new on the coast. There was the notorious Captain Kydd, and Henry Every, who wrecked havoc with their piratical activities and hampered the Malabar trade. However, seeing the success of the sea pirates and seeing their potential, in 1747 Ali Raja befriended and allied with the Angriya pirates against the Dutch. The Dutch feared this alliance and reinforced their garrison at Cananore expecting Angriyas to land in Cananore with the connivance of Ali Raja. Their fear came true when with Angriya's help Ali Raja attacked, overran, and plundered the country of Canara. Ali Raja dispatched 3,000 men with guns in small country crafts to ravage the area. They attacked Manjeshwar and landed their men to north of Mangalore, created havoc and overran Kollur. They carried off booty worth 40,00,000 pagodas. In the course of this aggression, some Brahmins were killed which was greatly mourned by the court of Bednur. In retaliation of this aggression, rice export from Mangalore to the Kolatiri country was stopped which resulted in acute food scarcity to the English at Tellicherry. The English remonstrated Ali Raja for allying with Angriya. Bombay President, and Council of the East India Company sent a sharp letter of remonstrance to Ali Raja. At the same time, the Dutch also warned Ali Raja against his association with the pirates. They deployed a naval unit to capture Angriya and ordered him to lay down his arms and surrender. But Angriya made his stand clear that whenever Ali Raja needed his assistance, he would be there to assist him against the Dutch. Ali Raja even built a hideout for the pirates on the Bank of River Valarpatam.[48]

However, in 1750, Ali Raja relented and made an application to renew the old company's friendship with the Dutch, which was granted to him on the condition that all the cardamom growing in his territory should be supplied to the Dutch Company. But to all intents and purpose this was just a ploy on the part of Ali Raja to momentarily calm down the Dutch. In fact, he was secretly weaving a plan to capture the Dutch Fort of Cananore with the help of the French in Mahe. Being aware of this act of treachery, the Dutch laid siege on Arakkal.[49]

Meanwhile, in the year 1750-51, the French at Mahè assisted the Kolatiri Prince against the Canarese and obtained a settlement in the province of Ramdilly. On the other hand, the English undertook to depose two Princes and to install another in their stead. But when their plan failed, they carried off the old King of Kolatiri as prisoner to Tellicherry. Later they had to set the imprisoned King free and make peace.

In 1752, Ali Raja made a new pepper contract with the Dutch Chief at Cananore and remained neutral in the dispute between the English and the Prince of Kolatiri. The following year, the Kolatiri Prince laid prohibition on all the estates of Ali Raja. The latter was greatly distressed about this and sought the Dutch Company's assistance. The Company, then, intervened, and all the disputes were settled. In 1753, Collastry and Ali Raja once again locked horns, but owing to the mediation by the Dutch matter was settled amicably. Around 1754, the Dutch entered into two pepper contracts, one with the Prince of Kolatiri for 300 candies of pepper, and the second contract with Adi Raja for 200 candies of pepper, which made the English jealous and they tried to prevent these contracts from being carried out. In the same year the French purchased the Portuguese fort at Mount Eli.[50]

In 1754, Ali Raja even turned against the Maldives and attacked the islands. As ruler of Cananore, he had held sway over the Arabian Sea for many centuries and the rulers of Maldives recognized him as their overlords. The islands of Maldives had long been known to sailors, travellers and conquerors. The name Maldives itself is derived from Sanskrit, Tamil and Malayalam, where *mala* means garland in Sanskrit, Malayalam and Tamil, and *dvipa* means island in Sanskrit, *Tivu* means island in Tamil, and *dvipu* means island in Malayalam. It was Portuguese, who popularized this name in Europe. The conversion of this island to Islam happened in the year AD 1153 when the last Buddhist monarch of Maldives Siri Bavanditta converted to Islam, and he adopted the Muslim name and title 'Sultan Muhammad Ali Adil'. As alluded in the earlier chapter, chieftain of Kolatiri Ali Moosa, the fifth ruler of the Arakkal house of Cananore conquered some islands of Maldives in AD 1183-4, thus, heralding close ties between Maldives and Arakkal. Ali Rajas as the rulers of Cananore subsequently came to be known, held their sway over this island. These islands originally comprised of settlers from Kerala, which is evident in the language, place names, poetry forms, dance forms relics of Hinduism underlying Buddhism local political organization and the like. There are occasions when the Maldivian princes revolted and paid a heavy price for it. In the year 1758, a Maldivian prince was kept as a prisoner in Cananaore.[51]

Meanwhile, conflicts continued between the French and English. The French soon realized that the English wanted to alienate the prince from them, so they made the latter visit them at Badagara and reinstated him in his palace. This incident infuriated the English. They became bitter and threatened Collastry with fire and sword. The prince was frightened and due to compulsion he made a new pepper contract with the Dutch Company servants. Later, the Prince broke all engagements with the English and entered into permanent contract with the Dutch in 1754. The Dutch Chief at Cananore Weijerman advanced a sum of Rs. 12,000, to the Prince on the above pepper contract.

At the same time in the year 1755, the Dutch entered into another solemn contract with Ali Raja by which he promised to supply them annually 400 candies of pepper, at the rate of Rs. 831/3. Ali Raja abided by the contract for three years, but later, he defaulted and he began to play truant and refused to supply the stipulated quantity of pepper and resorted to his old tricks. According to Dutch records, he had already lost his credibility by procastinating the pepper supply and, above all, he had even earned notoriety all over Malabar that one hears 'only evil things about him'.[52]

In 1756, hostilities commenced in Europe between England and France, and its echo reverberated on the Malabar Coast also. However, in Malabar, most of the time, the trade of the English and the French progressed at the expense of the Dutch. Meanwhile, Ali Raja invaded the fort belonging to the English at Maylure in Dharmapatam. But he failed to capture it. Seeing this, the prince regent (Kolatiri) severed his friendship with Ali Raja holding him responsible for the aggression on Maylure.

Ali Raja was in deep financial problems due to his incessant quarrels with the Dutch, the English, and the Kolatiri. Sensing this, the English decided to fish in troubled waters. They desired to exploit the situation to their benefit by helping Ali Raja with money to overcome his difficulties with the intention of trapping him later. The chief of Tellicherry, T. Hodge entered into an agreement with Ali Raja, and he was advanced a sum of Rs. 13,000 in return for supply of pepper at Tellicherry factory. It was précised then that in case of default, his ships would be seized. Apart from this, Ali Raja was compelled to assist the English against the French or any other Malabari incursion on them by deploying 300 armed Moplah soldiers whose expenditure would be met by the English.[53]

The English on their part tried to establish a trade monopoly in the area by driving the French away from Mahé. Eventually, they even succeeded in conquering Mahé and Pondicherry in the year 1761. The French at Mahé had to accept the terms of capitulation. The English totally destroyed Mahé settlement which was eventually recovered by the French in 1765. They incurred heavy loss for the reconstruction work and even toyed with the idea of abandoning Mahé on grounds of economic viability.[54]

Following the fall of Pondicherry, the French surrendered their forts in the north, except Mount Deli and Ramdilly (Ramanthali) to prince Capu Tamban of Kolatiri family. Handing over the charge of these forts to the Kolatiri prince by the French was disliked by Ali Raja, who in revenge, attacked the French fort of Ettikulam point at Mount Deli and mas-sacred the French garrison by annihilating twenty men. This fort was later handed over to the English.[55]

In 1762, the English withdrew their outposts and handed over Madakkara to the king regent of Kolathanadu (Kolatiri), which dealt a terrible blow to the ambition of the Ali Raja who realized that the English held Kolatiri in higher esteem than him. Thus, even though peace was established between the French and the English elsewhere, there was no peace in Arakkal and Kolatiri kingdom as fresh dissension was created between Ali Raja and the Kolatiri.

Ali Raja undertook an aggressive policy against the territory under the Kolatiris. He was also unforgiving towards the English for not safeguarding his interests. He realized only an open confrontation with Kolatiri can help him to achieve his ambition. He nurtured an ambition to become the sovereign of the entire Kolatiri kingdom. According to Dutch records, the supply of pepper from Kolatiri failed. The arrogance of Ali Raja reached such a point that he collected the revenue belonging to the Princes of Kolatiri. He started to disrespect the sovereignty of Kolatiri and the Malabari religion by purposely putting a 'golden knob' (spire/dome) on top of the Arakkal mosque in Cananore Bazaar to show his contempt for the worship of the 'heathens' defying the existing rules of the country, where you could not have a spire of gold on any edifice throughout the Malabar country, except at the three principle pagodas at Taliparambu, Kottayam and Pyachi.[56] The three temples that were allowed by tradition to have golden spires were the Rajarajesheshwara Temple of Taliparamba, the Trikkaikunnu Siva Temple of Kottayam, and Urppazhassikavu of Edakkad.[57]

Ali Raja, thus, hurt the religious sentiments of the Kolatiri people. Kolatiri took this as a personal insult and affront to his power and asked him to remove the golden spire immediately. But Ali Raja refused to do so. As he paid no respect to the mediation of the Dutch company for the golden knob Kolatiri approached the English for help against Ali Raja. Thus, the Prince of Kolatiri, along with his allies, aided by the English attacked Ali Raja and besieged him in his bazaar in Cananore. This quarrel continued for a long time. The hatred between the two had far-reaching consequences in the history of Malabar. The vacillating policy of Ali Raja and his inconsistent and unstable behaviour and frequent changing of camps created a climate of animosity towards him, compelling the English to refer to him as 'treacherous' as he was not a man of words. Nevertheless, on 28 August 1762, Kolatiri and Ali Raja entered into a peace treaty. However, friction continued unabated between them. The only consistent policy of Ali Raja was his hatred towards the Kolatiri.[58]

Long before, the Kolatiri Prince had faced financial difficulties. He appealed for assistance to the Dutch, their allies and the English, but his appeal went in vain. Unable to solve his financial woes, he finally went to Travancore and begged his uncle to settle the difference with the Moors. Here, it will be worthwhile to take note that whenever there was a problem in Kolathanadu, the Kolatiri always fled to Travancore seeking refuge and help, reason being there existed close blood relation between the Kingdom of Travancore and Kolathanadu. In fact, before the ascendance of Marthanda Varma to the throne of Travancore, it was the powerful Attingal Kingdom, which was the maternal house of the Raja of Travancore, and it was the Rani of Attingal who was entitled to give heirs to the Travancore Kingdom. According to tradition, the eldest son of the Rani of Attingal was the heir apparent to the throne of Travancore, and her eldest daughter was supposed to succeed her to the throne of Attingal. Any failure in the direct female descent required selection and adoption of two or more females usually from Kolathanadu to assure her succession. Thus, during the year July 1698, when the Queen of Attingal, Ashure (Aswathi) Tirunal passed away without leaving any heiress to succeed her, there was total confusion in the country till a new queen was installed by end 1699, who hailed from Kolathanadu. Besides, whenever Travancore kingdom ran out of heirs, it was customary to adopt princes from Kolathanadu. Hence there was a close relationship between the Kolatiri and the Travancore and Attingal Kingdom.[59]

However, peace was thus, restored once again. But the problem continued. Ali Raja is said to have lorded it over the country quite openly and had lost all fear of the Dutch and the Princes of the country. But in 1765, Ali Raja entered into an agreement with the English ensuring that he will not usurp the authority or trade rights of the Kolatiri in the region.[60]

Such persistent and never ending dissension between Ali Raja and Kolatiri had an unsettling effect in the Malabar country. The perpetual merry-go-round played by the English, the Dutch, the French, as well as Ali Raja and Kolatiri in Malabar was the most remarkable feature of this period. There seemed to be no permanent friends or permanent foes. Ali Raja proved to be a veteran in scuttling the camp of one for the other quite often, according to his needs and interests. This tarnished his image very much. Only one fact was constant in his dealings with the Europeans and Kolatiri, which was his appetite for pepper contract. In this volatile atmosphere, it was the Dutch who finally realized the futility of continuing the trade with Malabar, whereas the Kolatiri and Ali Raja did not have any fixed goals, except to make profits and assert their power in the region, especially in the case of the latter.

NOTES

1. J.B. Aquarone, *Joao De Castro. Gouverneur et Vice-roi Des Indes Orientales (1500-1548)*, vol. I, Paris, 1968, p. 231; W.W. Hunter, *A History of British India*, London, 1899, vol. 1, pp. 126-7; Ramakrishna Mukherjee, *The Rise and Fall of the East India Company*, Berlin, 1957, p. 59; James Forbes, *Oriental Memoirs*, vol. I, London, 1834, p. 187.
2. Auguste Toussaint, *L'Ocean Indien au XVIIe Siecle*, Paris, 1974, p. 121.
3. Martin Krieger, 'Danish country—Trade on the Indian Ocean in the 17th and 18th centuries', in K.S. Mathew (ed.), *Indian Ocean and Cultural Interaction (AD 1400-1800)*, Pondicherry, 1996, p. 123; John Bruce, *Annals of the Honourable East India Company*, vol. I, London, 1810, p. 136; Ishwari Prasad, *India in the Eighteenth Century*, Allahabad, 1973, pp. 65-6; S.P. Sen, *The French in India*, Delhi, 1971, p. 36; A. Galetti (tr.), *Dutch in Malabar*, Madras, 1911, p. 66.
4. For details see William Forster (ed.), *The Embassy of Sir Thomas Roe to the Court of the Great Mogul, 1615-1619*, Nandeln, 1899, 1967; J.B.P. More, *Origin and Foundation of Madras*, Chennai, 2014; A. Galleti, op. cit., Bombay letters received, 1694; Anjengo diaries, 1808; A.W. Handley, Resident Anjengo to Francis Warden, Chief Secretary to government, Bombay, 10 May 1808, pp. 304-9, Contract concluded with the Queen of Attinga, dated 29 June 1694; (translation from Malabar), IOL, London.
5. P.C. Alexander, *The Dutch in Malabar*, Annamalai, 1946, p. 4; Brian Gardner, *The East India Company*, London, 1971, p. 30; O.K. Nambiar, *An Illustrated Maritime History of the Indian Ocean*, New Delhi, 2013, p. 66.
6. J.P.I. Du Bois, *Vies des Gouverneurs Généraux avec l'abrégé de l'histoire des Établissements hollandais aux Indes Orientales*, La Haye, 1763, p. 204; Nagam Aiya, *The Travancore State Manual*, vol. 1, Trivandrum, 1906, p. 306; P.C. Alexander, *The Dutch in Malabar*, Annamalai, 1946, p. 4.

7. J. Van Lohuizen, *The Dutch East India Company and Mysore*, Raven Hage, 1961, p. 2; Auguste Toussaint, op. cit., p. 113.
8. John Fryer, *A New Account of East Indies and Persia*, vol. I, London, MDCCCCIX, pp. 132, 141; Brian Gardner, *The East India Company*, London, 1971, p. 39.
9. Pyrard de Laval, *Voyage de Pyrard de Laval aux Indes Orientales (1601-1611)*, Paris, 1998, pp. 409-10.
10. Ibid., pp. 409, 412.
11. Ibid., p. 216, Anjengo Factory Records, 1704-1749, Simon Cowse, *Anjengo to the Court of Directors*, June 1704, p. 5; A. Galletti, op. cit., p.143; James Forbes, op. cit., p. 212; Nagam Aiya, op. cit., p. 306.
12. Jean Henri Grosse, *Voyages aux Indes Orientales*, Paris, MDCCLVIII, 1757, p. 4; O.K. Nambiar, op. cit., p. 67; Philip Baldaeus, *A True and Exact Description of The Most Celebrated East India Coasts of Malabar and Coromandel and also of the Isle of Ceylon*, 1672, p. 624; K.P. Padmanabha Menon, *History of Kerala Written in the Form of Notes on Visscher 1857-1919*, vol. II, Delhi, 1983, p. 230; Alexander Hamilton, *A New Account of the East Indies*, vol. I, Edinburgh, MDCCXXVII, p. 291.
13. K.P. Padmanabha Menon, op. cit., p. 77; Philip Baldaeus, op. cit., p. 623; Francis Buchanan, *A Journey from Madras through the Countries of Mysore, Canara and Malabar*, vol. II, Madras, 1870, p. 196; Alexander Hamilton, op. cit., p. 291; Robert Sewell, *The Antiquarian Remains in The Presidency of Madras*, vol. I, Madras, 1882, pp. 241-2.
14. Alexander Hamilton, op. cit., p. 292; Philip Baldaeus, op. cit., p. 624; J.P.I., Du Bois, op. cit., p. 1; A. Galletti, *The Dutch in Malabar*, Madras, 1911, p. 143.
15. A. Galletti, op. cit., p. 147.
16. Sinnappah Arasaratnam, *Maritime India in the Seventeenth Century*, Delhi, 1994, pp. 100-1.
17. A. Gallettti, op. cit., p. 143; S. Arasaratnam, op. cit., p. 103.
18. Philip Baldaeus, op. cit., p. 622; T.I. Ponnen, *A Survey of the Rise of Dutch Power 1603-1678*, Trichnopoly, 1948, p. 194.
19. Abbé Carré, *The Travels of Abbe Carre in India and the Near East 1672-1674*, vol. I, Madras, 1990, pp. 706-7; John Fryer, *A New Account of the East India and Persia Being Nine Years Travels, 1672-1681*, vol. I, New York, 1967, p. 146.
20. Abbé Carré, Ibid., p. 154; Charles Fawcett, *The English Factories in*

India, 1670-1677, vol. I (new series), Oxford, 1936, pp. 289-90; K.K.N. Kurup, *The Ali Rajas of Cananore*, Calicut, 2002, p. 26.
21. Alexander Hamilton, op. cit., p. 292.
22. Thevenot, *Voyages de M De Thevenant contenant la relation de l'Indostan des Nouveaux, Mongols des autres peuples et Pays de l'Indes*, Paris, MDCLXXXIV, p. 263; Alexander Hamilton, op. cit., p. 295.
23. Manohar Malgonkar, *Kanhoji Angrey*, Bombay, 1959, p. 150, Samuel Mateer, *Native Life in Travancore*, London, 1883, p. 123; Leena More, op. cit., pp. 22, 42; John Bruce, *Annals of the Honourable East India Company*, vol. III, London, 1810, p. 195; Anjengo Factory Records 1704-49, Bombay letters received, 29 June 1694, p. 12; NAD and IOL; Anjengo Diaries 1808, A.W. Handley, Resident Anjengo to Francis Warden, Chief Secretary to Government, Bombay, 10 May 1808, pp. 304-9, MAB.
24. Robert Sewell, op. cit., p. 244; Secretariat Outward Letter Book 1699-1702, John Brabourne, Anjengo to Bombay Castle, 6 December, 1699, p. 11, MAB.
25. Alexander Hamilton, op. cit., pp. 294-5.
26. Alexander Hamilton, op. cit., p. 295; K.K.N. Kurup, op. cit., pp. 26-7.
27. Sir Charles Fawcett, op. cit., vol. III (new series), Oxford, 1954, pp. 383, 394, vol. I (new series), Oxford, 1936, pp. 289-90, K.K.N. Kurup, op. cit., p. 26.
28. Francis Buchanan, op. cit., vol. II, London, 1807, p. 422; E. Lennet de la Faralle, Mémoires (1725), quoted in A. Maritineau, *Les Origines de Mahé*, Paris, 1917, p. 11; Philip Baldaeus, op. cit., p. 622; K.K.N. Kurup, op. cit., p. 28; NAF 9368, *Notes Extraits des lettres d'un offcier de cavalier, qui a voyagé aux Indes Orientales*, 1776, p. 164, BNF, Paris.
29. Jacob Canter Visscher, *Letters from Malabar, Letter XIX*, by Herber Drury (tr.), Madras, 1862, pp. 119-20.
30. Tellicherry Consultations, vol. II, 1726-7, Madras, 1932, Diary dated 12 June 1727, p. 114, TNA; Tellicherry Consultations, 1726-7, vol. II, Diary dated 12 June 1727, Madras, 1932, p. 114, TNA; William Logan, *Malabar*, vol. I, Madras, 1989, p. 357; K.K.N. Kurup, op. cit., p. 31; Jacob Canter Visscher, op. cit., pp. 119-20.
31. Tellicherry Consultations, vol. III, 1727-8, Madras, 1933, Diary dated 19 February 1725, p. 61; Diary dated 19 February 1728, p. 64; Diary dated 21 June 1728, p. 127, TNA.
32. R.R.S. Chauhan, 'The Siddis in the Indian Ocean regions', in K.S.

Mathew (ed.), *Indian Ocean and Cultural Interaction* (AD *1400-1800)*, Pondicherry, 1996, pp. 25-51; K.K.N. Kurup, op. cit., p. 32.

33. William Logan, *Malabar*, vol. 1, Madras, 1951, p. 144.
34. Factory Records, Tellicherry, Sl. No. 1574, Letters sent, 19 July 1733, TNA, K.K.N. Kurup, *Ali Rajas of Cananore*, Calicut, 1995, pp. 32-3.
35. Tellicherry Consultations, 1731-2, vol. V, Diary, 11 May 1732, p. 55, TNA.
36. Tellichery Consultations, 1731-2, vol. V, Diary, 25 October 1732, p. 6, TNA; P. Groot and A. Galletti (trs.), *Memorandum of the Administration of the Coast of Malabar by the Right Worshipped Adrien Moens*, 18 April 1781, Madras, 1911, p. 144.
37. Tellicherry Consultations, 1732-3, vol. VI, Diary, 6 November 1732, p. 12 (Madras, 1933); K.K.N. Kurup, op. cit., pp. 33-4; Tellicherry Consultations, 1732-3, Diary, 8 June 1733, p. 37.
38. A. Galletti, *The Dutch in Malabar*, Madras, 1911, pp. 144-5; Letters from Tellicherry, 1732-3, vol. II, Letter, 19 May 1733, p. 55, TNA; K.K.N. Kurup, op. cit., p. 34.
39. Robert Sewell, *The Antiquarian Remains in The Presidency of Malabar*, vol. I, Madras, 1882, p. 243; Sathyan Edakkad, *Vasco Da Gama and the Unknown Facts of History*, Ramnattukara, 2010, p. 112.
40. Sanjay Subrahmanyam, *The Political Economy of Commerce, Southern India, 1500-1600*, Cambridge, 1990, pp. 57-8; James Heimann, 'Small Change and Ballast: Cowry Trade and Usage as a Example of Indian Ocean Economic History', *South Asia*, vol. 3, June 1980, pp. 48-69; A. Galletti, op. cit., p. 75; P. Groot and A. Galletti, op. cit., p. 145; William Logan, *Malabar*, vol. I, New Delhi, 1989, p. 370.
41. K.K.N. Kurup, op. cit., pp. 34-7; P. Groot and A. Galletti, op. cit.
42. Robert Sewell, *Archaeological Survey of South India; Lists of Inscriptions and the Sketch of the Dynasties of South India*, vol. II, Madras, 1884, p. 245; William Logan, *Malabar*, vol. I, op. cit., p. 362; William Logan, *A Collection of Treaties and Other Papers of Importance Relating to British Affairs in Malabar* (2nd edn.), Madras, 1989, pp. XXIV, XXV; K.K.N. Kurup, op. cit., pp. 35-7.
43. K.K.N. Kurup, op. cit., p. 37; William Logan, op. cit., p. 366.
44. William Logan, op. cit., p. 380; K.K.N. Kurup, op. cit., p. 38, Tellicherry Consultations 1746-7, vol. XVII A, Diary, 6 June 1747, p. 245 and Diary dated 10 June 1747, p. 246, TNA.
45. T.I. Poonen, *Dutch Hegemony in Malabar*, Trivandrum, 1978, p. 98;

K.M. Panikkar, *A History of Kerala, 1498-1801*, Annamalai, 1960, p. 24; Leena More, *English East India Company and Local Rulers in Kerala: A Case Study of Attingal and Travancore*, Tellicherry, 2003, pp. 127, 131; A. Galletti (tr. & ed.), *The Dutch in Malabar*, Madras, 1911, p. 53.

46. A. Galletti, op. cit., p. 24; T.I. Ponnen, op. cit., p. 105.
47. A. Galletti, op. cit., p. 147.
48. John Biddulph, *The Pirates of Malabar and an English Woman in India: Two Hundred Years Ago*, London, 1907, p. 48; K.K.N. Kurup, op. cit., p. 40; O.K. Nambiar, *An Illustrated Maritime History of the Indian Ocean*, pp. 54-5; O.K. Nambiar, *Our Seafaring in the Indian Ocean*, Bangalore,1975, pp.72-3; William Logan, op. cit., p. 391.
49. K.K.N. Kurup, op. cit., p. 40; A. Galletti, op. cit., p. 148.
50. Galletti, op. cit., pp. 146-7; Robert Sewell, op. cit., vol. I, 1882, p. 243; K.K.N. Kurup, op. cit., p. 40.
51. Galletti, op. cit., p. 170; V. Suryanarayan and V. Sudarsen, 'Development of Maritime traditions and their Impact on Cultural Evolution: A Case Study of Maldives', in K.S. Mathew (ed.), *Indian Ocean and Cultural Interaction (AD 1400-1800)*, Pondicherry, 1996, pp. 193-9; H. Dodwell (ed.), *The Private Diary of Anandaranga Pillai*, vol. IX, Madras, 1924, p. 363; K.K.N. Kurup, op. cit., pp. 39, 47.
52. Galletti, op. cit., p. 148; Sathyan, op. cit., p. 120.
53. K.K.N. Kurup, op. cit., pp. 40-1; A. Galletti, *The Dutch in Malabar*, Madras, 1911, pp. 147-8, Letters sent 1756-7, vol. II, Sl. No. 1583, p. 53, Diary of Tellicherry Factory, 7 March 1759, TNA.
54. S.P. Sen, *The French in India, 1763-1816*, Calcutta, 1951, p. 93; Alfred Martineau, *Les Origines de Mahe de Malabar*, Paris, 1917, p. xii; Cyril Antony (ed.), *Gazetteer of India: Union Territory of Pondicherry*, vol. I, Pondicherry, 1982, p. 7, cf. also, J.B.P. More, *Freedom Movement in French India*, Tellicherry, 2001.
55. Letters sent to Bombay 1763, vol. XVI, Sl. No. 1588, 29 October 1763, MAB.
56. Galletti, op. cit., p. 146; William Logan, op. cit., 1989, p. 400; Robert Sewell, op. cit., p. 243.
57. Sathyan, op. cit., p. 123.
58. Galletti, op. cit., p. 146; K.K.N. Kurup, op. cit., pp. 41-2; Sathyan, op. cit.
59. Edward Ives, *A Voyage from England to India*, London, 1773, p. 192; Maclean's Manual of Administration of the Madras Presidency, Madras, 1938, p. 36; Bombay letters received—1698, John Brabourne,

Anjengo to John Gayer, Bombay, 31 August 1698, p. 139, MAB; Secretariat outward letter book 1697-1699, Bombay Castle to John Brabourne, Anjengo, July 1698, p. 94, MAB; Shungoony Menon, *A History of Travancore*, Delhi, 1984, vol. I, p. 106; K.V. Krishna Ayyar, *A History of Kerala*, Coimbatore, 1965, p. 286.

60. A. Galletti, op. cit., p. 146; Diary of Tellicherry Factory, 13 August 1765, TNA; K.K.N. Kurup, op. cit., pp. 112-13.

CHAPTER 8

The Mysore Sultans and the Decline of Arakkal and Kolatiri

THE RISE OF HYDER ALI

In 1761, the Kingdom of Mysore, subject to the Nizam of Hyderabad, came under the sway of Hyder Ali Naik, who was a local man from a very modest origin, born in Kolar region. According to the Frenchman Legoux de Flaix, who was in Hyder's company, Hyder Ali's father was a Telugu called Tillaiappan. Hyder joined the Mysorean army and rose to become a *faujdar*. According to another account of the French captain, Claude Hugau based in Mahé in 1771, Hyder Ali's birth was very obscure and his ancestors were tanners by profession.

Hyder Ali had gradually established his reputation as a formidable soldier, when he was in the service of the Maharaja of Mysore as *faujdar* at Dindigul. He rose to prominence to become the commander of the Mysore forces. He began to attack and capture the neighbouring regions. In 1760, he captured the south Canara region. The very next year, he deposed Nanjaraj, the prime minister of the Mysore kingdom. He also reduced the young Mysore Raja into a prisoner and took over power into his own hands. He, thus, became the Sultan of Mysore. In doing so, he earned the displeasure of the traditional ruling dynasties of southern India, including the Nizam of Hyderabad, Nawab of Arcot and the Raja of Travancore. In the 1763, he attacked Ikkeri Nayak's army of Bednur region and defeated them. He annexed the territory of Bednur. Bednur was renamed as Hyder Nagar. Thus, the rich port and shipping of Canara coast fell into Hyder's hands. In 1765, Hyder Ali made a grant to the temple in south Canara. But the same Hyder had demolished the Shiva and Vishnu temples in Edakkad, Malabar in 1765-6, and two other old temples in Elangavur and Cherutaram, not far from Cananore, as reported by Sewell.[1]

In fact, it was the bustling harbours of Malabar and its flourishing trade facility, which motivated Hyder towards Malabar. He had heard about the famous Nair clans of Malabar who were fearless warriors with a spirit of independence, and who owed their allegiance to several chieftains and local rulers. He was aware that north Malabar comprised of several principalities like Kottayam, Palakkad, Calicut, and Kolathunad. Among them the most powerful was the Zamorin of Calicut and the Kolatiri Raja of Kolathanadu, who later came to be known as Chirakkal Raja. Apart from this, we know that there was a considerable Muslim community known as Mappilas at Cananore, whose chief Ali Raja owed allegiance to Kolatiris/Chirakkal Raja. Further south was the kingdom of Cochin and below was Travancore.[2]

HYDER ALI'S INCURSIONS INTO KOLATHANADU AND ITS CONSEQUENCES

In the year 1766, Hyder Ali received report from his secret agent Anant Rao about the political conditions prevailing in north Malabar, focusing on the brewing internal revolt between Kappu Thampan (Kolatiri Raja's nephew) and the King of Palakkad (Komiachan) against his kinsman Chirakkal Raja (Kolatiri). Moreover, Ali Raja, the Mappila chief of Cananore who was delighted at the rise of a Muslim chief in Mysore entered the fray by taking up the cause of Kappu Thampan and invited Hyder Ali to enter Malabar. Ali Raja had a tradition of inviting outsiders to interfere in the affairs of Kolathanadu. Earlier, he had invited the Kanarese chief.

Ali Raja's subjects were mostly Mappilas, comprising of 9,000 in number, who were armed with guns. Besides, he possessed the Maldives islands, whose inhabitants often refused to pay tribute to him. According to the Frenchman, who met Ali Raja in 1771, Ali Raja had a big fleet comprising of three ships of 200 to 300 tonnes and three galiots, mounted with 19 cannons, two *ghurabs* (merchant/war ship) with eight cannons and nine galvetts with nine canons. He used the wood found in his territory for the construction of ships. He traded with Mocha and Muscat as well as the eastern coast. He was also reputed to be a tyrant who used his fleet for piracy. The Frenchman asserted that Ali Raja was very industrious, active and hardworking who took care of everything in his territory.[3]

Ali Raja was also very pompous. For the marriage of his niece in November 1771, he threw a very big party to which was invited various dignitaries, including the French governor, Picot. All dignitaries gave Ali Raja costly gifts on the occasion. Thus, Ali Raja was running his own show in Cananore and Malabar, quite independent of the Kolatiri, who was always a menace to his power.

So, heeding to the invitation of Ali Raja, Hyder Ali reached Mangalore in 1766 with 40,000 infantry, 10,000 cavalry and 4 cannons and proceeded towards the kingdom of the Kolatiri. The door to Malabar was thrown wide open by Ali Raja and Hyder entered it with his powerful force. The Kolatiri Raja Udayavarma strongly defended himself, but ultimately he had to surrender to Hyder Ali. On 21 February 1766, Hyder captured Madayi fort. It is said that Kolatiri entered into an agreement with Hyder Ali at Madayi temple as a witness. According to the agreement, he had to pay to the Karnataka army 2,20,000 pagodas in instalments. From there, his army moved towards Cananore.

In the meantime, Ali Raja made his own political calculations in order to gain possession of the kingdom of Kolatiri. For this, he decided to make use of Hyder Ali. In this way he thought he could obtain the administration of Kolatiri kingdom as a reward from Hyder Ali himself. With this view, he went to meet Hyder Ali with presents and received promises of assistance.

Ali Raja rendered help to the invader with a ship and number of irregulars. Next, Hyder headed for the headquarters of Kolatiri at Valarpatanam. It is said that Ali Raja helped Hyder's troops in crossing the river by digging a canal connecting Pazhayangadi and Taliparamba rivers. This canal was later called 'Sultan Canal'. Ali Raja along with his army received Hyder, who wasted no time in going to Chirakkal palace demanding outstanding payment of two lakh rupees citing an old agreement between Kolatiri and Bednur, by which an amount of two lakh had to be paid to Bednur for not attacking his dominion. He insisted on getting back this money from Kolatiri, which was flatly refused.

The Kolatiri expected the French at Mahé to help him with some force to counter Hyder. The *pattamars* or the messengers, Annan and Vengudachelm Ayangar had informed the French at Mahé about the precarious situation of Kolatiri. The French had always maintained a good relationship with the Kolatiri. As a matter of fact, the French provided Kolatiri with arms and ammunitions, cartridges, European bedsheets, camphor and saffron for medical purposes. In his turn, the Kolatiri provided the French sandalwood and spices. He even gifted a rare mountain squirrel to the French governor at Mahé to please him. In spite of this good relationship, no help was forthcoming from the French. The French maintained strict neutrality during Kolatiri's conflict with Hyder Ali. Besides, neither did the Kottayam Raja nor the Kadathanad Raja dare to back Kolatiri at that time.

When the war broke out, Hyder Ali easily captured the Chirakkal palace on 6 March 1766. In the ensuing attack, Kolatiri Raja was killed. Hyder Ali adopted the seven-year old son of Kolatiri Raja, and christened him as 'Ayas Khan'. In the melee, the inmates of the palace including the successor Raja Ravi Varma fled and took shelter in 'Pithala' temple at Thiruvangad in Tellicherry. From there, Raja Ravi Varma proceeded to Travancore.

After capturing Chirakkal, Hyder handed over the administration of Chirakkal to Ali Raja. Thus, Ali Raja obtained his objective of governing Kolatiri kingdom by manipulating Hyder Ali. It is noteworthy that, it was Hyder Ali who officialized Ali as Ali Raja and made him into a ruler. Until then, no Malabari prince or king had recognized Ali Raja as a ruler. It was this consecration of Ali Raja by Hyder, which attracted the Muslims of the Malabar Coast right from Cape Comorin to Canara to pay their allegiance to Ali Raja.

On 15 March 1766, Hyder Ali reached Fort St. Angelo, Cananore and had discussions with the Dutch commander Crunel Barg. He requested support from the Dutch to drive out the English from this country. However, after taking stock of the situation Hyder Ali did not dare to encroach, the English East India Company's settlements at Dharmadam, Tellicherry, Thiruvangad, but went ahead and attacked Kottayam, its neighbouring region.[4]

In a nutshell, Hyder overran Chirakkal and Kottayam with ease, but in Kadathanad for the first time he faced stiff resistance from the Nair force, which was put down with brutality. He proceeded to Calicut where in an unfortunate turn of events Manavikrama Raja, the Zamorin of Calicut set fire to his palace and perished in the flame rather than submit to Hyder Ali. When the body of Zamorin was found, a number of his loyal admirers threw themselves into the flame and died along with their master. Seeing the danger and fearing an attack by Hyder, the Raja of Cochin offered his allegiance to the Mysore chief and agreed to be his tributary by paying a sum of two lakh rupees and eight elephants. Even the chief of Palakkad bowed their heads to the conqueror. Hyder took possession of all of Kolathanadu and the northern countries of Malabar. He occupied all the petty states as well as the Zamorin's dominions and thus, became master of the Malabar country between Cananore and Ponnani.[5]

Hyder Ali next turned his attention to Travancore. Taking stock of the situation, the Travancore Raja sought help from the English against Hyder and asked them to supply him arms and money. He even placed his troops at the disposal of the English as far as Calicut and Tinnevely.[6]

Hyder had an eye on Mahé especially its strategic position as a port on the western coast. In April 1766, Hyder Ali visited Mahé which was under the French control. The Mappilas of Mahé welcomed him and their co-religionists with open arms to the great displeasure of the Nairs. Ten years later, Hyder gifted the villages of Pallur, Pandakkal and Naluthura adjoining Mahé to the French. Until the incursion of Hyder Ali into Malabar, this region was untouched by Muslim conquest and had remained outside the influence of Muslim empires or kingdoms to its East and North.

Cordial relations had continued between Ali Raja and Hyder Ali. However, soon cracks appeared in their relationship as Hyder Ali was angry at Ali Raja's vengeful action against the Sultan of Maldives. Ali Raja had an old score to settle with the Maldives ruler. He defeated, blinded him and brought his eyes to Cananore and placed it before the Sultan. Hyder Ali was revolted and upset at this barbarous act. He promised to make amends and provided the Maldives king with all amenities. Hyder Ali was so much displeased with the actions of Ali Raja that he deprived him of the command of the fleet. Besides, Ali Raja was involved in the destruction of houses, buildings and temples in Neeliswaram.[7]

In 1768, most of the Rajas of Malabar, except Chirakkal Raja were given back their rights to their dominion. Meanwhile, the relatives of the Chirakkal Raja who were killed in the battle with Hyder Ali had taken shelter in Travancore. Chirakkal Raja's nephew, the next descendant to the throne was also in Travancore. He met Hyder Ali directly and requested him to give back the kingdom in return for payment of tax every year. He even wrote to the French about the atrocities committed by Ali Raja in his country and reminded them that the English were helping him against Mamalli Crao, (Ali Raja), while the French maintained neutrality in this conflict. It is noteworthy that Kolatiri rarely referred to Ali Raja as a Raja. Instead, he used the original ancestral name of the Ali Raja, i.e. Mamalli Crao alias Mamalli Kidavu meaning 'Mamalli's son'.

However, very soon in 1769, the Kolatiri, with the intention of patching up with Hyder Ali wrote to the French that he would pay Rs. 1,50,000 to the Nawab through the French to intercede on his behalf. Since he was short of money, he promised to advance Rs. 50,000 initially and the remainder he promised to settle in two instalments within a year. He also wanted to patch up with Ali Raja, who was in good terms with Hyder Ali at that time and wrote to the French that he would accede to all the demands of Ali Raja and also provide him with, sandalwood and spices at a diminished rate. Ali Raja was so happy with the overtures of Kolatiri through the French that he presented the latter governor at Mahé a tiger. But unfortunately the tiger broke out of the cage and Picot got it killed.

As a result, the Chirakkal kingdom got back its rights in 1774, at the expense of Ali Raja. It is noteworthy however that Ali Raja was negligent in paying tribute to Hyder Ali. So, Hyder Ali had no hesitation to take away the management of the Kolatiri kingdom from Ali Raja and hand it over again to the ruling prince on the condition that he paid the annual tribute, which had been earlier imposed on Ali Raja.

ACQUISITION OF CANANORE FORT AND RELATED EVENTS

When Hyder Ali was busy in Malabar, the Dutch were facing enormous loss in their pepper trade. The price of the Malabar pepper was higher than in the southern region of Kerala and they were unable to procure significant quantity of pepper. To make matters worse, there were constant conflicts within the Kolatiri palace and with the English which further weakened the Dutch. This pushed them to quit Malabar altogether and move to the Eastern archipelago. With this objective, they made preparations to dispose of Fort St. Angelo in Cananore which was in their possession since 110 years. Negotiations were carried out for selling the fortress. The Fortress of Cananore was accordingly disposed of before the departure of Senoff for a sum of Rs. 1,00,000 to Ali Raja in 1771, without the knowledge or consent of Kolatiri. He paid part of this sum and for the remainder amount he gave the Dutch a bond for Rs. 56,24,530/48 or 67,49,415 guilders. Further, as a guarantee he even pledged one of his vessels which lay in the river. The Dutch did not receive the remaining amount of the outstanding debt. Hence, they in a dispatch dated 24 September 1779 revealed their intention to sell the vessel pledged by Ali Raja.

Thus, the famous Fort St. Angelo situated in Cananore which was initially owned by the Portuguese and then, the Dutch finally passed down to the only dominant Muslim family of Cananore, the Arakkal house. After the possession of the fort, the Beevi or Ali Raja of Arakkal house of Cananore became more prominent. The territories of Ali Raja of Cananore comprised the *kirar* limits at Cananore and the Laccadive islands of Agatti, Kavaratti, Androth, Kalpeni, and Minicoy.[8]

Arakkal palace was just a kilometre away from the Fort St. Angelo's premises. From the ramparts of the Fort Angelo, the Arakkal palace and mosque were visible. On 11 April 1771, Ali Raja's treasure was deposited in the fort. He organized a great feast for the occasion and invited many guests including Picot, the French governor. On 10 September 1771, the marriage of his niece took place with a rich Mappila merchant. Ali Raja threw a lavish party, which lasted for eight days, invited various dignitaries of the region, and gifted presents to the Ali Raja, amounting to the value of 2,40,000 rupees. Food was also served consisting of rice, fish and water. Cannons were fired for the occasion from the ramparts of the fort. Governor Picot was also invited for this marriage. Picot chose to send a representative in his place.

About this time, Ali Raja was facing immense financial difficulties. On January 1776, he wrote to Picot the Governor of Mahé, asking him for money and promising to send him merchandise that he wanted. Picot declined to accept the demand. Again, in the month of August 1776, Ali Raja once again approached Picot for money. He pleaded with Picot to at least give him the little money he had. He promised to furnish him in return merchandises through his minister Congy Paquis. Picot was not in a position to help Ali Raja even this time. By January 1778, Ali Raja was neck-deep in debt. He informed Picot that he was sending Congy Paquis to collect 20,000 rupees. Picot again expressed his inability to advance that sum. In February, Ali Raja's finances were in dire straits. This time he pleaded with Picot that he absolutely needed money for his needs and subsistence. He even delivered a veiled threat that if his request was not fulfilled, he would be forced to look for other options. Picot told that he did not have the required money to lend him. In the month of March, Ali Raja wrote a letter to Bellecombe, Governor of Pondicherry asking him to advance him some money. When his request was not acceded to, Ali Raja stopped the boats (*manchus*) belonging to Bayaporta Congy Paquis in Cannanore from transporting rice to Mahé. Picot panicked thinking that Ali Raja would stop all boats transporting rice to Mahé as rice was essential for their survival. Picot came down from his high horse and pleaded with Ali Raja to allow boats to Mahé without any impediment, given the past friendship that prevailed between the French and Ali Raja. Around this time, Ali Raja fell sick. He requested the French at Mahé to send him a surgeon at once to cure him of his illness. This time the French obliged by sending Dr. Mace Launa.[9]

While things were unfolding thus, Hyder Ali exhibited a general tolerance towards other religions. In fact, with the emergence of Hyder Ali on the political scene of Mysore, the situation of Christian missionaries and Christians improved greatly. The Christian missionaries recognized Hyder as the most trusted friend of the French. Hyder did not persecute them, but provided them employment in his kingdom. His port always welcomed French vessels. Meanwhile, conversions were taking place to Islam from the poorer and lower Malabari castes in south Malabar and during the eighteenth century, it appears that many elite Malayalis of the higher castes in north Malabar also had converted to Islam. This may be partly at least due to the incursion of Hyder Ali into Malabar.

In the year 1778, Ali Raja passed away. He was said to be very cruel in character and a spendthrift who could not keep money. However, the intention of the Dutch Government to sell the vessel pledged by Ali Raja could not be realized as he passed away and was succeeded by his niece Joonoomabbe Adee Rajah Beevi. She was approached with a request to settle the pending amount. Though she gave a promise, she did not settle the payment. Beevi was displeased with the Dutch for putting up their pledged vessel for sale. However, the Dutch sold the vessel which fetched them Rs. 12,450. This amount was used to settle the account.[10]

CONFLICTS IN MALABAR AND HYDERALI'S DEATH

In 1778, war broke out between the English and the French back in Europe. In India also, the two powers were hostile towards one another. Pondicherry, a French territory was captured by the English in 1778. The French governor of Pondicherry wrote a frantic letter to Hyder Ali to take the French settlement of Mahé in northern Malabar under his protection. But Hyder was not interested. Soon after their victory in Pondicherry, the British wanted to attack Mahé. But the fear of Hyder deterred them momentarily. They, however sent forces comprising of three battalions of sepoys overland to Anjengo situated in Attingal kingdom to eventually capture Mahé. The Raja of Travancore was alerted and was asked to stand by with provision and other conveniences.[11]

Meanwhile, Hyder Ali ordered Sardar Khan to assist the French at Mahé in the war against the English. Even Kolatiri was ordered by Hyder Ali to assist the French in Mahé. The Beevi of Cananore was also dragged into this conflict between the English and French. Beevi and her husband promptly rendered all possible help with arms, ammunitions and soldiers to Sardar Khan. Hyder was enraged at the attempt of the English to capture Mahé, which was alleged to be under his protection. His main worry of Mahé being occupied by the English was because it was through Mahé, he derived his military supplies from the French. He even threatened the English that in the event of Mahé being attacked, he would retaliate by invading Arcot.[12]

In 1779, an English force was dispatched from Madras under Colonel Braithwaite to capture Mahè. The French garrison under its leader Mon. Picot de la Motte fought bravely but lost to the English. Mahé was captured in the month of March 1779. Before that in February 1779, Kolatiri paid to Hyder Ali through Picot a sum of 5,200 rupees and 200 *fardes* of rice, as demanded by Hyder Ali. This sum and rice was remitted to Picot by Bayaporta Congy Paqui.

This further victory estranged Hyder's relations with the English. Whereas on the other hand the Dutch at Nagapattinam on the Coromandel Coast and Cochin also united with Hyder to break up the friendship between the English and the Raja of Travancore. However, the English who had their headquarters in Tellicherry were confident of defeating them with the support of the Bekel Raja of north Malabar, who sent his horses for their assistance. Moreover, the Nizam of Hyderabad too offered to support them in their fight against the Dutch and Hyder.[13]

Around the year 1780, the Mysore army under the command of Sardar Khan encircled and blocked the Tellicherry fort and godown, which was ceded to the English in 1708 by the Chirakkal Raja. They also blocked the supply of food grains, thereby inducing severe famine inside the fort. Hearing the plight of the factors at Tellicherry, reinforcement was sent from Bombay in the year 1781 under the command of Colonel Humbertson with food and soldiers to assist the English. Both fought fiercely on land and sea. Hyder was hoping to get assistance from the French. In March 1781, French sent a fleet of five ships with 1,000 marines and 1,200 troops under the command of Admiral Pierre Andre de Suffren. Hyder was banking on their help and cooperation, but he was disillusioned with them as the French did not render any support. It was true that he went to war with the English on the Mahé issue heavily banking on help promised by the French which did not materialize.[14]

On 8 February 1782, the English under the command of Major Abington attacked the Mysore army. What ensued was a bloody battle. It was a do or die situation for the English who eventually defeated the Mysore army, captured 1,200 Mysore soldiers including their army chief Sardar Khan and imprisoned them in Tellicherry fort. Unable to face torture and humiliation by the English, Sardar Khan committed suicide inside the fort. Hearing this shocking news, Hyder Ali dispatched Magdum Ali to take up the command of the Mysore army in Malabar. But Magdum Ali lost his life in a clash with the English in Thrikaloor, twenty miles from Calicut on 5 April 1782.

After the death of Magdum Ali, Hyder appointed his son Tipu Sultan to head the Mysore army in Malabar. Hyder Ali met the French admiral Suffren during the month of July-August 1782. He was highly impressed with Suffren that he remarked that finally he had met someone who will help him to exterminate the English. But all the calculations of the English and the French went berserk as the monsoon lashed in, which compelled all the combatants to cease hostilities for the time being. Hyder encamped with his troops, sixteen miles north of Arcot. He had been suffering from cancer on his back for a long time and the disease got further aggravated with the fatigue incurred by his numerous campaigns. He died in his Camp at Narsingh Rayanapet near Chittor on 7 December 1782.

When Hyder's end was approaching his minister Purnaiya and Krishna Rao took every precaution to conceal the gravity of the malady from the army. Immediately after his death, messengers were dispatched on fleet camels to apprise Tipu of the event, and to urge his return at full speed. Hyder's body was embalmed and transported privately to Kolar in a coffin resembling a chest containing valuable spoils. Matters were so well arranged that the secret of his demise was kept for many days, not only from the English but from his own army. The French were particularly unhappy about the demise of Hyder Ali, as he was a steadfast and sincere friend of the French, and was considered as a hero back in France.[15]

It is noteworthy at this juncture that Hyder Ali was not the legitimate successor to the Mysore throne. This naturally created uneasiness among the ruling dynasties of southern India, which included the Nizam of Hyderabad, the Nawab of Arcot and the Malabar kings and princes alike. The former two were actually Muslims. In spite of that, they never accepted the ascension of Hyder Ali wholeheartedly. As far as the Kolatiri and the Travancore Raja was concerned, there was no question of accepting the supremacy of Hyder Ali. As a result, the Malabar kings and princes and the Nair militia bore the brunt of Hyder's fury. They were reduced and annihilated by Hyder's forces.

The Arakkal house took full advantage of Hyder Ali's incursion into Malabar. In fact, Hyder Ali's entry into Malabar was at the invitation of Ali Raja. It was no doubt done with the motive of countering the Kolatiri, who was an obstacle to the expansion of his power. This was a turning point in the history of Malabar and the Kolatiri kingdom. The Arakkal house reaped the benefits. The Arakkal chief was put in-charge of the Kolatiri kingdom by Hyder Ali himself. But the subsequent reinstatement of the Malabar princes including the Kolatiri in their dominions threw a spanner into the political calculations of Arakkal. The latter could do nothing against Hyder's wishes. Thenceforth, Arakkal's power was restricted to Cananore principality momentarily.

Thus, it has been well established that Hyder Ali was not against Hindus in general. As far as Mysore was concerned, he was tolerant towards his Hindu subjects and that his ministers and many officers were Brahmins like Poornayya. He had his own reasons for his action in Malabar. He was furious against the ruling class of Nairs and Nambudiris

Nambudiris for carrying out guerilla warefare against him. Frequent revolts by the Nairs prompted him to take stern action. Hyder himself had come to Manjeri to suppress the Nairs. He tried to disarm all the Nairs, except those who embraced Islam. Madanna and Srinivas Rao were given charge of the administration of Malabar. This very act reinforced the theory that the Mysore Sultan was not systematically against Hindus, given that he himself was of Hindu ancestry.[16]

TIPU SULTAN IN MALABAR AND ANNEXATION OF KOLATHANADU BY THE ENGLISH

Hyder was succeeded by his son Tipu Sultan to the throne of Mysore. Meanwhile, rumours were floating of a treaty of peace pending between the British and Tipu. Raja of Travancore feared Tipu so much, that he wanted his name to be added as an ally of the English in case of a treaty. On the other hand, English had concluded a treaty of perpetual peace and friendship with the Marathas to counter Tipu. In September 1783, England and France signed a peace treaty. Despite this, Tipu refused to stop hostilities though he accused the French of deserting an ally who had begun war for their sake. He also realized that he could never succeed without their assistance. In October 1783, information reached Travancore that Tipu along with a great part of his army and also a detachment of French troops, had recommenced hostilities at Mangalore and had captured several English officers.

Later troops of Tipu left Karwar for Tellicherry. Meanwhile, an English ship '*Superb*' with 300 travellers happened to be caught in a cyclone and was wrecked on the northwest of Cananore. On the whole, two officers and 200 men who were driven ashore near Mangalore were detained by Tipu and another hundred wrecked near Cananore were kept in irons as hostages by Arakkal Beevi. This time Tipu came to Cananore with his army at the request of Arakkal Beevi.

The English brigadier Norman Mcleod went there from Tellicherry to negotiate the release of the hostages in the dungeons of Fort St. Angelo. He held discussions with Arakkal Beevi and Tipu Sultan. But both of them refused to release the hostages. The English realized that the hostages could be freed only by capturing the fort. Subsequently, Mcleod decided to attack Cananore. Plans were drawn for the impending attack. Brigadier Mcleod sailed out from Tellicherry and reached Cananore on 9 December 1783. They launched a severe attack on the fort and the harbour, which was the main trade centre of Arakkal. Initially the Arakkal Beevi's army with the help of the Mysore forces defended themselves. But after the sixth day of the attack, on 14 December 1783, Arakkal forces laid down their arms and surrendered to the English. English lost 279 men and officers whereas Beevi's loss was much more significant. In Cananore, the 42 dependent fortresses were occupied by the English. Arakkal Beevi and the members of the royal family were taken as prisoners. The fort was pillaged and the Beevi was threatened with deportation. She was finally released after she had agreed to sign a treaty as dictated by Mcleod in 1784. By this treaty, her possessions were restored to her but she was required to pay a tribute of one lakh pagodas annually. She also had to pay an indemnity of one half lakh pagodas for the war expenses. Her forts were to be at the disposal of the Company, and all the merchandise and other properties in the town and in the forts were considered as lawful prize for the army. The Company was also given the monopoly to purchase all the pepper in the settlement at a reasonable price by Arakkal Beevi. In its turn, the Company promised to protect her from the Nairs, her 'natural enemies'.[17]

Thus, the English captured Fort St. Angelo and the harbour of Cananore, including Arakkal principality and their adjoining regions. This was a tremendous victory for the English. The English soldiers completely looted and pillaged the fort. However, Bombay Government had second thoughts, since Beevi was an ally of Tipu. They did not want to ignite further problems with Tipu. So they ordered restoration of Cananore back to Beevi. But it was only in April 1784, after the treaty of Mangalore, had been signed that the English, evacuated the place.

Subsequently, Beevi appeared before the committee who investigated into the looting and atrocities committed by Mcleod and his army. Actually, precious gold and silver objects, worth two lakh rupees were plundered from the Arakkal palace. In addition, they captured three of her vessels loaded with sugar, rice and sandalwood along with 25 country crafts anchored at the harbour loaded with 60,000 candies of coir, besides coffee, black pepper and 20 candies cardamom. The treasury of the Moideen mosque was also looted by Captain Lighten, who stole the goldplates intended for the minaret. Arakkal family got back their Fort St. Angelo and their palace. Tipu Sultan was furious when he heard about the capture and pillage by the English. He informed the commander of the Tellicherry settlement about the shocking way they plundered the Fort.[18]

Unlike his father, Tipu Sultan was more religiously inclined and was not favourably disposed towards Christians and missionaries. Tipu followed a different policy towards them. The French missionary records during the period contain general information regarding Tipu's approach towards the Christians. Tipu had his own reason for the shift in religious policy from that of his father. He hated the collusion of Christians in Canara and Mysore with the English who were his arch-rivals. These native Christians with the help of European missionaries, including some French openly sided with the English and worked as food suppliers, guards, spies or informers. This was regarded as a treachery by Tipu, especially his so-called friends, the French, who indulged in this missionary activity. He turned against them and resorted to massive conversion under threat of death. As a consequence, there was a massive migration of Christians from Mysore to the neighbouring countries. Many churches, convents and seminaries were destroyed. Even in Nawab of Arcot's territory, Tipu turned against the Christians who colluded with the English.[19]

Earlier in 1779, Tipu's general had captured Eli Mala. The Kolatiri Raja Rama Varma was afraid that Tipu Sultan who had reached Cotayangadi near Tellicherry would forcibly convert him to Islam. He decided to embrace voluntary death. He retired to Pycchi and procured a friendly Nair to shoot him dead. But before this act, he secured his sister and her two sons safe passage to Dharmapatanam and then to Travancore, as the Raja of Travancore was their blood relation. Tipu continued to nurse grievance against the State of Travancore for defying him by allying with the English, besides giving refuge to the rebel rulers and the Nayars of Chirakkal, Calicut, and Kolathanadu, whose custody was demanded by Tipu. It should be noted that the Kolatiri in due course came to be called Chirakkal Raja. In December 1785, Tipu's army marched towards Malabar. He arrived at Calicut via Tamasseri Pass in April 1786. He destroyed the town and removed its inhabitants to Nelluru, which he renamed as Farokhabad. It was situated on the Banks of Beypore River.[20]

Tipu's excesses in Malabar exasperated even the Muslims to such an extent, that they revolted against his government. In 1785, a powerful Mappila of Manchery rose in rebellion against the Sultan's government. Seeing this Ali Raja himself sought refuge in the English fort of Tellicherry in 1789.[21]

Meanwhile, in 1786, there was dissatisfaction brewing between Arakkal family and their islands of Amini, Kiltan, Kadamat and Chetalat regarding the trade policy pertaining to monopoly in coir trade especially. They protested and tendered their allegiance to Tipu. The latter seeing the strategic position of the islands in Arabian Sea refused to restore them to the Arakkal Beevi. This sent shock waves to the chieftains of Malabar, who even rose in revolt against Mysore power.[22] It is noteworthy that in his dealings with Arakkal Beevi, Tipu was not swayed by religious affinity, but rather by his own interests. However, in order to mend fences with the Beevi, Tipu compensated her with a *jagir* in Kolathanadu including Chalat and Kunnot worth Rs. 7,380.

In 1788, Tipu issued a proclamation, denouncing the

practice of polyandry existing in the country, and informed the people that if they did not desist from such a pernicious usage, they would be honoured with Islam. The Nairs and Nambudiris were particularly targeted for their 'obscene practices' and licentiousness. This was the pretext of Tipu to enter Malabar with 20,000 men, who created havoc in the region. The presence of Tipu Sultan in Travancore dislocated all the trade. The calamity lay not so much in the terror that he spread, but in the deliberate measure, he adopted against the traditional commerce of Malabar. He unleashed terror wherever he went. The entire country was laid to waste. As a result trade suffered. Hindu temples of the Nairs and Nambudiris, and Christian churches were equally desecrated by him. Towers of pagodas, palaces, houses of the nobles, of the rich and even sometimes the huts of the poor were committed to flames by this ferocious leader. Also, vast areas of pepper vines were destroyed by him. The Nairs and other Malabaris who resisted Tipu were forcibly circumcised. Many of them fled to the jungles.[23]

Nevertheless among Christians, Tipu made a distinction between Syrian Christians and other Christians. He spared the former as they did not side with the English. But he came down heavily on the Christians in the territories belonging to the Nawab of Arcot, who sided with the English, as well as the Kanara Christians. Thus, we can say that Tipu Sultan's ire against the Christians or Hindus was largely politically motivated. If the Nairs and Nambudiris who belonged to the ruling classes of Malabar and the Christians, especially Latin Catholics had sided with Tipu, instead of the English, he would have most certainly spared them too. But that was not the case. Therefore, they had to bear the brunt of Tipu's fury.[24]

One of the principal victims of Tipu's revenge was the Raja of Chirakkal, who was falsely accused of conspiring. He was attacked and killed and his body hung up after his death. In this raid, Tipu is said to have carried off large treasurers plundered from the temples of Malabar. The ancient Taliparamba Shiva Temple, called previously as Peruncellur Temple, 12 miles north from Cananore, was laid waste. Its sculptures and *gopurams* were destroyed. However, Tipu realized that he could not afford to antagonize the Mappilas of Malabar. He even proposed a marriage between his son Abdul Khaliq and the daughter of Beevi in 1789, which, however, did not materialize.[25]

On 29 December 1789, Tipu declared war against the Raja of Travancore, with the help of the French officer Count de Lally. As a counter, Lord Cornwallis officially declared war against Tipu Sultan for attacking Travancore in direct violation of the treaty of Mangalore. Fortunately, for the Raja of Travancore, southwest monsoon broke out with severity impending the progress of Tipu's troops. His arms and ammunitions were washed away. While Tipu was in Alwaye, he received report that British had declared war on Mysore and were marching towards his capital Seringapatam. This compelled him to withdraw his forces from Kerala and return back to Mysore.[26]

On 28 March 1790, an English army under Captain Byron reached Malabar Coast in a vessel called 'Phoenix' and captured a war boat of Tipu Sultan. Once again clashes broke out between the two. English captured Tipu's military barracks in Kathirur near Tellicherry along with the palace that he had acquired previously from Kottayam Raja. At the same time, they were planning to attack Cananore and were awaiting reinforcement from Bombay. Meanwhile, Arakkal Beevi had an inkling of the impending attack on them by the English. She realized that she could not withstand the attack of the English even if she had Tipu's help. So in order to avoid conflict she decided to enter into a peace treaty with the English, very much against Tipu's wishes.[27]

On 8 August 1790, Joonumma Beevi who was the ruler of Arakkal kingdom then came to an agreement with the English by which she agreed initially to allow the English to appoint their guards in the Cananore fort for its security. She, however, failed to comply with this agreement, as she thought that she signed the treaty under pressure. Nevertheless, the English forced her to send back the Mysore army. Meanwhile the English tried to forcibly enter Fort St. Angelo. But they were restrained by the Arakkal army. Beevi desperately recalled Mysore army for help. Very soon 8,000 Mysore troops reached Cananore and joined the Arakkal army. With their combined force they stopped the English from entering the fort.

The English were furious with Arakkal Beevi for not abiding by the agreement. The English commander in Tellicherry, Robert Taylor sought permission from Bombay to attack Cananore. In response on 22 November 1790, a fully equipped warship, Prince Royal came to Tellicherry from Bombay with orders to attack Cananore. First, they made arrangements for the security of Tellicherry Fort. On 28 November 1790, the English army first encircled and attacked the fort constructed by Tipu's army in Agaar at the Kuttikakam cape of Edakkad. Tipu was aware of the English forces movement and he moved to Cananore and settled down at the army camp of Arakkal built by Beevi to safeguard her borders. The house and the compound in this place was known as 'Kottayil'. The combined army of Tipu and Arakkal was no match to the superior weapons of the English. Beevi's husband too was killed. Numerous ships and boats of Arakkal were either destroyed or drowned in the cannon bombardment. Remaining ships and boats were eventually captured by the English. The English fired bombs from their cannons which were positioned atop their fort resulting in massive death and destruction. Unable to withstand this onslaught, the Arakkal-Mysore army surrendered to the English on 17 December 1790.[28]

The English, thus, captured Fort St. Angelo, Arakkal Palace and the entire Cananore town. They plundered the armoury and food stocks of the surrendered army. Apart from this, they captured the army camps and their weapon stockpiles belonging to Arakkal Beevi. In addition to this, they also took 5,000 Mysore soldiers as hostages. The British Captain Wiseman was appointed as the commandant of the Cananore Fort and town. He hoisted the British flag on Fort St. Angelo on 17 December 1790. Celebration was carried out by firing gun shots from cannons bewildering the Malabaris. A strong army was stationed for the security of the fort and its neighbouring region. In support, the British General Abercromby himself arrived at Tellicherry to conduct the operations in Cananore. His Majesty's ship 'Phoenix' with Captain Byron was engaged in the naval operations against Cananore. On 14 December, the siege began and the Beevi surrendered unconditionally to the superior authority of the English. Thus, the political power was handed over to the English who permitted the Beevi to continue to exercise justice to the inhabitants of Cananore according to their customs. On 14 February 1791, an assurance was also granted by Major Abercromby to Beevi of her being accorded personal protection against the power of Tipu. A shocking turn of events that occurred is that in return for the above assurance, Beevi consented to do everything in her power to reconcile and attach the Mappilas of Malabar coast to English interests and to enlist the support of the English in their war against Tipu.[29]

This was a turning point and a great achievement for the English as they were then able to surmount the traditional animosity of the Muslims towards them. Till a final agreement was reached, Beevi was given the right to collect taxes and carry on the administration. Side-by-side, the English also captured Lakshadweep which belonged to Beevi. A peace talk took place, but she did not participate as she was mourning her husband's death. Instead, she delegated a minister and the next descendant to the throne to attend the peace talks. Thus, after the capture of Cananore the entire Malabar was ceded to the English by Tipu with the rest of Malabar in 1792.[30] It appears that though in the beginning the Madras Government wanted to abolish the chiefship of Cannanore, later they reversed this decision and recognized the claims of Sultan Ali Raja to chiefship. Beevi was not totally unhappy with the turn of events. She gifted to Colonel Gordon and Mcleod two silver chairs after the cession of Cananore.[31]

On 20 April 1792, Major Down was appointed as the British commissioner to Cananore. Thenceforth, Cananore became the military centre for the English, instead of Tellicherry. According to the agreement signed by Beevi and the British on 28 October 1793, the former had to pay Rs. 15,000 yearly as tax to the English in order to continue the trade.[32] Tipu Sultan, on his part, realized that he could not rely on the French to oust the English. Tipu sent his ambassadors to the Turkish Sultan at Constantinople in 1794 and later to the King of Afghanistan in 1796 in an attempt to gain their support against his enemies. Tipu's hopes of obtaining French help finally came to an end when Napolean Bonaparte on his way to India at Tipu's request failed to defeat the English in Egypt.[33]

In 1796, another agreement was reached with the Beevi. The English decided to return Lakshadweep and some other regions to Beevi on condition that she had to pay taxes. This treaty was abided by her till 1865. When the Beevi defaulted in the payment of taxes, the agreement was cancelled and the British took up the right of collecting taxes. However, the British allowed *Malikhan* for the maintenance and expenses of Arakkal Beevi Bulea and the royal family. Thus, the famous Arakkal family was stripped of the power and had to live on *Malikhan* which the British provided. However, in 1797, all the forts of Cananore, Tellicherry and Palakkad under the control of the English were either renovated or rebuilt. After getting possession of Fort St. Angelo at Cananore, the English shifted their military base from Tellicherry to Cananore. Futhermore, they renovated and modified the old fort. They converted certain buildings inside the fort into armoury and storehouses of explosives. The spacious wide halls inside the fort which was occupied by the Portuguese and the Dutch during their heydays were converted into an ordinance depot filled with weapons, arms and ammunitions. All along the English, used Beevi as a puppet. Whenever possible under the pretext of the treaty, they forced her to pay money.

In one instance, Beevi pleaded with the English as she had paid 2,60,000 rupees to Mcleod as indemnity for her release. But in the records it was shown as if she paid only one and a half lakh rupees. She even produced all relevant documents to assert her claim. But nothing came out of this. The corrupt English tampered with the records to make money. They went about cutting her down to size for siding with the Mysore Sultan. Tipu himself lost his life in the course of his last battle with the English at Seringapatam in 1799.

Beevi was facing extreme financial crisis which was exploited by the English. She was forced to sign agreements with the English, which was detrimental to the interests of the Arakkal house. She had to swallow her pride and even admitted to pay Rs. 1,500 per annum as a *jumma* (revenue demand) on her properties in Cananore and the islands. She even agreed to pay the customs on all her articles of merchandise imported or exported, except upon the coir imports from the islands. She also surrendered the claim for one-fifth share of the revenue collections including the right and title over the *jagir* conferred by Tipu in exchange of Amindvi Group Islands.[34]

Beevi was compelled to execute such terms because the Governor-General in his instructions dated 27 July 1795 had already directed the abolition of her monopoly of trade with the islands. Even her claim over the *jagir* conferred by Tipu was not accepted by the commission on the grounds that it was only a temporary possession and also if it has to be restored it should be to Kolatiri, who was the actual owner of these fiefs. In truth, the English wanted to deny the said territory to both Beevi and Kolatiri for their own territorial ambition under the coverage of a legal consent.[35]

Actually, Malabar was ceded to the British by the Treaties of Seringapatam, dated 22 February and 18 March 1792. Except for Pazhassi Raja of Kottayam, who refused to pay the taxes to the British, all the others including Chirakkal and Arakkal fell in line. Some Nairs, nobles and others who resisted were arrested and exiled to Penang in Malaysia in 1802, which was then a British colony. Of these, only one by the name of Kishen Iyen was allowed to return to Tellicherry.

When the East India Company formally took over the administration of Malabar from Mysore after the death of

Tipu Sultan and the fall of Seringapatam in 1799-1800, they permitted the former chiefs and landlords to return from self imposed exile and reclaim their property and status wherever possible. Thenceforth, they acted as revenue collectors for the English. The various hereditary rulers of Malabar were even pensioned off by the English. The Kolatiri or Kola Swaroopam assets were partitioned. The property and wealth of the Kolatiris was awarded to the Chirakkal Kovilakam. On 6 August 1803, a court verdict ruled that the Chirakkal Raja was the legitimate successor of the Kolatiris. Ravi Varma Raja ruled Chirakkal from Valapatnam fort, until he abdicated in favour of the English. After abdication, he and his family lived in the old palace of Chirakkal, built earlier in 1683. Once assured of the Company's protection they became complacent and in the course of time much wealth and land were squandered off by the successors of Ravi Varma Raja.

An analysis of the foregoing events in a nutshell reveals that the English brought about the downfall of the Arakkal house. The pillage of Cananore by the English army brought a severe financial strain on the economic stability of the house. They had to pay ransom and other gratification to continue their existence. But by the third Mysore war Imbichi Beevi even lost her fortress which was confiscated by the Company. Furthermore, by entering into agreements related to the Laccadive Islands, she had surrendered her sovereignty to the English. Gone were the days of *rejador* and regent of the seas whose notoriety in seafaring was taken note even by the Europeans. Arakkal house was cut down to size and the ruler reduced to the status of a mere pensioner of the English.[36]

In later years, some Ali Raja Beevis were educated in Arabic and Islamic theology; few others were well versed in Hindustani and Persian language. One Beevi of Arakkal was a very modern lady who used to entertain foreign delegates at her palace. Buchanan described one such evening party thrown by the Beevi to the Europeans. Hodgson, the district collector of Malabar attended the party with Buchanan. Buchanan wrote:

we were received by the Beevi in her bedroom and the ladies were admitted to the chamber of her granddaughter. The dining room was very large and well lighted and the dinner was entirely after the English fashion. The quantity of meat put on the table as usual in India was enormous and the wines and liquors were very good. The young chief with the father and husband of the young lady, who have no kind authority received the company in the dining room but did not sit at the table. When dinner was served they returned to a couch at one end of the hall and smoked *hookas* until the company arose to dance. Appropriate toasts were given and these were honoured by salutes of guns from the Beevi's ships. Many fireworks were displayed, there was music both European and native. According to Buchanan the house of Beevi is very large and though not so showy as some of the Sultan's palace, is by far more comfortable and is in fact by much the best native house that I have seen.

From the above narration, it is very clear as to how the last Arakkal Beevi was classy and modern lady who used to entertain European guests at her palace. In Buchanan's words,

> the territory of Beevi is very small yet she pays revenue of 14,000 rupees as land tax and Company receives all the customs. She is allowed to collect all the other revenues. Though Laccadives are subject to her, but they are wretched islands producing no grains, only coconut and betel nuts and plantains. With so poor a territory and such a tribute the Biby could not support herself in the manner she does without the assistance of trade. She possessed several vessels that sail to Arabia, Bengal and Sumatra.[37]

Beevi of Cananore always maintained a smooth relationship with the English. During the second decade of the nineteenth century, the English supplied gunpowder to Beevi for the celebration of a marriage in her family. It is noteworthy that on 27June 1823, the Madras Governor sanctioned a re-mission of revenue to the amount of 1,500 pagodas per annum to Beevi of Cananore as a compensation for the loss of Amindvi islands, provided the latter renounced all other claims and acknowledged that the matter is closed forever.[38] As times went by, the wealth, power, prestige and properties of the Arakkal House and its numerous successors and descendants waned to such an extent that the Arakkal Palace today is completely in ruins, while in an old structure adjacent to the palace, the Arakkal Museum has been set up by some descendants of the family.

NOTES

1. Robert Sewell, *The Antiquarian Remains in The Presidency of Madras*, vol. I, Madras, 1882, p. 2; Legoux de Flaix, *Essai historique, géographique et politique d'Indostan*, vol. 1, Paris, 1807, pp. 51, 51fn, 52; Claude Hugau, *Le Voyage Extraordinaire d'un capitaine de dragons chez Hyder Ali Khan, 1769-1772*, Paris, 2001, p. 53.
2. Praxy Fernandes, *Tigers of Mysore: A Biography of Hyder Ali and Tipu Sultan*, Delhi, 1969, pp. 30, 199; Robert Sewell and S.K. Iyengar, *The Historical Inscriptions of Southern India*, Madras, 1932, pp. 302-4; J.B.P. More (ed.), 'Origin, Ancestry and Identity of Hyder Ali', in J.B.P. More, *Religion and Society in South india: Hindus, Muslims and Christians*, Nirmalagiri, 2006, pp. 11-28.
3. Praxy Fernandes, op. cit., Lewin Bowring, *Haider Ali and Tipu Sultan and the Struggle with the Mussalman Powers of the South*, Oxford, 1899, p. 30; Report of a Joint Commission from Bengal and Bombay appointed to inquire into the State and Constitution of the Province of Malabar, in the year 1792 and 1793, vol. 1, Bombay, p. 19, N.A.F. 9368; *Notes Extraits des lettres d'un offcier de cavalier, qui a voyagé aux Indes Orientales*, 1776, pp. 165-6, BNF, Paris.
4. Reports of a Joint Commission, op. cit., Denys Forrest, *Tiger of Mysore*, London, 1970, pp. 22, 24-5; Praxy Fernandes, op. cit., pp. 29-30; Paulin de Saint Barthelemy, *Voyages aux Indes Orientales*, vol. I, Paris, 1808, p. 225; Sreedhara Menon, *A Survey of Kerala History*, Kottayam, 1967, p. 285; Mohibbul Hasan, *History of Tipu Sultan*, Calcutta, 1951, p. 156; Lewin Bowring, op. cit., p. 139; A. Martineau, *Les origines de Mahe*, Paris, 1917, p. xii; A. Galetti, *The Dutch in Malabar*, Madras, 1911, p. 146; NAF, 9068, *Lettre de Prince Cherequel à Bernard Picot de la Motte (Gouverneur de Mahé)*, 21 Février 1766, p.7, BNF, Paris; NAF 9068, *Lettre de Prince Cherequel à Picot (Gouverneur de Mahé)*, 23 Février 1766, p. 7, BNF, Paris; NAF 9062, *Lettre de Picot au Prince Cherequel*, 23 Février 1768, p. 24, BNF, Paris; NAF 1907, *Lettre du Prince Cherequel à M. Repentigny*, Mahé, 16 June 1775, p. 3, BNF, Paris; *Lettre du Prince Cherequel à M. de*

Repentigny, 9 July 1775, p. 7, BNF, Paris; NAF 1908, *Lettre du Prince de Cherequel à M. Picot*, 16 June 1776, p. 1, BNF, Paris; NAF 9368, *Notes extraits des lettres d'un officer de cavalier qui a voyagé aux Indes Orientales*, pp. 167-8, BNF, Paris.

5. Denys Forrest, op. cit., p. 24; Lewin Bowring, op. cit., pp. 44-5; Shungoony Menon, *A History of Travancore*, vol. I, Delhi, 1984, p. 174.
6. Secretariat inward letter Book-1766, Chief Anjengo to Bombay Castle, 13 March 1766, p. 225, MAB; T.I. Ponnen, *Dutch Hegemony in Malabar*, Trivandrum, 1978, p. 160; A. Galletti, *The Dutch in Malabar*, Madras, 1911, p. 154; Shungoony Menon, op. cit., pp. 200-5.
7. E. Sicé, *Un mot sur la Répresentation des Etablissements Français de l' Inde à l'Assemblée Nationale*, Pondichéry, 1848, p. 8; J.B.P. More, *Freedom Movement in French India*, Tellicherry, 2001, pp. 5, 26; O.K. Nambiar, *An Illustrated Maritime History of the Indian Ocean*, New Delhi, 1992, p. 69; M.M.D.L.T. *History of Ayder Ali Khan*, vol. I, London, 1784, p. 98, NAF 9105; *Lettre du Roi de Neeliswaram to Picot*, June 1769, p. 14, BNF, Paris.
8. NAF, 9068, Picot 1777, *Correspondance avec Le Prince Colastry, Lettre de Prince Cherequel à M. Picot*, Mahé, 26 Février 1768, p. 24, BNF, Paris; William Logan, *Malabar*, vol. 1, Madras, 1989, p. 595; Sathyan Edakkad, *Vasco da Gama and the Unknown Facts of History*, Ramanattukara, 2010, p. 127; A. Galletti, op. cit., pp.147-8; John Fryer, *New Account of the East India and Persia being Nine Years Travels 1672-1681*, vol. I, New York, 1967, p. 144; O.K. Nambiar, op. cit., p. 72; NAF, 9068, *Lettre de Prince Cherrequel à M. Picot*, Mahé, 8 Avril 1769, p. 33, BNF, Paris; NAF, 9113, *Copie et traductions des lettres écrites et reçues d'Ali Rajah et d'autres Mapelese de la côte Malabar depuis*, 3 Janvier 1769 jusqu'au 1778, *Lettre de Picot à Ali Rajah*, 16 April 1773, p. 17, BNF, Paris.
9. NAF, 9113, Letter from Ali Raja to Picot, Mahé, 29 January 1776, p. 54; Letter from Picot to Ali Raja, 17 February 1776, p. 55; Letter from Ali Raja to Picot, 17 August 1776, p. 62; Letter from Ali Raja to Picot, 21 January 1778, p. 82; Letter from Picot to Ali Raja, 21 January 1778, p. 82; Ali Raja to Picot, 17 February 1778, p. 86; Picot to Ali Raja, 17 February 1778, p. 86; Ali Raja to Bellecomb, Governor General, Pondicherry, 28 March 1778, p. 92; Picot to Ali Raja, 6 May 1778, p. 93; Ali Raja to Picot, 24 August 1778, p. 94; Picot to Ali Raja, 25 August 1778, p. 94, NAF 9113; *Lettre d'Ali*

Rajah à Picot, 17 Septembre 1771, p. 34, BNF, Paris; Ali Rajah to Picot, Mahé, 11 Avril 1771, p. 32, BNF, Paris.

10. C. Adrian Mayer, *Land and Society in Malabar*, Oxford, 1952, p. 22; L. Robert Hardgrave, Jr., 'The Mapilla Rebellion, 1921: Peasant Revolt in Malabar', *Modern Asian Studies*, vol. I, II, 1977, pp. 59-60; see also Roland Miller, *Mappila Muslims of Kerala: A Study in Islamic Trends*, Madras, 1976, pp. 55-77; J.B.P. More, op. cit., p. 26; Adrien Launay, *Histoire des Missions de l'Inde: Pondichèry, Maissour, Coimbatore*, vol. I, Paris, 1898, pp. lix, liv, lv; J.B.P. More, 'Tipu Sultan and the Christians', in *Islam and Christian-Muslim Relations*, vol. 14, no. 3, July 2003, p. 315; A. Galletti, op. cit., pp. 148-9.
11. Military Department, Country correspondence, 1778, Fort St. George to the Rajah of Travancore, 23 December 1778, p. 367; Military Department, Country Correspondence, 1779, Fort St. George to the Rajah of Travancore, 20 January 1779, p. 15, TNA; S.P. Sen, *The French in India*, Delhi, 1971, p. 102.
12. Lewin B. Bowring, op. cit., p. 84; K.K.N. Kurup, *The Ali Raja's of Cannanore*, Trivandrum, 1975, p. 55.
13. Anjengo Residency Diary, 1782, John Hutchinson, Resident, Anjengo to Lord Macartney, Fort St. George, 22 February 1782, p. 9, TNA; Anjengo Residency Diary, 1782, John Hutchinson, Resident, Anjengo to Colonel Humberstone, Calicut, 3 April 1782, p. 23, TNA; O.K. Nambiar, op. cit., p. 74; K.K.N. Kurup, op. cit., p. 55; Anjengo Residency Diary, 1782, Colonel Humbertson to the Rajah of Travancore, 10 February 1782, p. 2, TNA; NAF 9111, *Copie du reçu fourni par M. Picot au Prince Cherequel pour le compte de Nabob Ayder Aly Kan*, 22 Février 1779, p. 27, BNF, Paris.
14. B. Sheikh Ali, 'French relations with Haider Ali and Tipu Sultan', International Seminar on Indo-French Relations and Indian Independence, 22-6 September 1997, Pondicherry, 1997, p. 17; Robert Sewell, *The Antiquarian Remains in The Presidency of Madras*, vol. I, p. 244.
15. Lewin B. Bowring, op. cit., pp. 104, 118; S.P. Sen, op. cit., pp. 102, 289; Adrien Launay, op. cit., vol. I, Paris, 1898, pp. 133-4, NAF 9368; *Lettre de M. Piveron Morelets, Goudalur à Commandant Suffren*, 6 January 1783 (Lettre no. 53); *Lettre à M. le Commandant Suffren de Piveron Morelets de Goudalur*, 18 Février, 1783, p. 467; Piveron Morelets à Suffren, p. 469, BNF, Paris.
16. M.G.S. Narayana, *Calicut*, Kozhikode, 2018, p. 225; J.B.P. More, 'Tipu Sultan and the Christians', in *Islam and Christian-Muslim Relations*, vol. 14, no. 3, July 2003.

17. Military Consultation, 1783, John Hutchinson, resident, Anjengo to I. Cox, Hippesley, acting resident, Tanjore, 9 October 1783, p. 4632, TNA; Mohibbul Hasan, *History of Tipu Sultan*, Delhi, 1951, 2005, p. 41; A. Martineau, *Bussy et l'Inde Francaise, 1720-1785*, Paris, 1935, p. 341; Anjengo Diary, 1783, Hutchinson, Resident, Anjengo to Bombay Castle, 14 September 1783, p.775; S.P. Sen, *The French in India*, Delhi, 1971, p. 102; K.K.N. Kurup, op. cit., p. 56; Military Sundry Books, vol. 61, letter dated 17 January 1784, pp. 766-7; Bombay commissioner's Diary dated 7 December 1792, The agreement was executed on 8 January 1784; C.U. Aitchison. *A Collection of Treaties, Engagements and Sanads*, vol. X, no. XXXIX, p. 124; Mohibbul Hasan, *History of Tipu Sultan*, Delhi, 1951, pp. 42, 36.
18. S.P. Sen, *The French in India*, Delhi, 1971, pp. 380-1; Military Consultation, 1784, John Hutchinson, Anjengo to the Rajah of Travancore, 22 March 1784, p. 1291, TNA; A. Martineau, op. cit., p. 424; Maistre de la Tour, *The History of Hyder Shah and Hyder Ali Khan Bahadur and of his son Tippoo Sultan*, London, 1855, p. 293; Mohibbul Hassan, op. cit., K.K.N. Kurup, op. cit., p. 67.
19. Mohibbul Hassan, op. cit., pp. 365-6, also see S.N. Saldanha, *The Captivity of Canara Christians under Tipu in 1784*, Mangalore, 1933; Mohibbul Hasan, op. cit., pp. 92, 352, 357-65; Roland E. Miller, *Mappila Muslims of Kerala: A Study in Islamic Trends*, Madras, 1976, p. 92; Adrien Launay, *Histoire des Missions de l' Inde, Pondichery, Maissour, Coimbatore*, vol. I, Paris, 1898, pp. 133-4.
20. Anjengo Diary, 1785, R.H. Boddam, Bombay Castle to John Macpherson, Fort William, 25 November 1785, p. 480, MAB; Kate Brittlebank, *Tipu Sultan's Search for Legitimacy*, Delhi, 1997, p. 25; Francis Buchanan, *A Journey from Madras through the Country of Mysore, Canara and Malabar*, vol. II, London, 1807, pp. 196, 557-8, 741-2; Robert Sewell. *The Antiquarian Remains in The Presidency of Madras*, vol. I, Madras, 1882, p. 242; Praxy Fernandes, op. cit., p. 97.
21. K.P. Padmanabha Menon, *History of Kerala*, vol. II, New Delhi, 1983, p. 542; Praxy Fernandes, op. cit., p. 96.
22. K.K.N. Kurup, op. cit., p. 58.
23. Military Consultation 1789, George Powney, Parvour to John Holland, Governor in Council, 14 December 1789, p. 3344, TNA; *Mahé, Etablisssement Français sur la côte de Malabar*, n.d., p. 79; T.W. Arnold, *The Preaching of Islam*, London, 1935, pp. 261-2; Ashin Das Gupta, *Malabar in Asian Trade, 1740-1800*, Cambridge, 1967,

p. 33; Leena More, *English East India Company and the Local Rulers in Kerala: A Case Study of Attingal and Travancore*, Tellicherry, 2003, p. 199.

24. J.B.P. More, 'Tipu Sultan and the Christians of Southern India', in J.B.P.More, *Religion and Society in South India: Hindus, Muslims and Christians*, Nirmalagiri, 2006, pp. 29-50.
25. Praxy Fernandes, *The Tigers of Mysore: A Biography of Hyder Ali and Tipu Sultan*, Delhi, 1991, pp. 98, 100; Robet Sewell, op. cit., p. 243; Mohibbul Hasan, op. cit., p. 366; MSS. vol. 996, *Lettre de M. Dubois à M. Boiret*, Pondichéry, 26 Mai, 1802, AME, Paris; Mss. vol. 995, *Lettre de l'Evêque de Dolicha*, Pondichéry, 14 Février 1795 à M. Chaumont, AME, Paris; Kesavan Veluthat, 'A Copper Plate Inscription from Peruncellur, North Kerala, India: AD 1145', in Mujeebu Rehman and K.S. Madhavan (eds.), *Explorations in South Indian History*, Kottayam, 2014, pp. 223-32.
26. Anjengo Diary 1790, Sober, Lieut. 10th Batallion commanding the detachment to John Hutchinson, Resident, Anjengo, 1 January 1790, p. 2; Anjengo Diary 1790, Cornwallis, Fort St. William to Fort St. George, 28 January 1790, p. 2; Denys Forrest, op. cit., p. 123; Lewin B. Bowring, op. cit., p. 143; Maitre de la Tour, op. cit., p. 273; C.K. Kareem, *Kerala under Hyder and Tipu*, Cochin, 1973; Kate Brittlebank, *Tipu Sultan's Search for Legitimacy*, Delhi, 1997, pp. 25, 94, NAF 9373; *Compte-rendu de l'entreprise de Tipu Sultan contre le Rajah de Travancore*, Pondichéry, le 7 Août 1790, pp. 321, 325.
27. Diary of the Malabar expedition, dated 17 December 1790, TNA; K.K.N. Kurup, op. cit., p. 60.
28. Mohibbul Hasan, op. cit. 194-5; Sathyan, op. cit., pp. 132-3.
29. Supervisor's Diary, dated 30 June 1794. See appendix XIV in K.K.N. Kurup, op. cit., p. 119; Diary of Tellicherry Factory, dated 31 March 1791, see appendix XIV, in K.K.N. Kurup, op. cit., p. 120; K.K.N. Kurup, op. cit., pp. 60, 115-20.
30. Robert Sewell, *Archaeological Survey of Southern India, Lists of Antiquarian Remains in the Presidency of Madras*, vol. I, Madras, 1882, p. 241.
31. See IOR/D/152F333, 1792-4, IOL; IOR/L/PS/6/529, Coll 21, October 1792—January 1864, IOL, London.
32. John Fryer, *A New Account of the East India and Persia being Nine Years Travels 1672-1681*, vol. I, New York, 1967, p. 144; *Mahé, Etablissement Français sur la côte de Malabar*, n.d., p. 117.

33. Mss. vol. 995, Lettre de Schwendiman, Pondichery, 11 Juillet 1799, AME, Paris; Sheikh Ali, 'French Relations with Haider Ali and Tipu Sultan: A record of Blunders', Paper presented at the International seminar of Indo-French relations and Indian Independence, September 1977, Pondichery, pp. 21-37.
34. C.U. Aitchison, *A Collection of Treatise, Engagements and Sanads*, vol. X, Mysore No. LV, pp. 166-7; K.K.N. Kurup, op. cit., p. 63; Mujeebu Rehman, 'The British Reports and Production of Colonial Knowledge: The Joint Commissioners' Report on Malabar 1792-3', in Mujeebu Rehman and K.S. Madhavan (eds.), *Explorations in South Indian History*, Kottayam, 2014, pp. 36, cf. also, K.K.N. Kurup, op. cit., pp. 120-9.
35. K.K.N. Kurup, op. cit., pp. 63, 120-9.
36. IOR/F/4/522/12464, October 1813-March 1815, pp. 96-9, IOL, London; M.G.S., Narayanan, *Calicut*, Kozhicode, 2018, p. 228; William Logan, *Malabar*, New Delhi, 1989, vol. I, pp. 473, 475, 490; K.K.N. Kurup, op. cit.; Vanidas Elayavoor, *Lore and Legends of North Malabar*, tr. Ashwin Kumar, Kottayam, 1996, pp. 426-8.
37. Francis Buchanan, *A Journey from Madras through the Countries of Mysore, Canara and Malabar*, vol. II, pp. 554-5.
38. Board Collections, From D. Hill, Secretary to Government, Revenue Department to the President and Member of Board of Revenue, 18 March 1823, vol. 862, IOR/F/4/866/22785, IOL; IOR/Z/F/4/40/C82, 1813-18, IOL, London.

CHAPTER 9

Conclusions and Observations

At the very outset, it needs to be emphasized that the west European colonizers like the Portuguese and English came first to the western or Malabar Coast of the Indian subcontinent. They established trade settlements, factories and forts in Surat, Goa, Cananore, Tellicherry, Calicut, Cochin and Anjengo, mostly with the permission of the local rajas or princes. Apart from Goa, where the Portuguese held a small territory, the Europeans had just factories and forts in other places, especially in the Malabar region. They were never in a position to conquer or penetrate deeper into the interior lands in Malabar especially from the coast.

Right from the time the Portuguese set their foot on the Malabar soil, the local kings or Rajas, along with their Nair militia and their Muslim seamen and warriors, who were mostly converts or descendants of converts from the local castes, with some admixture of Arab blood, had waged a relentless struggle against European penetration into Malabar. Even in Goa and Surat, the Europeans were restricted to their factories and settlements by the Mughal, Adil Shahi and Maratha forces. We have seen that the Kunjali Marakkars of Malabar who were at the service of the Samutiri, popularly known as or Zamorin of Calicut were a shining example of Malabari resistance to European penetration. Further north, the Kolatiri king and his Nair chieftains and militia, as well as the Ali Rajas of Cananore played a significant role in containing European penetration into Malabar, till the advent of the Mysore Sultans, which paved the way for the English army to invade Malabar from the east and subjugate it. A

Frenchman, who had visited Malabar at that time considered the Kolatiri ruler as more powerful than the Samutiri.[1]

Unlike in the Malabar Coast, where European penetration and colonization was restricted to their trading posts and forts by the Nair militia and the Moors, in the eastern coast of India, right from the Cholamandalam coast to Bengal, the resistance posed by Tamilians, Telugus and Bengalis were not vigorous enough to restrict the Europeans to their factories and forts. The eastern territories were actually ruled by descendants of the Mughals in Bengal, the Nizam of Hyderabad in the Deccan and the Nawab of Arcot in Tamil Nadu. The English outwitted all the European powers including the French and brought the territories on the eastern side of India under their control first through treaties and alliances with the local powers as well as through outright conquests.

The last power who stood on their way to subjugate the rest of south India was the Mysore Sultans and some *poligars* in southern Tamil Nadu. This they did in the late eighteenth century, by allying with the Travancore Raja and the Nawab of Arcot and doing away with the Mysore Sultans and the *poligars* once and for all. The kings or chieftains of Kolathunad, or north Malabar had no other alternative, but to rally behind the English. When they did not, they were suppressed and the rebels were transported even as far as Penang. The Kolatiri and Ali Rajas' power in north Malabar was curtailed and they were pensioned off. The entire region from the Zamorin's territory in the south up to south Canara in the north were annexed and made part of the Madras Presidency of British India in 1792.

In the earlier pages, we have traced the origin and early history of Cananore and north Malabar. During the early Chera period, the north Malabar region was ruled by chieftains like Nannan. They were not subject to the Chera kings, which meant that they were independent rulers of *Damiriké* or Tamilakam, as noted by Ptolemy and the Peutinger tables. Nannan's name has been mentioned in the ancient Sangam literature. Cananore which was mentioned as Naura in

Ptolemy's work seems to have been part of Nannan's chiefdom.

During the second Chera period, the preceding chieftains gave way to the rise of the Mushika dynasty. There is no clear evidence that this dynasty, which has been described extensively in the Sanskrit work of Atula, the court poet of the Mushikas, were subject to the Chera Perumals of south and central Malabar. However, there were some interactions between the Mushikas and Cheras. But there is no conclusive evidence that the Mushikas were in any way tributary to the Cheras. There is also no indication of the existence of Cananore in Atula's work. But the Arab traveller al-Idrisi who was on the Malabar Coast in the eleventh century seems to have mentioned the town of Cananore as Jirbattan.

In the subsequent thirteenth or fourteenth century, the Mushikas in their turn seems to have given way to the Kolatiri kings in northern Malabar. There is also no conclusive evidence to prove that the Kolatiri kings were subject to the Chera kings or even the Zamorins of Calicut. They seem to have been always independent rulers though there might have been interactions and even marital relationship with the neighbouring kingdoms.

It was the Kolatiris, who allowed Europeans to settle in their country for trade purposes. The Kolatiri like the other Malabar rulers down south took care to restrict the Europeans to their forts and trading posts. The latter were never allowed to expand in the interior lands. For this purpose, the Kolatiris relied on their Nair militia as well as the Muslim seafarers. The latter also indulged in trade with foreign countries on behalf of the Kolatiri and took charge of the finances of the country. Thus arose the Mamales of Cananore, the prime trading family of Cananore, which for a long time served as the seat of the Kolatiri kingdom.

These Mamales in later days were succeeded by the Ali Raja, who was given the responsibility of lording over the coastal strip of Cananore as well as some islands off the Malabar Coast. As they were the prime traders as well as seafarers, the Europeans very soon struck a relationship with them for purposes of trade. But in the course of time, especially when the Dutch sold the Fort St. Angelo to Ali Raja, and with the advent of the Mysore Sultan into Malabar, they became extremely powerful that they began to challenge the supremacy of the Kolatiri king, their mentor.

Ali Rajas seem to have originated during the thirteenth century or before from Cananore. Actually, Ibn Battuta had noted in his accounts of the fourteenth century that a prince of Cananore or Jurkannan/Jurfattan had converted to Islam. Ali Rajas might be the descendants of this Prince. It was this conversion which was later confounded with the conversion of Cheraman Perumal, which never happened. Tradition also holds that a Kolatiri princess married a Moor, which gave rise to the Ali Raja. The Kolatiri princess actually belonged to the family of Arrigeru Calanngaravittil of Darmadam, as noted by the minister of the Ali Raja in one of his letters. Thus, the Ali Rajas were related to the Kolatiri king, unlike the Kunjali Marakkars of the Zamorin. The latter were probably children of the Chinese seamen and local women, who were Islamized, giving rise to a new breed of off-springs known by the name *tchini betchengan* (sons of Chinese, or Chinese boys). It was believed that this new hybrid race were feared and respected all over the coast, to the extent that the pirates would not attack any of their vessels at Calicut.[2] Traces of Chinese connection with the local populations are visible even today in the physical appearance of many Malayalis, both Hindu and Muslim in coastal Malabar.

Arrigeru Calanngaravittil seems to have given rise to what came to be known as the Arakkal house of Cananore. Actually, Arakkal is just a shortened form of Arrigeru Calanngaravittil 'Arri' + 'Cal' or 'Arr + Cal', which in course of time became Arakkal. Arakkal house continued to follow the matrilineal system of Hindu succession, in memory of their Nair ancestors who converted to Islam. This matrilineal succession was unheard of in other Muslim countries and was contradictory to the Shariat rules. Sanction for this practice seems to have come from the Caliph himself. This once again demonstrates that the Arakkal dynasty was related to the Kolatiris since ancient times.

Besides, the Arakkal rulers, both males and females, were called as Ali Rajas. But according to the documents discovered in French archives, a French officer in his report has noted, this was because the Ali Rajas originally belonged to the sect of Ali. In the light of this findings, the claims by historians that Ali was a corruption of *azhi* (sea) or *alai* (waves) is erroneous

As time went by, the rift between the Arakkal House and the Kolatiris kept widening. In this tussle for power, Ali Raja made use of the northern Canarese chiefs to counter the Kolatiris. He actually invited them into Malabar to cut Kolatiri to size. Later, when Mysore, came under the control of Hyder Ali and Tipu Sultan, Ali Raja invited them once again into Malabar, which lead very much to the weakening of the Zamorin and the Kolatiri. But before Ali Raja could take full advantage of the situation, the English in pursuit of the Mysore Sultans penetrated Malabar, which put an end to the dominance of the Malabar kings and princes, including the Ali Rajas in north Malabar. They were pensioned off and their domains annexed and made part of the Madras Presidency of British India. Thus, Malabar was conquered from the eastern lands, and never from the western coast.

Today, the descendants of Arakkal and Chirakkal (Kolatiri) are still there in Cannanore and the region surrounding it. But they are no more a power to be reckoned with. Some of their family members have even taken to government jobs. The Arakkal palace is in ruins, while the family itself lives in modern constructions in Cananore or in Tellicherry. There is a warehouse sort of building of the olden days which has been converted into a museum called Arakkal Museum, where you find especially the *Tamburatti Vilakku*, given by Chirakkal to Arakkal as well as the stately chair meant for Cheraman Perumal. However, the Arakkal mosque built near the dilapidated palace is still erect and well maintained. Till date, no steps have been taken for the restoration or renovation of the palace. However, the Chirakkal palace is still evident, shorn of its former pomp and splendour, in which some descendants of Kolatiri live today.

Today, we find the Muslims in great numbers in north Malabar, especially in urban areas like Tellicherry and Cannanore. The old Juma Masjid in Cananore has been renovated. It is found in Cananore city, which is the old area where the Arakkal wielded power since sixteenth century, where we find a high concentration of Muslims even today.

Since the annexation of north Malabar by the English in 1792, it was a district of the Madras Presidency of British India known as the Malabar district. In August 1947, when India became independent, it continued to be part of Madras Province. But in 1956, when the Indian States were reorganized on a linguistic basis, the Malabar district parted company with Madras and became part of the new Kerala State.

NOTES

1. M. Dellon, *Relations d'un voyage des Indes Orientales*, Tome I (French), Paris, MDCLXXXV, pp. 134-5.
2. R.H. Major, *India in the 15th Century, Abd er Razzak*, London, MDCCCLVII, p. 17.

Bibliography

ARCHIVES

Archives des Missions étrangeres, Paris.
India Office Library and Records, London.
National Archives of India, New Delhi.
Tamil Nadu State Archives, Chennai.
Maharashtra State Archives, Mumbai.

LIBRARIES

Bibliothèque Nationale de France, Paris.
Calicut University Library, Calicut.
Centre d'Etudes de l'Inde, Paris.
Connemara Library, Chennai.
Madras University Library, Chennai.
Royal Asiatic Society, Mumbai.
Bombay University Library, Mumbai.
Nehru Memorial Museum & Library (currently The Prime Ministers Museum and Library Society), New Delhi.

BOOKS

Ahmad, Maqbul, S., *India and the Neighbouring Territories in the Kitab Nuzhat Al Mushtaq Fikhtiraq al-Afaq of al-Sharif-al-Idrisi*, Leiden, 1960.

——, *An Account of India and China by Sulayman-al-Tajir et al.* compiled in AD 851, Shimla, 1989.

Aitchison, C.U., *A Collection of Treatise, Engagements and Sanads*, vol. X, Mysore, 1973.

Aiya, Nagam V., *The Travancore State Manual I*, Trivandrum, 1906.

Alexander, P.C., *The Dutch in Malabar*, Annamalai, 1946.

Ali Sheikh, B., *British Relations with Haider Ali*, Mysore, 1963.

Ames, Glenn, J., *The Journal of the First Voyage of Vasco da Gama to India, 1497-1499*, Leiden, 2009.

Antony, Cyril (ed.), *Gazetteer of India: Union Territory of Pondicherry*, vol. I, Pondicherry, 1982.

Aquarone, J.B (tr.), *D Joao De Castro, Gouverneur et Vice Roi des Indes Orientales (1500-1548)*, 2 vols., Paris, 1968.

Arasaratnam, S., *Islamic Merchant Communities of the Indian Sub-continent in South East Asia*, Kuala Lumpur, 1989.

——, *Maritime India in the Seventeenth Century*, Delhi, 1994.

Arnold, T.W., *The Preaching of Islam*, London, 1935; Lahore, 1961.

Astley, Thomas (compilor), *A New General Collection of Voyages and Travels Consisting of the Most Esteemed Relations Which have been hitherto Published in Many Languages Europe, Asia, Africa and America*, vol. I, London, MDCCXLV.

——, *A New General Collection of Voyages and Travels in Europe, Asia, Africa and America*, vol. IV, London, 1968.

Aiyyar, Krishna K.V., *The Zamorins of Calicut*, Calicut, 1938.

——, *A History of Kerala*, Coimbatore, 1965.

Badger, George Perry (ed.), John Winter Jones (tr.), *The Travels of Ludovico Di Varthema in Egypt, Syria, Arabia Deserta and Arabia Felix in Peris, India and Ethiopia: AD 1503 to 1508*, London, MDCCCLXIII.

Bahauddin, K.M., *Kerala Muslims: The Long Struggle*, Trivandrum, 1992.

Balakrishnan, K., *Kannur Fort*, Kottayam, 2008.

Baldaeus, Philip, *A True and Exact Description of the Most Celebrated East India Coasts of Malabar and Coromandel and also of the Isle of Ceylon, Translated from the High Dutch Printed at Amsterdam*, 1672; London, 1703; New Delhi, 1996.

Barbosa, Duarte, *A Description of the Coasts of East Africa and Malabar*, tr. Henry E.J. Stanley, London, 1767.

——, *The Book of Duarte Barbosa*, tr. M.L. Dames. 2 vols., London , 1921.

Barros , Joao de, *Decadas de Asia*, vol. I, Lisboa, 1778.

Bartolomeo, Paolia Da San, *A Voyage to the East Indies*, London, tr. William Johnston, 1800.

——, *Voyages aux Indes Orientales*, vol. I, Paris, 1808.

Beauchamp, Henry, K. (tr. and ed.), *Hindu Manners and Ceremonies by Abbe J.A. Dubois*, Oxford, 1906.

Beaumont de Saunier, *Voyage de Innigo de Biervillas Portugais, A la cote de Malabar, Goa, Batavia et autres lieux des Indes Orientales*, Paris, MDCCCXXXVI.

Biddulph, John, *The Pirates of Malabar and an English Woman in India Two Hundred Years Ago*, London, 1907.

Biervillas de Innigo, *A la cote de Malabar, Goa, Batavia et autres lieux des Indes Orientales*, Premier partie, Paris, MDCCCXXXVI.

Birch, Gray de Walter (tr.), *The Commentaries of the Great Afonso D'Alboquerque*, London, MDCCCLXXVII; London, 1875; London, MDCCC.LXXX.

Birdwood, George, *Report on the Old Records of the India Office*, Calcutta, 1891.

Bouchon, Genevieve, *Les Musalmans de Kerala à l'époque de la découverte Portugaise*, Genève, 1973.

——, *Mamale de Cananor—Un adversaire de l'Inde Portugaise (1507-1528)*, Paris, 1975.

——, *L'Asie du Sud à l'époque des Grand Decouvertes*, London, 1987.

——, *Regent of the Sea, Cannanore's Response to the Portuguese Expansion*, tr. from French by Louis Shackley, Delhi, 1988.

——, *Albuquerque. Le Lion des Mers d'Asie*, Paris, 1992.

Bowring, Levin, *Haider Ali and Tipu Sultan and the Struggle with the Mussalman Powers of the South*, Oxford, 1893.

Boxer, C.R., *The Portuguese Seaborne Empire, 1415-1815*, London.

Briggs, John (tr.), *History of the Rise of Mahomedan Power in India till the year* AD *1612*, from the original Persian of Mahomed Kasim Ferishta, London, 1829.

Brittlebank, Kate, *Tipu Sultan's Search for Legitimacy*, Delhi, 1997.

Brown, Truedell, S. *Onesicritus: A Study in Hellenistic Historiography*, Berkeley, 1949.

Bruce, John, *Plans for the Government and Trade of Great Britain in the East Indies*, London, 1813.

——, *Annals of the Honourable East India Company*, 3 vols., London, 1810.

Buchanan, Francis, *A Journey from Madras through the Countries of Mysore, Canara and Malabar*, 3 vols., Madras, (London, 1807).

Burnell, A.C. (ed.), *The Voyage of John Huygen Van Lischoten to the East Indies*, vol. I, London, 1885.

Caldwell, Bishop R., *A History of Tinnevelly*, New Delhi, 1982 (reprint).

Caldwell, Revd. Robert, *A Comparative Grammar of the Dravidian or South Indian Family of Languages*, New Delhi, 1987 (reprint).

Caminatayer, U. Ve. (ed.), *Patirruppattu*, Madras, 1980.

Camoens, *His Life and His Lusiads: A Commentary*, 2 vols, London, 1881.

Carré, Abbé, *The Travels of The Abbé Carré in India and the North East 1672-1674*, vol. I, Madras, 1990; vol. 1, London, 1947; 2 vols., New Delhi, 1990.

Cassou, Jean, *La Decouverte du Nouveau Monde Vue d ensemble*, Paris, 1966.

Castanheda, Fernao Lopes de, *The First Book of the Historie of the Discoverie and the conquest of the East Indias enterprised by the Portingales*, tr. into English by Nicolas Lichefield, London, 1582.

Cekkilar, *Periya Puranam*, Madras, 1884.

Courtier, John Le, *Letter Chiefly from India Containing an Account of the Military Transactions of the Coast of Malabar During the late War Together with a Short Description of the Religion, Manners and Customs of the Inhabitants of Hindustan*, London, 1790.

Dale, Stephen, *Islamic Society in South Asian Frontier: The Mappillas of Malabar, 1498-1922*, Oxford, 1967.

D' Albuquerque, Alfonso, *Commentaries*, tr. & ed. Walter de Grey Birch, 4 vols., London, 1875-1884.

Dames, M.L. (tr. & ed.), *Book of Duarte Barbosa*, 2 vols., London, 1918-21, 1967, 1989 (reprint).

Danver, F.C., *Report to the Secretary for India in Council on the Portuguese Records relating to the East India contained in the Archivo Da Terre Do Tombo and the Public Libraries at Lisboa and Erora*, London, 1891.

——, *Portuguese in India*, 2 vols., London, 1894.

——, *Report on the Portuguese Records Relating to the East Indies*, New Delhi, 1991 (first published in 1892).

Das, A. Gupta, *Malabar in Asian Trade, 1740-1800*, London, 1914.

Day, Francis, *The Land of Perumals*, Madras, 1863.

De Castro, Xavier (tr.), *Voyage de Pyrard de Laval aux Indes Orientales (1601-1611)*, Paris, 1998.

Dellon, *Nouvelle Relation d'un voyage fait aux Indes Orientales*, Amsterdam, MDCXCIX.

——, *Relation d'un Voyage des Indes Orientales*, Tome I, Paris, MDCLXXXV.

Dikshitar, Ramachandra, *Studies in Tamil Literature and History*, Madras, 1936.

Divakaran, Kattakada, *Kerala Sancharam Keralathe Samagrahamayi Ariyaan*, Trivandrum, 2018.

Dodwell and J.F. Price (trs.), *The Private Diary of Ananda Ranga Pillai, 1736-1761*, Madras, 1904-1908.

Dowson, John and Elliot (eds.), *The History of India as told by its own Historians. The Mohammedan Period*, 8 vols., London, 1867.

Du Bois, J.P.I., *Vies des Gouverneurs Généraux avec l'abrégé de l'histoire des Établissements hollandais aux Indes Orientales*, La Haye, 1763.

Dunn, E. Ross, *The Adventures of Ibn Battuta, a Muslim Traveller of 14th Century*, California, 1986.

Du Val (ed.), *Voyage de Francis Pyrard de Laval, trois parties*, Paris, 1679.

Duperron, Anquetil, *Voyage en Inde, 1754-1763*, Paris, 1997.

Duyvendak, J.J.L., *The True Dates of the Chinese Maritime Expeditions in the Early 15th Century*, vol. XXXIV, Leiden, 1939.

——, *Ma Huan Re Examined*, Amsterdam, 1933.

Edakkad, Sathyan, *Vasco da Gama and the Unknown Facts of History*, Ramanattukara, 2010.

Elayavoor, Vanidas, *Lore and Legends of North Malabar*, tr. Ashwin Kumar, Kottayam, 1996.

Fawcett, Charles, *The English Factories in India 1670-1677*, vol. I, Oxford, 1936 (new series).

——, *The English Factories in India, Bombay, Surat and Malabar Coast*, vol. III, London, 1954.

Ferrand, Gabriel, *Les Classiques de L'Orient Voyage du Marchand Arabe Sulayman en Inde et en Chine Rédigé en 851 suivi de Remarques par Abu Zayd Hassan (vers 916)*, Traduit de l'Arabe, Paris, 1922.

Forbes, James, *Oriental Memories*, vol. I & II, London, 1813.

Forrest, Denys, *Tiger of Mysore*, London, 1970.

Foster, William, *Early Travels in India, 1583-1619*, New Delhi, 1985.

Francesco, Cardim Antonio, *Relation de la Province du Japon ecrite en Portugais*, Paris, MDCXLVI.

Frederick, Charles Denvers, *The Portuguese in India being a History of the Rise and Decline of their Eastern Empire*, vol. 1, London.

Fryer, John, *A New Account of East Indies and Persia being Nine Years' Travels, 1672-1681*, vol. I, London, 1909; New York, 1967.

Gabriel, Theodore, *Hindu-Muslim Relations in North Malabar, 1498-1947*, New York, 1996.

Galletti, A. (tr. & ed.), *The Dutch in Malabar*, Madras, 1911.

Ganesh, K.N., *Keralathinte Innalekal*, Thiruvananathapuram, 1996.

Gangadharan, M., *Mappila Padanangal*, Calicut, 2007.

Goulard, Simon (tr.), *Histoire de Portugal contenant des entreprises, Navigations et gestes mémorables des Portugallois, tant en la conquête des Indes Orientales par eux découvertes , qu' ès guerres d' Afrique et autre exploits depuis l'an 1496 sous Emmanuel I, Jean III et Sébastien I.* Paris, 1587.

Gray, Albert (tr.), *The Voyage of Francis Pyrard of Laval*, 3 vols., London, 1887-1890.

Grosse, John Henry, *A Voyage to East Indies*, London, 1757.

——, *Voyages aux Indes Orientales* (tr. G. Hernandez), London, 1758.

Grunlee, William Brooks (ed. & tr.), *The Voyage of Pedro Alvares Cabral to Brazil and India*, London, 1938.

Gundert, H. (ed.), *Keralolpatti*, Mangalore, 1843; Trivandrum, 1961.

—— (ed.), *Kerala Parama or History of Malabar from AD 1498 to AD 1631*, Mangalore, 1868.

——, *A Malayalam and English Dictionary*, Germany, 1970.

Gupta, Ashin Das, *Malabar in Asian Trade, 1740-1800*, London , 1914.

——, *Indian Merchants in the Age of Partnership, c. 1500-1800, The World of the Indian Ocean Merchant 1500-1800.* Collected essays of Ashin Das Gupta, ed. Uma Das Gupta, New Delhi, 2001.

Gurukkal, Rajan and Raghava Varier, *Cultural History of Kerala*, Thiruvananthapuram, 1999.

Guyon, Abbé, *Histoire des Indes Orientales Anciennes er Modernes*, 3 vols., Paris, 1699.

Hamilton, Alexander, *A New Account of East Indies*, Edinburgh, MDCCXXVII, New York, 2001.

Hasan, Mohibbul, *History of Tipu Sultan*, Calcutta, 1951.

Hirth, F. and Rockhill, W.W. (tr.), *Chou-fan-chi* by Chau-Ju-Kua, St. Petersburg, 1911.

Hunter, W.W., *A History of British India*, London, 1899.

Huntingford, G.W.B. (tr. & ed.), *The Periplus of the Erythrean Sea*, London, 1980.

Husain, Mahdi, *The Rehla of Ibn Battuta*, Baroda, 1976.

Hourani, G.F., *Arab Seafaring in the Indian Ocean in the Ancient and Medieval Times*, Princeton, 1951.

Hugau, Claude, *Le Voyage Extraordinaire d'un capitaine de dragons chez Hyder Ali Khan, 1769-1772*, Paris, 2001.

Innes, C.A. and Evans, F.B., *Malabar Gazetter*, 2 vols., Trivandrum, 1997.

Iyengar, P.T. Srinivasan, *History of the Tamils from the Earliest Times to 600 AD*, Madras, 1989.

Iyer, Anantha, Krishna, L.K. *The Cochin Tribes and Castes*, 2 vols., Madras,1912.

Iyer, K.V. Subramanya, *Historical Sketches of Ancient Deccan*, Madras, 1917, 1909.

Jaubert, A. (tr.), *La Géographie d'Edrissi*, II, Amsterdam, 1960.

Jayne, K.G., *Vasco Da Gama and his Successors, 1460-1580*, London, 1910.

Johnston, William (tr.), *Bartalomeo, Fra Paolina, A Voyage to the East Indies*, London, 1800.

Jones,Winter John, *The Travels of Ludovico di Varthema in Egypt, Syria, Arabia Deserta and Arab Felix in Persia, India and Ethiopia*

AD 1503-1508, London, MDCCCLXIII, New York, 1963; New Delhi, 1997.

Kail, O.C., *The Dutch in India*, New Delhi, 1899.

Khurdadbeh, Ibn, *Arabic Classical Accounts of India and China*, tr. from original Arabic with commentaries by S. Maqbul Ahmad, Shimla, 1989.

Koumareeshwari, S. (ed.), *Agananuru, Purananuru, Sanga Ilakkiyam*, vol. 3, Chennai, 2012.

Koya, S.M. Mohamed, *Mappilas of Malabar*, Calicut, 1983.

Krishnamachariar, M., *History of Classical Sanskrit Literature*, Delhi, 1970.

Kumaran, M.P., *Kolathupazhama*, Thrisur, 1998.

Kunjan Pillai, P.N. Elamkulam, *Studies in Kerala History*, Kottayam, 1970.

Kunju, A.P. Ibrahim, *Medieval Kerala History*, Trivandrum, 1975.

——, *Mappila Muslims of Kerala, Their History and Culture*, Trivandrum, 1989.

Kurup, K.K.N., *The Ali Raja's of Cannanore*, Trivandrum, 1975.

——, *Aspects of Kerala History and Culture*, Trivandrum, 1977.

——, *Kannurile Ali Raja Vamsham*, Calicut, 2008.

Kurup, K.K.N. and E. Ismail, *The Saga of Iringal*, Vatakara, 2011.

Latourette, Kenneth, *The History of the Expansion, The History of the Expansion of Christianity*, vol. III, New York, 1971.

Launay, Adrien, *Histoire des Missions de l' Inde: Pondichèry, Maissour, Coimbatore*, vol. I, Paris, 1898.

Levathes, Louise, *Les Navigateurs de l'empire Celeste La flotte Imperial du Dragon 1405-1433* (tr.), Isabelle Leymaris, New York, 1994.

Lee, Rev. B.D., Samuel, *Ibn Battuta, The Travels of Ibn Battuta*, translated from the abridged Arabic manuscipt copies preserved in the Public Library of Cambridge with notes and illustrations of the History, Geography, Botany, Antiquities occurring throughout the work, London, 1829.

Legoux de Flaix, *Essai historique, géographique et politique d'Indostan*, vol. 1, Paris, 1807.

Logan, William, *Malabar Manual*, Madras, 1951; New Delhi, 1989.

—— (ed.), *A collection of Treaties Engagements and Other Papers of Importance Relating to British Affairs in Malabar*, vol. III, Madras, 1891.

Maclean, *Manual of the Administration of the Madras Presidency*, Madras, 1938.

Maffei, Jean Pierre, *L'Histoire des Indes Orientales et Occidentales*, Paris, 1665.

Ma, Huan, *Ying Yai Sheng Ian* (*The Overall Survey of the Ocean Shores*, Translated from Chinese text edited by Feng Ch'eng-Chun with Introduction, Notes and Appendices by J.V.G Mills, Thailand, 1971.

Maistre, de la Tour, *The History of Hyder Shah and Hyder Ali Khan Bahadur and of his son Tipoo Sultan*, London, 1855.

Major, R.H. (ed.), *India in the Fifteeen Century being a Collection of Narratives of Voyages to India in the Century Preceding the Portuguese Discovery of the Cape of Good Hope from Latin, Russian and Italian Sources*, London, MDCCCLVII.

Majumdar, R.C., *The Classical Accounts of India*, Calcutta, 1968.

Martineau, A., *Les Origines de Mahe*, Paris, 1917.

——, *Bussy et linde Francaise, 1720-1785*, Paris, 1935.

Mateer, Samuel, *Land of Charity*, London, 1871.

——, *Native Life in Travancore*, London, 1883.

Mathew, K.S., *Portuguese Trade with India in the 16th Century*, Delhi, 1983.

—— (ed.), *Indian Ocean and Cultural Interaction* (AD *1400-1800)*, Pondicherry, 1996.

——, *Maritime Malabar and the Europeans*, Kolkata, 2003.

Malgonkar, Manohar, *Kanhoji Angrey*, Bombay, 1959.

Manavikrama, Kovilakatt, *Zamorin of Calicut*, *Kerala Caritram*, Kottakal, 1924.

Mathru, P.R.G., *The Mappila Fisherfolk of Kerala*, Trivandrum, 1977.

Mayer, C. Andrian, *Land and Society in Malabar*, Oxford, 1952.

McCrindle, J.W. (ed.), *The Commerce and Navigation of the Erythraen Sea*, London, 1870.

——, *Ancient India as described by Megasthenes and Arrian*, Delhi, 1926.

——, *Ancient India as described by Ptolemy*, New Delhi, 1884.

Menon, Achyuta Chelnat, *Ballads of North Malabar (Vatakkan Paatukal)*, *Madras*, 1935.

Menon, C. Kunnirama, *The Literature of Ballad and Song in North Malabar*, Madras, 1913.

Menon, Padmanabha, *History of Kerala*, vol. I, Ernakulam, 1924.

——, *History of Kerala written in the form of notes on Visscher's letters from Malabar*, Madras, 1989.

Menon, Shungoony, *A History of Travancore*, Delhi, 1878, 1984.

Menon, A. Sreedhara, *Kerala District Gazetters*, Trivandrum, 1962.

——, *A Survey of Kerala History*, Kottayam, 1967; Madras, 1984.

Miller, E. Roland, *Mappila Muslims of Kerala: A Study in Islamic Trends*, Madras, 1976.

Minorsky, V., (tr.), *Hudud al-Alam, 'regions of the world', a Persian Geography*, AD *372*-AD *982*, London, 1970.

—— (tr.), *Sharaf al-Zaman Tahir Marvazhi: On China, the Turks and India*, London, 1942.

Mohammad, P.A. Saythu, *Kerala Muslim Charithram*, Kozhikode, 1951.

More, J.B.P., *Political Evolution of Muslims in Tamilnadu and Madras, 1930-1947*, Hyderabad, 1997.

——, *Freedom Movement in French India, The Mahé Revolt of 1948*, Tellicherry, 2001.

——, *Origin and Early History of the Muslims of Keralam* AD *700*-AD *1600*, Calicut, 2011.

——, *From Arikamedu to the Foundation of Modern Pondicherry*, Madras, 2014.

—— (ed.), *Offerings to the Muslim Warriors of Malabar*, Chennai, 2015.

More, Leena, *English East India Company and the Local Rulers in Kerala: A Case Study of Attingal and Travancore*, Tellicherry, 2003.

Morelet, Arthur (tr.), *Journal du Voyage de Vasco da Gama*, Lyon, 1864.

Muthathu, Vaikathy Pachu, *Thiruvithamkur Charitram*, Cochin, 1867.

Nagaswamy, R., *Mirror of Tamil and Sanskrit*, Chennai, 2012.

Nainar, M.H., *Arab Geographer's Knowledge of Southern India*, Madras, 1942.

Nair, C. Gopalan, *Wynad its Peoples and Traditions*, Madras, 1911.

Nair, P.K. Parameswaran, *History of Malayalam Literature*, New Delhi, 1967.

Nambiar, O.K., *An Illustrated Maritime History of the Indian Ocean*, New Delhi, 1992.

——, *Our Seafaring in the Indian Ocean*, Bangalore, 1975.

Nambutiri, N.M., *Kerala Samskaram Akavum Puravum*, University of Calicut, 2002.

Narayanan, M.G.S., *Perumals of Kerala: Political and Social Conditions of Kerala under the Cera Perumals of Makotai (*AD *800-1124)*, Calicut, 1996.

——, *Aspects of Aryanizatiion in Kerala*, Trivandrum, 1973.

——, *Re-Interpretations in South India History*, Trivandrum, 1977.

——, *Kozhikodu Charithrathill Ninnu Chila Edukal* (Malayalam), Kozhikode, 2011.

——, *Kozhikodinde Katha*, Ottapalam, 2001.

Nayar, C. Gopalan, *Malayalatile Mappilamar* (Malayalam), Mangalore, 1917.

Neill, Stephen, *A History of Christianity in India, The Beginnings to AD 1707*, Cambridge, 1984.

Nightingale, Pamela, *Trade and Empire in Western India, 1784-1806*, Cambridge, 1970.

Nilakantan, M.M., *Adi-Keralam*, Voyages (legendary history of Kerala), Calicut, 1933.

Nieuhoff, John, *A Collection of Voyages and Trades*, vol. II, London, MDCCIV.

Oaten, E.F., *European Travellers in India*, Madras, 1991.

Osorivis, Jerosme, *Histoire de Portugal Contenant Les Enterprises, Navigations and Gestes Memorables des Portugallois Tant En La Conquete des Indes Orientales*, Paris, MDLXXXVII.

Panikkar, K.M., *Malabar and the Portuguese*, Bombay, 1929.

Parry, J.J., *Trade and Dominions: The European Overseas Empire in the 18th Century*, London, 1977.

Pearson, M.N., *The Portuguese in India*, Cambridge University, Bombay, 1987.

——, *The New Cambridge History of India*, vol. I, Cambridge, 1981.

Pelliot, Paul and A.C. Moule, *Marco Polo (Description of the World)*, vol. I, London, MCMXXXVIII.

——, *Marco Polo, Le Divsement du Monde, Les Livres des Merveilles*, Paris, 1996.

Philips, *An Account of the Religion, Manners and Learning of the People of Malabar in the East Indies*, London, 1717.

Pillai, P.N. Kunjan, Elamkulam, *Studies in Kerala History*, Kottayam, 1970.

Pillai, K.N. Sivaraja, *Chronology of the Early Tamils based on the Synchronic Tables of their Kings, Chieftains and the Poets Appearing in the Sangam* Literature, Madras, 1932.

Pillai, T.K. Velu, *A History of Travancore*, Trivandrum, 1935.

Pirès, Tomé, *The Suma Oriental, 1512-1515* (tr. from Portuguese by Armanda Cortesao), 2 vols., Nendeln, 1944, 1967; New Delhi, 1990 (reprint).

Poonen, T.I., *Dutch Beginning in India Proper-1580-1615*, Madras, 1933.

——, *Dutch Hegemony in Malabar and its Collapse AD 1663-1795*, Trivandrum, 1978.

Prasad, Ishwari, *India in the Eighteenth Century*, Allahabad, 1973.

Ramunny, Murkot, *Ezhimala: The Abode of the Naval Academy*, New Delhi, 1993.

Raynal, Abbé, *A Philosophical and Political History of the Settlement and Trade of the Europeans in the East and West Indies*, vol. II, London, 1783.

Rawlinson, H.G., *Intercourse between India and the Western World*, Cambridge, 1916.

Rehman, Mujeebu and K.S. Madhavan (eds.), *Explorations in South Indian History*, Kottayam, 2014.

Ravenstein, E.G. (tr. & ed.), *A Journal of the First Voyage of Vasco da Gama, 1497-1499*, London, 1898.

Reinaud, M., *Relation Des Voyages fait par les Arabes et Les Persans dans L'Inde et l'Chine*, Tome I et Tome II, Paris, 1845.

Renaudot, E., *Ancient Accounts of India and China by Two Muhammadan Travelers in the 9th Century* AD, London, 1733.

Rheede, Henrik Adriaan van, *Dutch Records*, Madras, 1911.

Rheede, Henrik, Adriaan van, *Memoire written in the year* AD *1677*, Madras, 1911.

Robson, Iliff (tr.), *History of Alexander and India*, Books I-IV in 2 vols., Cambridge, Harward, 1929, 1946, 1954, 1961, 1967.

——, Books V-VII, in 2 vols., Cambridge Massachusettes, 1933, 1949, 1958, 1966.

Rowlandson, Lieut M.J. (tr.), *Tohfut-ul-Mujahideen*, an Historical Work in Arabic language by Sheikh Zain-ud-Din, London, MDCCCXXXIII.

Saint-Barthélémy, Paulin de, *Voyage aux Indes Orientales*, Trois, vols., Paris, 1808.

Saldanha, S.N., *The Captivity of Canara Christians under Tipu in 1784*, Mangalore, 1933.

Sastri, Nilakanta, *The Colas*, Madras, 1975 (reprint).

——, *A History of South India*, Madras, 1966.

Saussure, de Léopold, 'Commentaire des instructions Nautiques de Ibn Majid et Suleyman al-Mahri' in Gabriel Ferrand (ed.), *Introduction à l'Astronomie Nautique Arabe*, Paris, 1928.

Sayyid Mohamed, P.A., *Caritra Keralam*, Kottayam, 1957.

Schoff, W.H. (ed. & tr.), *The Periplus of the Erythrean Sea*, New York, 1912.

Sekhar, A.C., *Evolution of Malayalam*, Poona, 1953.

Sen, Surendranath, *Indian Travels of Thevenot and Careri*, New Delhi, 1948.

Sen, S.P., *The French in India*, Delhi, 1971.

Sewell, Robert, *A Sketch of the Dynasties of Southern India*, Madras, 1883.

——, *The Antiquarian Remains in The Presidency of Malabar*, vol. I, Madras, 1882; vol. II, Madras, 1884.
——, *Archaeological Survey of Southern India*, vol. 2, Madras, 1882.
——, *A Forgotten Empire*, New Delhi, 1962.
Sewell, Robert and S.K. Iyengar, *The Historical Inscriptions of Southern India*, Madras, 1932.
Shekar, A.C., *Evolution of Malayalam*, Poona, 1953.
Shokoohy, Mehrdad, *Muslim Architectures of South India: The Sultanate of Ma' bar and the Traditions of the Maritime Settlers on the Malabar and Coromandel Coast*, Tamil Nadu, Kerala and Goa, UK, 2003.
Spies, Otto, *An Arab Account of India in the 14th Century* being a Translation of the Chapters on India from Al Qalqashandi's Subh-ul-A'sha, Delhi, 1935.
Sridharan, M.P., *Papers on French Colonial Rule in India*, Calicut, 1997.
Stanley, J. Henry, (tr.), *The Three Voyages of Vasco Da Gama and his Viceroyalty* (from the Lendas da India of Gaspar Correa), New York, 1963.
——, *A Description of the Coasts of East Africa and Malabar in the beginning of the 16th Century by Duarte Barbosa*, translated from an early Spanish Manuscript in the Barcelona Library with notes and preface.
Subrahmanyam, Sanjay, *The Career and Legend of Vasco da Gama*, Cambridge, 1997; Delhi 1998.
Suryadinata, Leo (ed.), *Admiral Zheng He and South East Asia*, Singapore, 2005.
Tan Ta Sen, *Cheng Ho and Islam in South East Asia*, Singapore, 2009.
Tavernier, Jean Baptiste, *Les Six voyage de Jean Baptiste Tavernir Ecuyer Baron d' Aubonne en Turque en Perse et aux Indes*, Paris, 1843.
Temple, R.C. (ed.), *The Travels of Peter Mundy, 1634-1637*, London, 1919.
Thevenot, *Voyages de M. Thevenot Contenant La Relation de l'Indostan des Nouveaux. Mongols et des autre peuples et paye des Indes*, Paris, MDCLXXXIV.
Thomas, P., *Christians and Christianity in India and Pakistan*, London, 1954.
Thurston, Edgar, *Castes and Tribes of Southern India*, vol. II, Madras, 1909; New Delhi, 1993.
Tibbetts, G.R. (tr.), *Arab Navigation in the Indian Ocean before the coming of the Portuguese, being a translaton of Kitab al Fawa'id fi usal al-bahr wa'l-qawa'id of Ahmad bin Majid al-Nadji*, London, 1971.

Tiele, P.A. and A.C. Burnell (eds.), *The Voyage of John Huygen Von Linschoten to the East Indies*, vol. I, London, 1885.

Toussaint, Auguste, *L'Ocean Indien au XVIIIéme Siècle*, Paris, 1974.

Unni, N.P., *History of Mushikavamsa*, Trivandrum, 1980.

Varma, Chirakkal Rama and Elaya Raja, *Malayalatile Nayanmar*, Kuthuparamba, 1913.

Variyar, V.N.S., *A Brief Abstract of the Kerala Mahatmayam*, Calicut, 1880.

Veluthat, Kesavan, *Brahman Settlement in Kerala*, Calicut, 1978.

——, *The Political Structure of Early Medieval South India*, New Delhi, 1993.

Vincent, William, *The Commerce and Navigation of the Ancients in the Indian Ocean*, vol. I, London, 1807.

——, *The Periplus of the Erythrean Sea*, vol. II, London, 1807.

Visscher, Jacob Canter, *Letters from Malabar*, Madras, 1862.

Warmington, E.H., *The Commerce between the Roman Empire and India*, New Delhi, 1995.

Wheeler, J. Talboys, *A History of English Settlements in India*, Calcutta, 1878.

Whitway, R.S., *The Rise of Portuguese Power in India, 1497-1550*, London, 1899.

William, Johnston (tr. from German), *A Voyage to the East Indies*, London, MDCCC.

Wilks, Mark, *Lieut. Colonel, Historical Sketches of the South of India. An attempt to trace the History of Mysoor: From the Origin of the Hindoo Govt.of that State to the Extinctions of the Mohammedan Dynasty in 1799*, vol. I, Madras, 1869.

Wilson, H.H., *Mackenzies Collections: Descriptive Catalogue of the Orient Manuscipts and other Articles Illustrative of the literature, History, Statistics and Antiquities of the South of India collected by the late Lieut.Col.Colins Mackenzie Surveyor General of India*, vol. I, Calcutta, 1828.

Yule, Henry (ed.), *The Book of Marco Polo*, vol. II, London, 1903.

—— (tr. & ed.), *Cathay and the Way Thither*, 2 vols., London, 1866.

——, *Hobson-Jonson, A Glossary of Colloquial Anglo Indian Words and Phrases and of Kindred Terms, Etymologiccal, Historical, Geographical and Discursive*, London, 1903.

Zvelebil, K.V., *A History of Indian Literature. Tamil Literature*, Wiesbaden, 1974.

ARTICLES

Aiyer, S., 'An Unidentified Territory of South India', *Journal of Royal Asiatic Society*, II, 1922.

Cherian, A., 'The Genesis of Islam in Kerala', *Indica*, 6(1), March 1969, pp. 1-13.

de Saussure, Leopold, 'Commentaire des instructions Nautiques de Ibn Majid et Suleyman al-Mahri, in Gabriel Ferrand (ed.), *Introduction à l'Astronomie Nautique Arabe*, Paris, 1928.

Fawcett, F., 'War songs of the Mappilas of Malabar', *Indian Antiquary*, XXX, November-December 1901, pp. 499-508, 528-37.

Ganesh, K.N., 'Writing the History of Pre-Modern Kerala: A Study in the Transtition of Historical Consciousness', in Mujeebu Rehman and K.S. Madhavan (eds.), *Exploratiions in South Indian History*, Kottayam, 2014, pp. 43-70.

Hardgrave, L. Robert, Jr., 'The Mapilla Rebellion, 1921: Peasant Revolt in Malabar', *Modern Asian Studies*, I, II, 1977.

Harrison, J.B., 'Five Portuguese Historians', in C.H. Philips (ed.), *Historians of India, Pakistan and Ceylon*, London, 1961.

Jouveau-Dubreuil, 'The Temple of Augustus in the South of India', *The Quarterly Journal of the Mythic Society*, 19, 1929.

Khan, Shaukat Ali, 'Indo-Arab Relations before Muhammad bin Qasim', in P.M. Joshi (ed.), *Studies in the Foreign Relations of India*, Hyderabad, 1975, pp. 135-44.

Kieniewicz, Jan, 'The Portuguese Factory and Trade in Pepper in Malabar during the 16th Century', *Indian Economic and Social History Review*, vol. IV, no. I, March 1969.

Krieger, Martin, 'Danish Country: Trade on the Indian Ocean in the 17th and 18th Centuries', in K.S. Mathew (ed.), *Indian Ocean and Cultural Interaction (AD 1400-1800)*, Pondicherry, 1996.

Kunju, A.P. Ibrahim 'Mappilas of Malabar', *Silver Jubilee Souvenir*, Feroke College, Feroke, 1974, pp. 45-9.

——, 'Origin and Spread of Islam in Kerala', in Ashgar Ali Engineer (ed.), *Kerala Muslims: A Historical Pespective*, Delhi, 1995.

Maqbul, Ahmed, 'Al-Masudi on the Kings of India', *Al Masudi Millenary Commeration Volume*, Aligarh, 1960.

Meile, Pierre, 'Les Yavanas dans l'Inde Tamoul', in *Melanges Asiatiques*, Paris, 1940-1.

More, J.B.P., 'Some Maritime Aspects of the Indian Ocean Region, 1660-1760', in K.S. Mathew (ed.), *Indian Ocean and Cultural Interaction (AD 1400-1800)*, Pondicherry, 1996.

——, 'Origin, Ancestry and Identity of Hyder Ali', in J.B.P. More, *Religion and Society in South India: Hindus, Muslims and Christians*, Nirmalagiri, 2006, pp. 11-28.

——, 'Tipu Sultan and the Christians of Southern India', in J.B.P. More, *Religion and Society in South India: Hindus, Muslims and Christians*, Nirmalagiri, 2006, pp. 29-50; *Islam and Christian Muslim Relations*, Birmingham, vol. 14, no. 3, July 2003, p. 315.

——, 'Social Structure and Identity of Muslims of Mahé in North Malabar', in Valsamma Sebastian and Vinodkumar Kallolickal, (eds.), *Concerns Issues and Perspectives in History*, Ernakulam, 2011, pp. 42-67.

——, 'From Vasco da Gama to Sheikh Zainuddin's Tohfut-ul-Mujahideen', in Mujeebu Rehman and K.S. Madhavan (eds.), *Explora-tions in South Indian History*, Kottayam, 2014, pp. 243-63.

More, Leena, 'Early Hindu-Muslim Resistance to Colonialism in Kerala', in J.B.P. More (ed.), *Religion and Society in South India: Hindus, Muslims and Christians*, Nirmalagiri, 2006, pp. 51-70.

More, Leena and J.B.P. More 'Some Aspects of Modern Medicine and Muslims in the Tamil Country' in Charles Dias (ed.), *Kerala Spectrum: Aspects of Cultural Inheritance*, Cochin, 2006, pp. 317-32.

Noushad, M.K. and Muhammed Shihad, 'The Mappila Raja: The Rise of Arakkal Dynasty in Malabar, Kerala', in *Kannur Muslim Heritage Congress*, 2019, Kozhikode, 2019, pp. 410-11.

Otten, J. Henry, 'The Mappilas', *The Minaret*, VII, 1951, pp. 7-10.

Rahim, Abdul, 'Islam in Negapatanam', *Bulletin of the Institute of Traditional Cultures*, Madras University, July-December 1974.

Rajesh, K.P., 'Agro-Pastoralism and the Early Chiefdom of Ezhimala, North Kerala', in Mujeebu Rehman and K.S. Madhavan (eds.), *Explora-tions in South Indian History*, Kottayam, 2014, pp. 191-214.

Rao, Gopinatha, 'Extracts from the Mushaka Vamsam and Mushaka Vamsa: A Study', *Travancore Archaelogical Series*, vols. I, II, no. 10.

Ravenstein, E.G., 'The Voyages of Diogo Cao and Bartholomeu Dias, 1482-8', in *The Geographical Journal*, vol. xvi, 1900, pp. 625-55.

Rehman, Mujeebu, 'The British Reports and Production of Colonial Knowledge: The Joint Commissioners' Report on Malabar 1792-93', in Mujeebu Rehman and K.S. Madhavan (eds.), *Exploratiions in South Indian History*, Kottayam, 2014, pp. 355-71.

Rockhill, W.W., *Chau Ju Kua* (Notes on the Relation and Trade of China), T'oung-Pao, vols. XV-XVI, Leiden, 1914-1915.

Thapar, Romila, 'Early Mediterranean Contacts with India: An Overview', in F. De Romanis and A. Thernia (eds.), *Crossings: Early Mediterranean Contacts with India*, New Delhi, 1997.

Veluthat, Kesavan, 'A Copper Plate Inscription from Peruncellur, North Kerala, India: AD 1145', Mujeebu Rehman and K.S. Madhavan (eds.), *Exploratiions in South Indian History*, Kottayam, 2014, pp. 223-32.

Warren, W.P., 'Islam in Southern India', *The Moslem World*, XXI, 1931, pp. 352-62.

MISCELLANEOUS

Ali, Sheikh, 'French Relations with Haider Ali and Tipu Sultan: A record of blunders', paper presented at the International Seminar of Indo-French relations and Indian Independence, September 1997, Pondicherry, *Tamil Lexicon*, Madras, 1982.

Mahé, *Etablissement Français sur la côte de Malabar*, n.d.

More, J.B.P., 'Cannanore and Malabar: Some Historical Aspects', unpublished paper.

Leena, P.K. (Ph.D. unpublished Thesis), 'The History of the English East India Company's settlement at Anjengo', Calicut University, 1989.

Paul, Jose, 'Vasco Da Gama's discovery of a maritime route to India-The Myth and Realities'—Paper presented in the 'International Seminar on Maritime Malabar and the Europeans (1500-1962)', Tellicherry, 2002.

Purram, Nampuri, *Cellura Mahatmayam*, A Work on the Saiva sanctuary of Taliparamba in Chirakkal Taluk in Original Malayalam and Sanskrit Verse Report of a Joint Commission from Bengal and Bombay appointed to inquire into the State and Constitution of the Province of Malabar, in the year 1792 and 1793, vol. 1, Bombay.

Index